Symbols Used in this Book

🚗 .... Parking

♿ .... Wheelchair Access

👫 .... GuidedTours

🚶 .... Self-guided Tours

🧗 .... Walking Trails

🎁 .... Gift Shop

🌮 .... Picnic Area

🔺 .... Camping

☕ .... Concessions

🍴 .... Restaurant

🛏 .... Accommodations

🦜 .... Bird Watching

🏆 Museums that are primarily of interest to local residents.

🏆 🏆 Museums worth visiting if you are in the area.

🏆 🏆 🏆 Museums worth going out of your way to see.

🏆 🏆 🏆 🏆 Museums that are definite tourist attractions, worth making a special trip to see.

🏆 🏆 🏆 🏆 🏆 Museums that are destination museums or world class tourist attractions

HERITAGE HUNTER'S GUIDE
TO
ALBERTA MUSEUMS

Roberta Hursey

**Brightest Pebble
Publishing Co. Ltd.
1996**

Dedicated to
Chief Scout, Robert A. Hursey

First Printing, May 1996 by:
Art Design Printing Inc., Edmonton Alberta, Canada

Cover design by Art Design

First published in 1996 by
Brightest Pebble Publishing Co. Ltd.
7604 - 149 Avenue
Edmonton, Alberta, Canada
T5C 2V7
Phone (403) 457-7496   Fax (403) 475-0243

Canadian Cataloguing in Publication Data

Hursey, Roberta, 1939

Heretage Hunter's Guide to Alberta Museums

Includes bibliographical references and index

ISBN 0-9699669-3-8

1. Museums—Alberta—Guidebooks.
2. Alberta—Guidebooks.
3. Alberta—History.
I. Title.

AM21.A43H87 1996 069'.097123   C96-900369-2

Heritage Hunter's Guide to Alberta Museums

CONTENTS

ACKNOWLEDGMENTS

A number of people have generously given their time and assistance throughout the development of this guide book. Several "scouts" accompanied me on visits to museums and shared their insights. I am most grateful to my "chief scout," Dr. Bob Hursey, who travelled with me on several trips photographing the museums we visited, helping with all the driving, sharing his insights on countless audio tapes, and never complaining about my strange itineraries. Most of all, he provided continuing support and encouragement throughout the project. I would also like to thank other "scouts"—Elizabeth Macpherson, Margaret McInall, Ruth Burwash, Gil Freschauf and Susan Weir—who accompanied me on various site visits.

Without assistance from the Alberta Museums Association, this book would not have been possible. Dr. Adriana Davies, Executive Director, has been most supportive throughout the project, giving me access to the Alberta Museum Association's directory database. A special thanks goes to Eric Waterton, Head of Museum and Community Relations, Alberta Community Development, whose advice on setting up site visits and information about emerging museums was most helpful.

Several people have taken the time to review sections and chapters of the guide book: Dr. Paul Voisey, History Department, University of Alberta, critiqued the Introduction and gave me some interesting insights into more recent historical research. Thanks goes to various museum and tourism people for reviewing chapters about their communities: Morris Flewwelling, Michael Dawe, and Valerie Miller at Red Deer Museum; Wendy Martindale, Red Deer Tourist Association; Cecile McCleary and staff at Galt Museum in Lethbridge; Tom Willock and Donny White at Medicine Hat Museum; James Tirrul-Jones and Elizabeth Macpherson, Musée Héritage Museum, St. Albert; June Honey and Bruce Ibsen, City of Edmonton Archives; Edmonton historian A. J. "Alex" Mair; Lindsay Moir, Glenbow Museum; Lynn Cartwright, Museum of the Highwood, High River; Marsha Regensburg and Michael Payne, Historic Sites and Archives Service, Alberta Community Development; Rose Bendfeld, Heritage Park, Ft. McMurray; Lisa Paice, Fort Chipewyan Bicentennial Museum; Germaine Champagne and Marie Marchand, Musée Historique de St. Paul Museum; Peter Goertzen, Grande Prairie Museum, Fran Moore, DeBolt Museum and other members of the Spirit of the Peace. Any errors, however, are entirely my responsibility.

Without the generous financial support from the Alberta Historical Resources Foundation in providing a grant for research and writing, I would not have attempted to take on a project of this magnitude.

Thanks also to Phyllis Schmidt for reading and editing the manuscript several times and providing expert advice and publisher James Musson, for his patience and congeniality in involving me in each step of preparing this guide for publication.

To my daughters, Alex, Barb and Cathi, thanks for your encouragement when I really needed it. And to my friend, Anne Pope, thanks for giving me the idea for this guide book years ago.

Muttart Conservatory, courtesy of Muttart Conservatory, Edmonton, Alberta

USING THE HERITAGE HUNTER'S GUIDE

Are you a heritage hunter?

If you enjoy travelling to a new place and discovering what makes it unique from all other places, you are a heritage hunter. If you find visiting museums an engaging way of learning about the human and natural history of a place, you are a heritage hunter who will want to use this guide book time and time again.

The purpose of the *Heritage Hunter's Guide to Alberta Museums* is to put you on the trail discovering places where you can enjoy learning about Alberta's rich historical, natural, and cultural heritage. My scouts and I have attempted to blaze the trail and provide you with a compass and some signposts along the way.

Before we start, here are a few terms and definitions: *Heritage* refers to the legacy of the land, people, events and activities that make up the unique character of a particular region. *Museum* in this guide refers to non-profit, permanent establishments that are open to the public and are administered in the public trust for purposes of conserving, preserving, researching, interpreting, and exhibiting Alberta's heritage.

This guide gives information about museums that enrich our knowledge of Alberta's heritage and are open and accessible to the public. These include local history museums, provincial museums, multidisciplinary museums, natural history museums, historic and archeological sites, historic parks, villages and buildings, Native and multicultural museums and centres, art museums and galleries, military and police museums, technological and industrial museums, zoological parks, botanical gardens, planetariums, and science centres.

You may want to use this guide together with an Alberta Official Road Map. In this guide, we have arranged museums by community along main highways. Phone numbers of museums and seasons of operation are listed. Every attempt has been made to ensure that the information in this guide is accurate. However, to avoid disappointment, call the museum ahead of time or check at the visitor centre in the community to confirm hours of operation.

INTRODUCTION

ALBERTA'S LAND

If you spend some time driving around Alberta, you will notice its rich variety of land forms, vegetation, and climate. Alberta has five distinct natural regions, more than any other province in Canada. If you are travelling west through southern Alberta, you will pass through shortgrass prairie into forested foothills and on to the snow-capped Rocky Mountains. Travelling from the southern to the northern border of Alberta, you will pass from shortgrass prairie through two more natural regions: aspen parkland and the boreal forest. Between each of these regions are transition zones that contain plants and wildlife common to both regions.

Many geological forces have created Alberta's landscape. Long before the Canadian Rockies began to emerge, Alberta had been covered several times by shallow seas. Most of Alberta's bedrock is sedimentary rock, formed from organic and inorganic sediments deposited at the bottom of ancient seas. The conventional oil, natural gas, and coal that we extract from layers of sedimentary rock were once the living organisms of ancient coral reefs and forests.

Let's imagine we were able to travel back in time to about 100 million years ago. What did today's Alberta look like? We would discover that it had a much warmer climate. Much of the land was a vast river delta with vegetation similar to what you would find today in the southeastern United States. A shallow sea covered the southeast corner of the province. Rivers originating from mountains along the western border meandered in a northerly direction and eventually joined the Arctic Ocean.

Dinosaurs and other reptiles roamed the deltas and uplands. Mammals were around during this period, but they were very small—seldom larger than a house cat. All were marsupials (primitive mammals, like opossums) that carried their young in a pouch. Some insects were considerably larger than today's. The dragon fly had wings spanning three feet. Pterosaurs (flying reptiles) dominated the air. We know about these early life forms because their skeletons, foot prints, and other traces have been found imbedded in rocks throughout the province. Some of these magnificent creatures died under conditions that caused their skeletons to be preserved and their bones replaced, cell by cell, with minerals.

About 60 million years ago, events that still remain one of the world's great mysteries caused the dinosaurs, flying reptiles, and many other species of animals and plants to become extinct in a relatively short time. Alberta's climate became much cooler and drier. Many plants, such as cycads, ferns, redwoods and cypress succumbed in the cooler climate. Small mammals, with their protective fur, not only survived but began to evolve into many new species, becoming larger and filling the niches that dinosaurs once occupied. Flightless birds disappeared. Many birds able to migrate to warmer climates were able to survive. In later ages, receding glaciers and new rivers would carve deep valleys and canyons, exposing rocks with the remains of Alberta's ancient life.

Many of Alberta's museums offer the heritage hunter the opportunity to learn more about Alberta's palaeo-history. **The Royal Tyrrell Museum** in Drumheller and its **Tyrrell Field Station** at Dinosaur Provincial Park have perhaps the most impressive exhibits and collections of Late Cretaceous dinosaur fossils. You will also want to visit the **University of Alberta's Paleontology Museum** for its magnificent collection of palaeozoic invertebrates, the oldest fossils found in the province.

Beginning in the Eocene period, some 40 to 60 million years ago, the Rocky Mountains began to emerge. Forces deep beneath the earth's surface pushed up older rocks and exposed ancient sediments of primarily limestone and dolomite. The Rocky Mountains are still growing on the average of a few inches each year.

Alberta's climate during the Eocene period became increasingly colder and drier. Alberta experienced at least two, possibly three, glacial periods. The last glacial period (Wisconsin) began approximately 35,000 years ago. An ice sheet up to 1500 meters thick covered all but the highest mountain peaks and parts of the Cypress Hills and Porcupine Hills. As these mighty rivers of ice began to melt and recede about 14,000 years ago, they carved out U-shaped valleys in the mountains and deposited millions of tons of ground-up rock and gravel on the prairies. This glacial material forms the basis of some of our richest soils.

Throughout the prairies you can see monuments to the Ice Age in the form of erratics (large granite and quartzite boulders) that were left behind by the receding glaciers, many hundreds of miles from where the rocks originated. The largest of these can be seen just west of Okotoks on Highway 7. Pockets of melting ice formed many of Alberta's lakes. In the wake of the melting glaciers, animals and plants again began to colonize the land.

The **Provincial Museum of Alberta** and the **University of Alberta Geology Museum** have exhibits featuring the glacial geology and life during Alberta's Ice Age. Fossil skeletons and models of giant Quaternary mammals give us a picture of life during Alberta's Ice Age.

ALBERTA'S PEOPLE

Alberta's Original Inhabitants

The first people arrived in Alberta about 10,500 years ago. Small groups of nomadic hunters came from Siberia and crossed the Bering land bridge into Alaska and Yukon and migrated down into British Columbia and Alberta. These hunters followed herds of woolly mammoths, giant elk, bison, and other large ungulates. Some archeologists contend that there was an ice-free corridor through Alberta, between the Rocky Mountains and the continental ice sheet. So far, the oldest traces of human occupation in Alberta, dating back about 10,500 years, have been found in the Vermilion Lakes area near Banff. The arrival of the first people coincided with the disappearance of many of the giant Pleistocene mammals. These mammals may have been hunted out or were unable to adapt to the increasingly warmer and drier climate.

What do we know about these early people? They probably traveled in family groups and lived in teepee-like structures made of hides and poles and anchored down by stones. Dogs were used to pull loads, and sometimes they served as emergency food. Besides hunting, these people foraged for roots and berries and snared smaller game. Highly inventive, these men and women fashioned their weapons, tools, clothing, and shelter from the natural materials around them. Projectile points, charred bones, and medicine wheels found throughout the province, have given us glimpses of how the first inhabitants might have lived for thousands of years.

Buffalo, or bison, once covered the North American Plains in the millions. Now they exist only in small herds in national parks, game farms, and other places where they are either protected or raised for meat. Bison belong to the family *Bovidae*. Alberta has two subspecies: the Plains and Wood Bison.

For the Plains People, the buffalo was a general store on the hoof. A whole culture formed around the buffalo, which was as much a mystical being with spiritual powers as a main form of subsistence. They believed that the buffalo was a gift from the sun, and their Sun Dance each summer was largely centred around the buffalo. Plains Cultures used every part of the buffalo: the flesh for food; the bones for tools; the hide for clothing, saddles and teepees; the sinews for thread; and the stomach to heat water and stones for cooking. The hair was woven into ropes and then used as a whip or fly swatter. In areas where there was no wood for fires, the people collected dried buffalo dung. Women made pemmican, a highly nutritious food made from buffalo meat, cut into strips, dried, pounded, mixed with berries and fat, and stored in a rawhide storage container called a *parfleche*. Pemmican was useful when travelling or when fresh meat was not available.

Blackfoot Medicine Woman at Gleichen. (Provincial Archives of Alberta A3941)

Writing-on-Stone Provincial Park and **Head-Smashed-In Buffalo Jump World Heritage Site** provide excellent places for the heritage hunter interested in learning more about Alberta's earliest peoples. **Nose Creek Valley Museum** in Airdrie and **Grand Prairie Pioneer Museum** also have large collections of archaeological artifacts that pre-date the arrival of Europeans to North America.

Native History before Arrival of Europeans

Alberta's Plains and Northern Forest Natives lived a self-sufficient, nomadic life style. For much of the year they lived in family groups and bands. Each tribe controlled a general territory, and battles often erupted over boundaries. They developed well-established trade routes along a network of trails and rivers. They traded with bands and tribes to the east and west of the Rockies.

Both groups had sophisticated hunting and foraging techniques that required group cooperation and ingenuity. Because the Plains Indians depended on the large herds of migrating bison for subsistence, the acquisition of the horse in the early 1700s dramatically changed their hunting techniques and improved their ability to follow the bison herds. Northern Forest Natives subsisted mainly on moose, fish, deer, and caribou and used dogs for carrying their belongings. Alberta's Native peoples had, and still have, a rich oral history and spiritual life based on thousands of years of their close association with nature.

Fur Trade Explorers

Two fur trade companies were to have a major influence on the history and development of Alberta. The Hudson's Bay Company (HBC), founded in 1670 and based in London, had concentrated its fur trading activities in eastern and central Canada for over 100 years before venturing into the western prairies. Many of the eastern and central regions had been trapped out, and the time had come to exploit the prairies. In the 1780s, the newly formed North West Company (NWC), based in Montreal, began to establish fur trading depots at the head of Lake Superior. From there they established posts further west.

The market for furs in Europe, particularly beaver hats, fueled the competition between the rival companies. Even before fur traders from Europe and Eastern Canada actually arrived in Alberta to trade with native trappers, trading activities farther east profoundly impacted upon the movement and displacement of native groups in and around Alberta. Eastern tribes like the Cree and Assiniboine migrated west to trap for furs. They brought European guns and iron goods with them and drove tribes such as the Beaver, Slavy, Kootenai, and Blackfoot from their traditional territories.

The HBC sent Anthony Henday to the western prairies to establish new trade markets. He traveled with Cree traders and arrived in Alberta in September 1754. He visited one of the Blackfoot camps near present day Red Deer, but he was unsuccessful in convincing the Blackfoot to trade with the Company.

In 1778, Peter Pond, working for the NWC, founded the first trading post in Alberta, on the Athabasca River near Fort Chipewyan. He built posts at Fort Chipewyan on Lake Athabasca and Fort Vermilion on the Peace River. Both posts formed what are today the oldest communities in Alberta.

The NWC had established several posts along the Peace and Athabasca rivers by the time Alexander Mackenzie, another Nor'wester, completed his epic journey across the North American continent from the Atlantic to the Pacific in 1792.

The chief traders and management of the companies were generally of Scottish and English background. The middle men, often Cree, traded directly with the local bands; craftsmen and laborers came from a variety of cultural backgrounds. Both companies hired French Canadians or Métis (mixed bloods) to convey supplies and furs to their destinations. The Hudson's Bay Company generally contracted hearty men from the Orkney Islands to build the clinker-style York boats, which plied the river highways.

The fur traders took Native women as country wives. These women served as ambassadors and interpreters in trade negotiations with tribes and formed an essential work force, dressing hides and making pemmican and snowshoes. The descendants of this partnership became a distinct society, unique to the Canadian West. The Métis adopted a blend of both Native and European lifestyles, working seasonally for the fur companies, going on an annual bison hunt in the summer, and farming along their river lots.

Musée héritage museum in St. Albert, **Jasper-Yellowhead Museum** and **Musée Historique de St. Paul Museum** have exhibits that feature the history and contributions of the Métis people in their communities.

During the 1790s, fierce competition between the two companies led to the establishment of posts throughout northeastern and central Alberta. The Hudson Bay Company sent David Thompson and Peter Fidler to survey the Athabasca and the Saskatchewan rivers. Within 20 years, over a dozen fur trade posts dotted Alberta's landscape. When fierce competition for furs became financially ruinous, the companies amalgamated in 1821 under the Hudson's Bay Company name.

If you are interested in learning more about Alberta's fur trade history, you will want to visit **Rocky Mountain House National Historic Site**, **Fort Edmonton** (a replica of the 1842 fort), **Fort Assiniboine Museum**, **Fort George-Buckingham House Interpretive Centre** near Elk Point, and the restored buildings at **Historic Dunvegan Provincial Historic Site** near Fairview. Many Alberta museums like the **Glenbow Museum** in Calgary and the **Provincial Museum of**

Alberta, Edmonton, have significant collections related to the fur trade era. The more adventurous Heritage Hunter should plan a visit to **Fort Chipewyan Bicentennial Museum** and **Fort Vermilion,** a hamlet with several buildings dating back to its fur trade history.

Arrival of Missionaries

Christianity and civilization went hand-in-hand in the minds of missionaries who began arriving in Alberta in the mid-1800s. Robert Rundle, a Methodist minister from England, was the first permanent missionary to settle in Alberta, in 1840. He spent eight years preaching among the Cree and Assiniboine. His successor, Benjamin Sinclair, started the first mission at Pigeon Lake in 1848. Other Methodist missionaries came in the 1850s: Henry Steinhaur, an Ojibwa convert from Ontario, tried to get natives to adopt an agricultural lifestyle. In 1863, George McDougall and his son, John, started the Victoria mission on the banks of the North Saskatchewan river, about 100 miles downstream of Edmonton.

The Roman Catholic missionary Father Jean-Baptiste Thibault founded a mission at Fort Chipewyan in 1842 and one at Lac Ste. Anne in 1844. He was soon followed by the Oblates of Mary Immaculate, a French-based order. Father Alexander Taché began his missionary work in Fort Chipewyan in 1847. Missions were also started at Lac La Biche in 1853, and one at Fort Dunvegan in 1866. Father Albert Lacombe, perhaps the most famous of these early Oblates, arrived in Alberta in 1852 to take over the mission at Lac Ste. Anne. The Grey Nuns, the first Sisters, arrived at Lac Ste. Anne in 1859. They were the first educated white women to settle in Alberta.

The 19th century missionaries attempted to change the traditional lifestyle of native people and "civilize" them. The missionaries' efforts to convert Natives to Christianity and adopt an agricultural way of life based on European values experienced little success, especially among the Plains Indians, until after the demise of the buffalo herds in the 1870s.

To learn more about Alberta's missionaries, you will want to visit **Lac La Biche Mission**, near the town of Lac La Biche; the **Father Lacombe Chapel** and **Vital Grandin Centre** in St. Albert; **Historic Dunvegan**, near Fairview; and **Victoria Settlement** near Smoky Lake.

The North West Mounted Police

The dream of having a transcontinental highway linking eastern Canada with the Canadian West began as early as the 1850s. A group of influential expansionists lobbied the British government to acquire Rupert's Land from the Hudson's Bay Company. They challenged HBC's claims that western Canada was unsuitable for agriculture.

In 1857 the British House of Commons sent a scientific expedition led by Captain John Palliser. Notable geologist and naturalist, Dr. James Hector, was a member of the Palliser Expedition. From 1858 to 1860, various teams travelled throughout Alberta to gather geological data, explore the suitability of agriculture, and determine the feasibility of building a wagon road across Canada to the Pacific. The Palliser Expedition reported that, with the exception of the southeastern corner, Alberta did have agricultural potential. His report prompted negotiations between the Canadian and British governments to purchase Rupert's Land from the HBC. In 1869, the HBC sold most of its land for £300,000, with the proviso that HBC continue its fur trade activities as a private corporation.

The newly purchased Rupert's Land encompassed over 1.5 million square miles (3.9 million square kilometres), and, for a period in the 1870s, the Canadian government had no effective control over western Canada. This opened Alberta to exploitation by whisky traders from Montana who began trading whisky to natives for their goods. The Plains Indians population had already been reduced by smallpox in the 1780s, the 1830s, and 1869-70. The systematic destruction of buffalo herds in the U.S. northern plains profoundly affected Alberta's Indians, who depended upon the herds for their existence. Now the disastrous effects of the whisky trade threatened the remaining Native people with physical and moral destruction.

In 1873, partly to lay undisputed claim to the newly acquired lands to keep Americans from usurping control over the area, the Canadian government passed an act providing for the establishment of the North West Mounted Police (NWMP). When, in the summer of 1873, American frontiersmen massacred some 30 Assiniboine men, women, and children in the Cypress Hills, Prime Minister John A. MacDonald dispatched about 300 troops, led by Commissioner George A. French and Colonel James Macleod, to the area. The newly formed NWMP began an epic journey, beginning in July 1874, across southern Saskatchewan and Alberta, arriving in October at Fort Whoop-Up, a whisky post on the Bow River. All but one whisky trader had left the fort, having had prior warning of the arrival of the NWMP.

The NWMP established its first fort on an island in the Oldman River. It was named Fort Macleod after Col. Macleod. Two weeks later, another column of NWMP arrived at Fort Edmonton. Soon after, Fort Saskatchewan was established downstream at the junction of the Sturgeon and North Saskatchewan Rivers. In August 1875, Fort Calgary, established at the junction of the Bow and Elbow Rivers, became the third NWMP post.

Alberta's NWMP joined forces with volunteer militias during the Riel Rebellion of 1885. Although Riel's uprising mainly took place in Saskatchewan, the massacre at Frog Lake, where nine men were killed, struck fear in the hearts of white settlers. Alberta's joint field forces, including two units of the NWMP, mobilized to provide protection against Alberta's Métis and Indians if they joined Riel. The Native communities, however, did not take part in the uprising. Leaders, like Chief Crowfoot of the Blackfoot, believed that the resistance would fail and they would be worse off than they were.

Several Alberta museums have superb NWMP artifacts and exhibits depicting the arrival of the NWMP and its role in keeping order in the province. **The Fort Museum** at Fort Macleod is a living history museum, with restored buildings set in a replica of the original fort. Numerous NWMP and RCMP collections can be seen. **Fort Calgary, Fort Whoop-up** in Lethbridge, and the **Fort Saskatchewan Museum** also have exhibits and collections that feature the history of the NWMP and RCMP.

Rise of the Ranching Industry

The dream of a transcontinental railway was foremost in John A. MacDonald's mind when he became Canada's first prime minister in 1857. A railroad would link Canada from coast to coast and provide transportation for settlers to fill the empty prairies after the signing of the Indian treaties. The loss of the buffalo herds had brought the Plains Indians to the brink of starvation. In 1877, the Blackfoot Confederacy and other plains tribes signed Treaty 7 and moved onto reserves. The need for beef to feed the Natives and the NWMP troops provided new markets for a growing ranching industry.

Ranchers began running cattle in southern Alberta as early as the late 1870s. The industry predominated throughout the 1880s and 1890s. Large ranches such as the Cochrane, the Oxley, and the Walrond ranches, owned by retired politicians and British aristocracy, sprang up along the foothills west and south of Calgary. The arrival of the Canadian Pacific Railway in 1885 enabled ranchers to ship cattle to Eastern Canada and Europe. In the 1890s Great Britain became an important market for western calves. The railway, however, presented ranchers with a mixed blessing. While expanding the market for cattle, the railroads also brought land-hungry settlers to homestead farms in southern Alberta. A new strain of hardy wheat and dryland farming techniques made it possible in good years to grow crops on land that had been thought only suitable for ranching.

If you are interested in learning more about Alberta's ranching history, you will want to visit **Cochrane Ranch** in Cochrane. **The Museum of the Highwood** in High River and **Medicine Hat Museum** have exhibits and artifacts featuring Alberta's ranching history.

Railways Across Alberta

The Canadian Pacific Railway arrived in Alberta in June of 1883. Towns like Medicine Hat, Lethbridge, and Calgary already existed, but the coming of the CPR gave an economic boost and unprecedented growth to these communities. Other towns grew along the right of way; the location of CPR tracks determined where towns would be built. To be missed by the railway sounded the death knell to many communities. Red Deer and Edmonton were linked to the CPR by 1891, when the Calgary and Edmonton Railway ended at Strathcona (South Edmonton).

Much of central and northern Alberta would have to wait for a new century for a transcontinental railway. The Grand Trunk Pacific (GTP) and the Canadian Northern Pacific (CNoR) began to lay track through Alberta between 1905 and 1911 in a race that would eventually cause both companies financial grief and unnecessary duplication of tracks west of Edmonton and over the Yellowhead Pass. The GTP and CNoR faced financial collapse by 1916 and required substantial government funding. Finally in 1923, the Canadian National Railways absorbed these companies into one massive network.

The Edmonton, Dunvegan & B.C. Railway reached the isolated Peace River district in 1916 and the Alberta & Great Waterways Railway reached Waterways (Fort McMurray) in 1921. Hard times and mismanagement forced these companies into bankruptcy creating a provincial-wide political scandal. It seemed that it was more profitable to build railways than to run them. Finally in 1930, the Northern Alberta Railway was formed from failed companies; and for 40 years the NAR served towns like Grande Prairie, McLennan, Peace River, Lac La Biche, and Fort McMurray with a vital link to Edmonton and the outside.

Museums that feature railway history in their collections and exhibitions are far too numerous to list here. The majority of local history museums in Alberta have railway artifacts. The **Alberta Railway Museum**, **Fort Edmonton Park**, **Heritage Park Historical Village** in Calgary, and the **Alberta Prairie Railway Excursions** in Stettler offer rides on historic steam trains. The Quick Reference has a list of other railway museums in Alberta.

Locomotives #1395 and #6060 at Alberta Railway Museum. (R.L. Hursey)

Homesteading in "The Last Best West"

The first Dominion Lands Act of 1872 provided free 160-acre homesteads (a quarter section) to settlers. Land was surveyed into townships of 36 sections—one mile square. These sections were marked by monuments at the corners, four pits three feet square, 18 inches deep, about five feet apart. An iron post was driven at the centre of the system of pits and the post marked with a chisel on its southwest face displayed the number of the section, township and range. Settlers paid a ten-dollar filing fee and agreed to break 15 acres of land in three years to acquire full title to the land. Latecomers and homesteaders, wanting to expand their holdings, bought land from the railway companies.

At first the Dominion Government encouraged people primarily of British origin from eastern Canada and Great Britain to settle the

Canadian West. In 1881, the Dominion Lands Survey completed the subdivision of lands around Edmonton and Fort Macleod. However, settlement of the prairies was slow until after the completion of the Canadian Pacific Railway (CPR) through southern Alberta in 1885. The CPR advertised for settlers to homestead in the West. Settlement would mean increased business for the CPR in shipping and in the sale of its land holdings. After 1896, the Dominion government switched its emphasis on U.S. and European settlers to those from poorer parts of the world that could provide cheap labour. The CPR steamship lines advertised cheap passage.

Thousands of immigrants came, many in groups that filled boxcars with personal belongings and tools to begin homesteading the "Last Best West." In southern Alberta, wheat was the major crop. Farms tended to be larger and more mechanized. In the more wooded areas, with its shorter growing season, mixed farming prevailed and farms tended to be smaller. By the 1890s, Alberta's landscape became a patchwork quilt of ethnic communities. The stitching that held these communities together was the railroads.

One of the last areas of major settlement was the large arable lands of the Peace River country. North of Edmonton, nearly 500 kilometres of forests, muskeg swamps, sand hills and primitive trails formed a formidable barrier blocking this rich area of arable land from prospective settlers. At the turn of the century, only the most hardy of pioneers—missionaries, trappers and fur traders— had found the land appealing. In 1908, settlers travelled by wagons and cabooses pulled by oxen and horses. They took the Chalmers Trail through the Swan Hills to Lesser Slave Lake and overland from Grouard to Peace River Crossing. Depending upon the weather and trail conditions, the trip could take up to two months. In 1911, after the completion of the Grand Trunk Pacific railway to Edson, settlers began using the Edson-Grande Prairie Trail to get to the Grande Prairie region.

Alberta's Ethnic Heritage

In any major Alberta city, you can visit a local shopping mall and hear a half dozen or more languages spoken in one afternoon's shopping. Alberta attracts people of every race, religion, and social level from all over the world. Today most of the immigrants settle in Alberta's urban centres. In the 1880s and early 1890s, immigrants were primarily of British or American origin, seeking arable land to homestead. Many came in large groups.

In 1886 a group of Mormons arrived from the United States and settled in the area of Cardston, named after their leader, Charles Ora Card. They became the first successful group of farmers in Alberta.

A much larger group of colonists formed what is known today as the Barr Colony. About 2000 of them under the leadership of Isaac Barr came to the Lloydminster area from Britain in 1903. Almost all of them came from urban working class backgrounds with no farming experience. They were poorly organized and ill-equipped for the hardships they would experience.

Between 1892 to 1913, immigrants from northern and eastern Europe began to settle in central Alberta. Alberta's population expanded from 73,000 in 1901 to 374,000 by 1911. These immigrants came for a variety of reasons, but mostly to improve their economic and social standing or to escape religious and political persecution. The Doukhobors were the largest group of colonists to come to western Canada as a group. Over 7000 of these religious non-conformists and pacifists fled Russia to escape religious persecution and military conscription. They first settled in Saskatchewan, but after the government took away their land in 1907 for refusing to take the oath of allegiance, which was against their religious beliefs, and for not cultivating the required land under the Homestead Act, they began to move into the interior of B.C and the Crowsnest Pass area of Alberta. These two governments were more congenial to their way of life.

Ukrainian-Canadians comprise the largest ethnic group other than those of British and American origin. They came in three waves beginning in 1891. The first, from 1891 to 1914, consisted primarily of peasants from the provinces of Bukovyna and Galicia. The second, between the world wars, saw approximately 170,000 Ukrainians making Canada their home. The third wave followed the Second World War. Many of these were displaced persons.

The Scandinavians settled mostly in central Alberta in small communities centred around their churches. French-speaking settlers from Quebec and the northern United States settled in communities in north central Alberta and the Peace River area. Two groups came directly from France: immigrants from Brittany took up homesteads around St. Vincent and St. Paul; another group settled around Trochu. Ukrainians took up homesteads in the townships northeast of Edmonton beginning in 1892, joining many of their former neighbors, German-speaking settlers from the province of Galicia. Communal religious groups like the Hutterites and Mennonites also came in large numbers to homesteads in Alberta. Not all immigrants settled on farms; many took up their former trades or established businesses in Alberta's urban centres.

Since the First World War, the pattern of ethnic settlement in Alberta became far more diverse. Many newcomers came from Mediterranean countries and Asia. They settled mostly in urban areas. Today, Alberta continues to attract immigrants from all over the world. There are over a hundred recognized ethno-cultural peoples living in Alberta.

Most of Alberta's community museums have historic houses, exhibits, and artifacts that reflect their rich multicultural heritage. The **Multicultural Heritage Centre** in Stony Plain offers cultural programs throughout the year to all ages. Edmonton has three Ukrainian-Canadian museums. There are two historical villages: the **Historical Village at Shandro** near Smoky Lake and **Ukrainian Cultural Heritage Village**, 40 kilometres east of Edmonton. Both have many restored historic buildings from the Ukrainian-Canadian communities of north-eastern Alberta. **Stephansson House** near Innisfail and the **Markerville Creamery** focus on Icelandic settlement. The **Dickson Store** in Dickson features the culture of Danish settlers. In Calgary, the **Chinese Cultural Centre** has an excellent art museum, and the centre itself is a replica of the Temple of the Sun in Beijing. The **Beth Tzedec Synagogue's Heritage Collection** reflects the rich culture of Calgary's Jewish community.

Alberta's Agricultural Heritage

Until the end of the Second World War, agriculture was Alberta's largest industry. In 1901, 75 percent of Albertans lived in rural areas. By 1941, it had dropped to 61 percent and to 52 percent by 1951. By 1961, more Albertans lived in urban centres. Of the 214 museums that are members of the Alberta Museums Association, approximately 170 are local history museums. Most of them concentrate on the history of agriculture in their community. Some go beyond simply showing static displays of farm equipment and machinery and portray the living agricultural history of the province. During the summer many communities celebrate Heritage Days and host threshing bees, tractor competitions and parades. Pioneer Plowmen and Threshermen's Clubs throughout the province restore and maintain vintage farm equipment.

The **Reynolds-Alberta Museum** in Wetaskiwin has an impressive collection of horse-driven and mechanized farm equipment. Some were uniquely designed for, and manufactured in, Alberta. A few of the more successful museums to bring to life Alberta's agricultural past include the **South Peace Centennial Museum** at Beaverlodge, **Pioneer Acres of Alberta** at Irricana, and the **Prairie Acres Heritage Village and Farm Equipment Museum** near Picture Butte.

Growth of a Province

From the time Canada purchased Rupert's Land from the HBC in 1869, Alberta was part of the Northwest Territories. On September 1, 1905, Alberta celebrated achieving provincial status. Edmonton became the capital, and the Honorable A.C. Rutherford was appointed the first premier. The first legislative assembly met on the third floor of McKay Avenue School in Edmonton. construction on the Alberta Legislature Building began in 1909 and was completed in 1913. The building perched on a plateau overlooking Fort Edmonton, the major supply depot and regional government for the HBC for over a century. Two years later the last remains of this historic fur trade fort were demolished.

Alberta Legislative Building with Fort Edmonton in the foreground.
(Provincial Archives of Alberta B6610)

The **Alberta Legislature Building** has daily tours for visitors and school groups. Tours are also available at **Government House. The Edmonton Public Schools Museum** (McKay Avenue School) has restored the third floor as the first provincial legislative assembly. **Rutherford House**, on the University of Alberta campus, was the home of A.C. Rutherford, the first premier of Alberta and first president of the university.

Growth of Urban Centres

The first decade of the 20th century experienced years of growth and expansion in urban centres around the province. Many people became wealthy from new businesses, real estate speculation and coal mining interests. This was the period of building expansion; new schools and hospitals were erected to meet the needs of a growing population. Fire-resistant brick and sandstone buildings replaced wooden structures, considered fire hazards. Municipal police and fire departments evolved from small volunteer groups to highly skilled organizations. Improved roads and mass transportation provided better access between urban and rural areas. The newly elected legislative assembly began to pass important acts that created a provincially owned telephone system and founded the University of Alberta.

From the turn of the century to the beginning of the First World War, Alberta experienced an era of growing cultural refinement as urban centres founded libraries, built movie houses and theatres, and organized exhibitions and art and music societies. But the period had its down side. It was also a time of intense discrimination by earlier Anglo and French settlers against newcomers from Eastern Europe; religious intolerance between Protestants and Catholics grew, as did the demoralization of native peoples as their ability to determine their own destinies was taken away from them by governments and religious groups. A real estate crash in 1912, a depression in 1913, and the threat of war in Europe dried up investments. Alberta suddenly had an unemployment problem, and many families had to go on welfare.

The **Alexander Galt Museum** in Lethbridge and the **Medicine Hat Museum** are municipal museums that effectively present their urban histories. Living museums like **Heritage Park Historical Village** in Calgary and **1910 Street** at Fort Edmonton Park have preserved and restored many turn-of-the-century heritage houses, churches, and public buildings. Since its creation in 1987, the **Alberta Main Street Programme** has assisted communities like Lacombe, Medicine Hat, and the Municipality of Crowsnest Pass in restoring and maintaining turn-of-the-century buildings along their main streets.

Two Wars and a Depression

When the Great War broke out in Europe in August 1914, Alberta solidly supported the war effort. The province had one of the highest number of enlistments. Many Albertans, especially of British background, enlisted out of patriotic fervor; others who had lost their jobs joined to be gainfully employed. The war, in part, solved Alberta's unemployment problem. Of the 45,136 who served overseas, 6,140 were lost. Thus Alberta suffered one of the highest numbers of mortality per capita of any province.

Good times did not immediately follow the end of the war in 1918 and 1919. There were few jobs for returning veterans and they deeply resented business people who profited from the war. The influenza epidemic of 1918 killed 4,000 of the 38,000 Albertans who contracted the disease. Hundreds of children lost both parents and were placed in orphanages run by church groups. Coal miners went on strike over low wages and lack of safety in the mines. Farmers suffered from poor grain prices in the 1920s and complained about the tariff policy and the high costs charged by elevators.

In the 1920s, farmers for the first time entered politics on a large scale. The United Farmers of Alberta defeated the Conservatives and Liberals in the 1921 election and formed the government. Farmers also established the Alberta Wheat Pool in 1923, giving farmers an opportunity to maximize their profits. The Pool's grain elevators sprang up in small towns throughout Alberta, becoming distinctive features on the prairies.

Women, tired of being powerless, began to agitate for political rights. Their efforts peaked in 1929, when a group of Alberta women known as the "Famous Five," succeeded in a landmark case in getting women legally recognized as "persons" under the British North America Act and allowing women to be appointed to the Senate.

The return to a modest prosperity finally came to Alberta in the late 1920s. The oil fields around Turner Valley and Black Diamond were becoming profitable and provided new opportunities for employment. The population of Edmonton and Calgary began to expand for the first time since the boom years. Farmers began to mechanize. Cars, improved roads, radios, and telephones brought an end to some of the isolation of rural life.

The Great Depression of the 1930s struck the western prairies particularly hard. After years of drought and falling grain prices, farmers found themselves in a vulnerable position. Banks began to foreclose on farms, and many were forced to leave the land their families had once homesteaded. With no money to afford gas for their automobiles, farmers hitched their cars to horses. Bennett buggies, as they were called, became a common feature on the prairies. Unemployment reached an all-time high in 1933 and 1934. Soup kitchens and bread lines became common sights in urban centres. Many men took to the rails, hoping to find work out of the province.

Photo of Hunger march, Calgary, 1932. (Provincial Archives of Alberta A9216)

William Aberhart, high school principal, lay preacher, founder of the Prophetic Bible Institute in Calgary and charismatic radio announcer, began a meteoric rise in politics. In 1934 he founded the Social Credit Party, a unique blend of politics, religion, economics, and social consciousness. In 1935, the Social Credit Party formed the new provincial government, defeating the UFA. To increase the spending power of the average Albertan, Aberhart promised to give $25 a month to Albertans that qualified. Although this money never materialized, the Social Credit Party—under Aberhart and his successors, Ernest Manning and Harry Strom—remained in power from 1935 to 1971, longer than any other political party in Alberta.

Alberta and the Second World War

Aberhart's programs did little to pull Alberta out of the Depression. The Second World War had a much larger impact. Beginning in 1938 after Hitler invaded Poland, thousands of Albertans enlisted in the Canadian Armed Forces. Many had not worked in years. While the war seemed to be solving the unemployment problem, it created a new one. No longer were there enough men to fill critical jobs. Women began doing non-traditional work left by men going overseas or to jobs more essential to the war effort.

Alberta's contributions to the war effort went far beyond those men and women who served overseas. Its location in the middle of the continent, away from strategic bombing sites, made it an ideal place to train pilots. Edmonton's airport, which had provided air service to the North for twenty years, became the western Canada headquarters for the British Commonwealth Air Training Program (BCATP). Seventeen of Canada's 105 flight training centres were established in Alberta in places like Calgary, Claresholm, Vulcan and Nanton. From 1938 to the end of the war, a total of 131,553 pilots and air and ground crews (55 percent were Canadian) had received training at BCATP bases.

Edmonton also became a vital centre in the Northwest Staging Route following the Japanese attack on Pearl Harbor and Russia's joining of the Allied Forces. Hundreds of airplanes, originating from eastern Canada and the United States, landed at Edmonton en route to Alaska and the Soviet Union. In 1942, fear of a Japanese invasion of Alaska and Canada encouraged the construction of an all-weather road from Canada to Alaska. American engineers and supplies were flown in and out of Edmonton and shipped by railroad to Dawson Creek, the beginning of the Alaska Highway. The Lovat Scouts, a British regiment, did their high mountain reconnaissance training at Jasper National Park.

Following the Japanese attack on Pearl Harbor, Japanese-Canadians—many of whom had lived in Canada for generations—were evacuated from the west coast of British Columbia. Alberta became the dubious host to relocation camps. Canadian conscientious objectors and German prisoners of war were sent to camps established throughout Alberta.

To learn more about Alberta's role in the Second World War, you will want to visit the **Museum of the Regiments** and the **Aero Space Museum** in Calgary, the **Alberta Aviation Museum** at the Edmonton Aviation Heritage Centre, the **Lancaster Air Museum** in Nanton, and the **Canadian Aviation Hall of Fame** in Wetaskiwin.

Leduc #1 and the Boom Years

In the years following the end of the Second World War, Albertans returned to peacetime endeavors. Servicemen returned to take up their lives where they left off. Husbands, wives, and children reacquainted themselves with each other. Women were encouraged to vacate their war-time jobs for returning veterans, to marry, stay at home, and have children. Still, there were not enough jobs for the returning veterans. Many accepted government loans to go back to school to learn a trade or pursue a university degree.

By the early 1950s, the post-war baby boom created a demand for more housing, hospitals, and other services. Before the war, Alberta's population reached about 800,000. By 1951, that had grown to almost 950,000.

In 1947, Leduc #1 gushed its rich fountain of oil and was soon followed by Leduc #2. These were not the first oil wells in Alberta. The first was drilled at Waterton Lakes in 1901. Turner Valley, southwest of Calgary, launched Alberta's first oil boom in 1914. But the Leduc wells introduced a major change in Alberta's economy. The province was no longer dependent upon agriculture alone. The existence of oil sands was known since Natives and fur traders mended their birch bark canoes with tar that seeped out of the banks along the Athabasca River. In the 1960s and 1970s, government and oil companies financed mega projects like the Great Canadian Oil Sands and Syncrude near Fort McMurray to extract the bitumen from the oil sands and refine it into a synthetic crude oil that was then shipped to Edmonton's refineries for further processing. At the time, the oil sands seemed the answer to Canada's long-term energy needs.

Alberta's prosperity attracted many new people to the province. By 1961 Alberta's population grew to about 1,332,000. The 1960s also marked a shift from an agricultural to an urban society. This new economic prosperity brought back a feeling of optimism not experienced since the boom years prior to the First World War. Albertans were eager to buy the new manufactured domestic products that came on the market after the war. Much of what had adorned the home during the Depression years became emotional surplus. The collections in many of Alberta's museums that emerged in the 1960s are of the material culture—clothing, furniture, toys, decorations, automobiles, and farming equipment—that reminded people of the years they struggled in poverty.

Albertans Today

Who are Albertans today? Today's cultural map of Alberta is very different from what it was at the turn of the century. In the 1911 Census of Canada, people of "British" origin made up 51 percent of Alberta's population of 374,295. Other ethnic groups included people of French, German, Scandinavian, Native, and Eastern European background. Today those who claim British origins still comprise most Albertans, but many other ethnic groups make Alberta their home. Canada's 1986 Census listed 60 different ethnic groups. In the last 20 years many immigrants from Asian countries, namely from India, Pakistan, China, Japan, and Southeast Asia, have immigrated to Alberta. This ethnic diversity has had a profound influence, not only upon the urban and rural settlement of Alberta, but on its cultural heritage. Diverse languages, architecture, religions, arts, festivals and cultural activities add to Alberta's unique character.

"Wop" May and Vic Horner. Mercy flight from Edmonton to Fort Vermilion, 1929. (Provincial Archives of Alberta A11,797)

ALBERTA'S MUSEUMS

Did you know that there are about 230 museums in Alberta? And that in 1993, 6.7 million people visited Alberta's museums? Did you know that some 9,000 people work in Alberta's museums, and 70 percent of these are volunteers?

Alberta's museums include local history museums, archives, historic sites and buildings, halls of fame, pioneer villages, art galleries/museums, interpretive centres, Native and multicultural centres, multidisciplinary museums, police and military museums, science centres, technology and occupational museums, nature centres, zoos, and botanical gardens. About 80 percent of Alberta's museums are local history museums. For all their diversity, these museums share a dedication to the preservation and presentation of Alberta's natural and cultural heritage.

The oldest museum in Alberta is the Banff Park Museum, founded in 1895, with collections that date from the 1880s. The present facility was built in 1903. Most of Alberta's museums originated between 1960 and 1980, when the federal and provincial governments provided grants at an unprecedented rate to communities to write local history books, gather collections and build museums. Two events—Canada's Centennial Year of 1967 and Alberta's 75th Anniversary in 1980—stimulated the growth and development of Alberta's museums. These events helped to create in Albertans a new awareness that they had a fascinating history to be proud of and one that needed to be shared with others.

The size of a museum does not necessarily determine the quality of its collections nor its visitor appeal. Some of the most interesting museums are hardly larger than a private home—and sometimes *are* someone's home. Be on the look out for these small museums as you travel around Alberta.

Although many museums are open only during the summer months on a regular basis, you can always arrange a visit to most museums by calling for an appointment. You may discover in your travels that many of Alberta's local history museums have similar artifacts reflecting a shared agricultural and technological history. However, each community has a different story, or many stories, to tell about its land and people. You will find that the staff or volunteers who work in local history museums are some of the most friendly and helpful people on this planet.

GLOSSARY OF MUSEUMS

Archives are institutions that collect and preserve documents on paper, photographs, motion picture film and audio-visual tapes. Many local history museums have archives.

Art Galleries/Museums. These are non-profit institutions that collect, preserve, conserve, research, interpret, and exhibit two- and three-dimensional artwork. Private galleries that operate for profit to sell artist's works are not included in this guide.

Ecomuseum. The term is derived from the Latin *eco* or *oeco*, meaning "household," "habitat," or "vicinity." An ecomuseum encompasses an entire community—its architecture, people, industries, businesses, and social institutions. In an ecomuseum, the people who live in a place are the interpreters of their own history and social institutions; thus each ecomuseum is unique. One of the purposes of an ecomuseum is to provide economic opportunities that are offered by tourism. For example, the towns and villages that are part of the Municipality of Crowsnest Pass are part of the Crowsnest Ecomuseum.

Halls of Fame are usually institutions that pay tribute to people who have been outstanding in their field or have given exceptional service to their community, province, or nation. Collections are usually associated with the person, such as photographs, memorabilia, letters, awards, and personal diaries. Examples include the Canadian Aviation Hall of Fame, Wetaskiwin; Olympic Hall of Fame, Calgary; and the Appaloosa Hall of Fame, Claresholm.

Historic Sites. Natural and Historic Sites are designated areas that have special significance to Alberta's or Canada's heritage. These sites focus on important historic events, places, and people. Natural and historic sites differ from traditional museums in that the collection—whether it be a house, a group of buildings, an archaeological site or natural area—is preserved in its place of origin. Federal, provincial and municipal governments generally operate these sites and many have interpretive centres near them.

Interpretive Centres exist mainly to interpret an historic site, a person or group of people, an industry, or a nature area. The collections exist mainly for public education and exhibition and often contain replicas as well as actual artifacts or specimens. Interpretive centres include aboriginal, multicultural, nature, industrial, occupational, science, and technology centres.

Local history museums. A local history museum is an institution that has collections related to a particular community or region. Its main purpose is to preserve and communicate the heritage of the community to the community. Most local history museums began as historical societies and are generally operated by volunteers.

Multidisciplinary Museums have collections pertaining to a variety of fields and academic disciplines. Objects are often collected for purposes of study and research. Curators who are in charge of the collections generally have a degree in a specialized field. Multidisciplinary museums include institutions like the Provincial Museum of Alberta, Glenbow Museum, and the University of Alberta Museums and Collections.

Museum. A museum is a non-profit institution that exists to preserve, conserve, research, interpret, and exhibit objects for purposes of educating and delighting the public.

Science Centres/Museums. Science centres and museums are educational and entertainment centres that promote science as an important part of our everyday lives. Collections are mostly objects and specimens that explain a particular scientific principle or field of study. Most of the programs and exhibits are aimed at school-aged children. The Edmonton Space and Science Centre, Calgary's Planetarium, the Energeum and the Alberta Science Centre are examples of this type of facility.

Technological/Industrial Museums. These museums collect and preserve artifacts pertaining to a particular technology or industry such as transportation, agriculture, communications, commercial, and industrial technology. The Alberta Railway Museum, Alberta Aviation Museum, Reynolds Alberta Transportation Museum, the Grain Academy Museum, Edmonton Telephone Historical Information Centre, and Fort McMurray Oil Sands Interpretive Centre are but a few of Alberta's diverse technological and industrial museums.

Occupational Museums. These are museums that focus on a particular type of work or profession. Examples of these are the Edmonton Police Museum and Archives, the Alberta Forest Service Museum, and the Alberta Association of Registered Nurses Museum.

Traditional museums are object-centred institutions in which the collections have been removed from their place of origin and reside in another facility to preserve, research, exhibit and interpret. Most museums in Alberta are traditional museums.

World Heritage Sites are natural and historic sites that have been designated by UNESCO as places having international importance. World Heritage Sites in Alberta include Wood Buffalo National Park, Dinosaur Provincial Park near Patricia, and Head Smashed In Buffalo Jump near Fort Macleod.

Zoos, Botanical Gardens, Nature Parks and Conservatories. These are classified as museums because they have living collections that are preserved, conserved, researched, interpreted, and exhibited for the purposes of public education and enjoyment. Private game farms and wildlife parks that are operated primarily for profit are not included in this guide book.

Russian Orthodox Church at Historical Village at Shandro (R.A. Hursey)

Remington-Alberta Carriage Centre-Cardston (R.A. Hursey)

TRACKING ALBERTA'S HERITAGE

MUSEUMS BY REGION

Now that you are ready to start exploring Alberta's marvelous heritage, you will want to be armed with information to help you plan your trips. That is the intention of this section of the guide. Each chapter is arranged in one- to three-day road trips. Included is an overview of the human and natural history of the communities and districts and any interesting features my "scouts" and I have observed during our excursions.

Following each overview is a directory of the museums in the area, arranged alphabetically by community. General information includes the mailing address, location, governing body, season of operation, phone number(s), minimum visiting time, and admission information. The exact charges have not been included, as these are subject to periodic change. Museums that have admission fees average from $2 to $5 per person. However, most Alberta museums do not charge admission and depend upon donations from their visitors. Specific information about each museum includes brief descriptions of the facility, its collections and any special features to be noted. Because many museums change the hours of operation from year to year, specific hours have not been included in this guide book. It is best to call ahead or check at the local visitor centre to find out the hours of operation.

Symbols Used in this Book

Parking 🚗   Wheelchair Access ♿   Guided Tours 👥
Self-guided Tours ↱   Walking Trails 🚶   Gift Shop 🎁
Picnic Area ⛱   Camping ⛺   Concessions 🍴   Restaurant 🍽
Accommodations 🛏   Bird Watching 🦅

🏆 Museums that are primarily of interest to local residents.

🏆 🏆 Museums worth visiting if you are in the area.

🏆 🏆 🏆 Museums worth going out of your way to see.

🏆 🏆 🏆 🏆 Museums that are definite tourist attractions, worth making a special trip to see.

🏆 🏆 🏆 🏆 🏆 Museums that are destination museums or world class tourist attractions

1

CROWSNEST PASS AREA—HIGHWAY 3

If you are beginning your exploration of Alberta's heritage in the southwest corner of Alberta, prepare yourself for an adventure. The area is not only rich in mining history and geology, but it is one of the most scenic drives you can find anywhere. The Crowsnest Pass area along Highway 3 starts at the Alberta-British Columbia border, where Crowsnest Mountain stands guard to the gateway of a beautiful valley. If you are a fly fisherman as well as a heritage hunter, this area will truly be paradise-on-earth. The Crowsnest River is one of the best fly fishing streams in western Canada.

My scout and I were entranced by this land of strong winds, awe-inspiring mountains, trout streams, and the string of mining towns that appear frozen in its coal mining past. Appearances, however, are deceptive. These are not ghost towns; they are vibrant communities that make up the Municipality of Crowsnest Pass. The people of Coleman, Blairmore, Frank, Hillcrest, and Bellevue have weathered good times, when coal was king, and the bad times, when mines closed down.

Although the mines no longer operate, the five communities are developing a thriving tourism industry under the guidance of the Ecomuseum Trust and the Alberta Main Street Programme. Proud of their coal mining heritage, the people of Crowsnest Pass are telling their own fascinating story.

The communities had their beginnings in 1898. Rich coal deposits in the Crowsnest Pass region attracted American developers in the 1890s. The Canadian Pacific Railway, wary of these investors, decided to run a line from Lethbridge through Crowsnest Pass to the British Columbia interior. The railway, completed in 1898, provided a market for the coal and brought an influx of businesses, investors and miners to the area. Entrepreneurs H.L. Frank and C.P. Hill founded the mines of Frank and Hillcrest. These mines attracted immigrants from all over Europe—mostly Great Britain, France, Belgium, Czechoslovakia, and Italy—forming distinct ethnic communities.

A series of disasters wracked the area. On April 29, 1903, the whole side of Turtle Mountain slid down upon Frank, burying part of the community of 600 people with millions of tons of limestone. About 70 people were killed. An explosion at the Bellevue mine on December 9, 1910, caused the deaths of 31 miners. Then on June 19, 1914, Canada's worst mining disaster occurred when methane gas ignited, causing an explosion at the Hillcrest Mine that killed 189 of the 235 men who were on shift. You cannot fail to see the results of the Frank Slide disaster as you drive through the area.

Frank, Alberta the day after the slide (Glenbow Archives, Calgary, Alberta NA 411-9)

Frank Slide Interpretive Centre brings to life this once thriving community of 600 people and tells the tragic story of the disaster through exhibits and a moving multimedia slide presentation. The centre overlooks the rubble—a mute testament to the many lost lives. A few kilometers east of the interpretive centre is a turnoff to the **Hillcrest Cemetery**, where the remains of 189 miners are buried together in three mass graves.

The Remarkable Survival of Baby Marian

One of the most miraculous survivals of the Frank Slide was baby Marian Leitch. When the side of Turtle Mountain tumbled down on the Frank community at 4:10 a.m., April 29, 1903, baby Marian Leitch miraculously survived the disaster that instantly killed her parents and four brothers. She was flung from the top story of her home, clear of the rubble that killed most of her family. In the dawn hours, rescuers pulled her two sisters from the destruction. They had escaped with a few bruises, but the baby was nowhere to be found. Later, a neighbor woman heard the cries of baby Marian and found her in a hay pile several yards from the house.

For those seeking more adventure, take a tour into the **Bellevue Underground Mine,** but not if you're claustrophobic.

At the turn of the century, Bellevue had its share of mining accidents, but before closing in 1961, the mine was considered one of the safest coal mines in Canada. Today you can share some of the miners' experiences. You will don a hard hat equipped with a battery powered light. A well-trained interpreter will lead you through the tunnel entrance into a strange world of darkness, where temperatures vary little from summer to winter. You will learn about the beginnings of coal mining in Crowsnest Pass, the evolution of coal mining technology, and the mine's fascinating history.

While you are in the Crowsnest area you will want to visit the **Coleman Journal Building**, where you will see an early handset press in operation. The owner of the newspaper never upgraded to linotype machines, and when he died in 1970, his widow closed the building, leaving intact all the presses and equipment. Also plan on spending some time wandering **Blairmore's Main Street**; many of the buildings have been restored to their former grandeur. For information about other local sites of interest, you can inquire at the **Crowsnest Pass Ecomuseum Trust** in Blairmore.

Emilio Picariello, Rumrunner

From 1916 to 1923, Alberta was a dry province. The possession of liquor for other than scientific, medical or sacramental purposes was considered illegal. Prohibition launched a new illicit industry of bootleggers and rumrunners. The Alberta Provincial Police (APP) was formed in 1916 largely to control the illicit trade of booze. Because the force was small (only 125 men), poorly organized, and not adverse to some bribery among the ranks, the APP was mostly ineffectual in dealing with the bootleggers and rumrunners.

Emilo Picariello, a Sicilian who immigrated to Canada at the turn of the century, moved to Crowsnest Pass around 1911. His hotel in Blairmore became a front for the largest rum running operation in southern Alberta. Picariello ran liquor from B.C. to Alberta and Montana with a fleet of McLaughlin-Buicks specially equipped with extra storage for booze and bumpers reinforced with concrete for plowing through APP barricades.

On September 21, 1922, Picariello and his son, driving separate cars, were stopped by the APP at a roadblock. His son was shot and wounded as he tried to run off. When Picariello heard a rumor that his son died, he and a Mrs. Florence Lassandro (a friend of his son), armed with revolvers, shot and killed an unarmed APP constable, Steve Lawson. Picariello and Lassandro were arrested for murder; they were convicted and later hanged at the Fort Saskatchewan Prison in May of 1923. The highly publicized Picariello-Lassandro case was instrumental in bringing an end to prohibition in Alberta. Voters feared future incidents of violence and wanted the government, rather than criminals, to control the sale of liquor. In a November 1923 referendum, Alberta voters ended the eight years of prohibition.

MUSEUMS IN THE MUNICIPALITY OF CROWSNEST PASS

☛ Bellevue Underground Mine
Box 1440, Blairmore, AB T0K 0E0
Visible from Highway 3, the entrance to the mine
is off the access road into Bellevue.
Governing body: Crowsnest Pass Ecomuseum Trust, Blairmore
Open May to September. 10:00 a.m. to 5:30 p.m.
☎ 403-562-8831 * *Admission fee charged* * *Visiting time:* one hour

West Canadian Collieries Ltd. established Bellevue mine in 1903. A guided walking tour through a mine tunnel of the Bellevue coal mine brings to life the history of this mine, which operated from 1903 to 1961. Wear a miner's helmet and lamp and learn about how miners worked and the equipment they used. Be sure to wear sturdy shoes and dress warmly, as the mine is cool, even in mid-summer. Plans are to expand the tour of the mine shafts within the next few years.

☛ Coleman Journal Building
Box 1440, Blairmore, AB T0K 0E0
Downtown Coleman, across from Crowsnest Museum.
Governing body: Privately owned.
Open June to September, daily ☎ 403-562-8831
Admission fee charged *Visiting time:* one half hour

In this historic building the Coleman Journal newspaper was printed from 1921 to 1970. Learn about how hand-set printing was done on a 1930s printing press from an interpreter trained in early newspaper printing.

☛ **Crowsnest Museum**
Box 306, Coleman, AB T0K 0M0 * 7701 18th Avenue, Coleman.
Governing body: Crowsnest Historical Society
Open May 24 to Labour Day ☎ 403-563-5434
Admission by donation * *Visiting time:* one half hour
🍷 🚗 🎁 🍴 ▬

Located in the former Coleman High School, this local history museum has many interesting collections, especially related to coal mining and community history. Descriptive labels could be improved, however. But if you have lots of time to spend looking at quantities of artifacts, you will probably enjoy this museum.

☛ **Crowsnest Pass Ecomuseum**
Box 1440, Blairmore, AB T0K 0E0
13437 - 20 Avenue, Blairmore
Governing body: Crowsnest Pass Ecomuseum Trust Society
Open Year round, Monday to Friday 9:00 a.m. to 5 p.m.
☎ 403-562-8831 * *Admission by donation*
Visiting time: one half hour
🍷 🍷 🚗 ♿ 🍴 ▬

Located in the Old Courthouse in Blairmore, this is the headquarters of the Crowsnest Pass Ecomuseum. The aim of the Crowsnest Pass Ecomuseum Trust is to preserve and develop the historical and cultural diversity of the Crowsnest Pass through recreation, education, and tourism. This is the place to go to find out all there is to see and do in the area and about the existing and future historic sites in the area. The Trust will arrange group tours. Ask about the self-guided Historical Driving Tour brochures of the historic buildings in the four communities of Crowsnest Pass.

☛ **Frank Slide Interpretive Centre**
Provincial Historic Site
Box 959, Blairmore, AB T0K 0E0
One kilometer off Highway 3 between Blairmore and Bellevue.
Governing body: Historic Sites and Archives Service, Alberta Community Development
Open May 15 to Labour Day ☎ 403-562-7388
Admission fee charged * *Visiting time:* one hour
🍷 🍷 🍷 🍷 🚗 ♿ 🚻 🎁 ⛲ ♨

The museum overlooks the site of the rockslide of 1903 that buried much of the town of Frank and took 70 lives. The

Interpretive Centre's exhibits and an excellent multi-media show tell the tragic story of the rockslide and give the visitor a picture of Crowsnest Pass during the heyday of coal mining.

Frank Slide Interpretive Centre (R.A. Hursey)

☛ **Leitch Collieries Provincial Historic Site**
Box 959, Blairmore, AB T0K 0E0
On Highway 3 in the Municipality of Crowsnest Pass.
Governing body: Historic Sites and Archives Service, Alberta Community Development.
Open May 15 to Labour Day weekend **Visiting time:* one half hour
☎ 403-562-7388 * *Admission by donation*

Leitch Collieries was established in 1907 and was the largest mine in the early history of Crowsnest Pass. The company closed in 1915 due to financial problems and a decline in the coal market. The site is partially restored—mostly stabilized so that further deterioration will not occur. A trail leads to the remains of a once active and thriving mine operation. Although the outdoor interpretive signs tell the story of the company, they are not always oriented to the sites described and may cause some confusion. This is a very nice spot to stop for a picnic.

2

WATERTON LAKES NATIONAL PARK & AREA

As you drive east of the Crowsnest Pass area along Highway 3, the mountain valley widens into foothills and prairie grassland. You are entering one of the windiest parts of Alberta. In fact, you will pass by a major wind power experimental station near Pincher Creek and see huge power-generating structures bearing little resemblance to the historic prairie windmills.

Westerly breezes blow through this region most of the year. In summer, hawks and eagles ride the thermal winds that buffet and bend lodgepole pines into fantastic shapes and turn the grass into an ocean of golden waves. In the winter, warm chinook winds give reprieve through the coldest season. Cattle ranchers welcome chinooks as old friends, for the winds periodically melt the snow off the range and allow cattle to graze.

A chinook (pronounced shi-NOOK) is a warm, dry wind that sweeps down the eastern slopes of the Rocky Mountains after a Pacific storm. Air ascending the western slopes loses most of its moisture. As the air drops down the eastern slopes, pressure increases, creating warm, dry winds. You can sometimes see the effects of this warm air pushing up clouds to form a chinook arch.

Doukhobor women pulling a breaking plow near Pincher Creek. Many immigrants could not afford a draft animal. (Provincial Archives of Alberta P452)

East of Crowsnest Pass, Doukhobor settlers established the towns of Cowley and Lundbreck. About 7,000 Doukhobors, a pacifist, vegetarian religious group, came to Canada from Russia in 1899 to escape religious persecution and military conscription. They became the largest single group of immigrants to arrive in Canada at the time. Doukhobors, who settled in the Crowsnest Pass area, lived communally in thirteen colonies, growing wheat and vegetables. Today, they no longer live communally, but continue to keep alive their beliefs in the sacredness of life, pacifism, and vegetarianism.

Turning south on Highway 6, you enter the town of Pincher Creek, gateway to Waterton Lakes National Park. In the late 1870s, trading companies from Fort Benton, Montana, moved herds of cattle up into the Pincher Creek area to sell to the NWMP, stationed at an outpost near Waterton Lakes, and to the starving Peigans, who no longer had buffalo to hunt. Alarmed that so much money for beef was going south of the border, the Canadian government amended the Dominion Lands Act in 1881 to permit the leasing of large grazing areas for ranching. Most of the ranchers were politically powerful and wealthy investors from eastern Canada and Great Britain.

In 1883, the first German immigrants to Alberta settled in Pincher Creek. The discovery of major natural gas fields in 1947 has brought new prosperity to the local area.

Pincher Creek, 1883. (Provincial Archives of Alberta B2425)

To learn more about the history of Pincher Creek and the surrounding area, you will want to visit the **Pincher Creek & District Museum**. The museum includes an historical park that features a log church associated with Father Lacombe and a log house that belonged to Kootenai Brown. The **Oldman River**

Antique Equipment and Threshing Club displays early farm equipment during the summer months. In July, the club presents its annual threshing, ploughing, and seeding demonstrations.

> *Tracks and Traces:* Pincher Creek got its name from an incident involving a group of prospectors from Montana, who camped by the creek one night back in the early 1860s. One of them lost a very valuable tool, his pair of pincers. The rusted pincers were found in 1875 by a member of the NWMP detachment that arrived in the area to establish a post.

Driving east of Pincher Creek on Highway 3, you enter the reserve of the Peigan band. The Peigan are part of the Blackfoot Confederacy that includes the Blood, the Sarcee, and the Blackfoot. The **Oldman River Dam** is visible from the highway. This large earthen dam has been the centre of controversy for years between many environmentalists and members of the Peigan Nation on one side and the provincial government and farmers in need of water to irrigate crops on the other.

East of the dam you enter the town of Brocket, headquarters of the Peigan Nation. At Brocket, the **Oldman River Cultural Centre** displays a collection of native tools, beadwork, and other artifacts related to the history of the Peigan Nation.

If you are heading south from Pincher Creek on Highway 6 to Waterton Lakes National Park, you will be driving through some of the most spectacular scenery in Alberta. Here the Rocky Mountains thrust up right out of the prairies. My scout and I had many Kodak moments along this route. Entering Waterton Lakes National Park is like entering a time warp. This is land sacred to the Blackfoot who wintered here, long before Europeans arrived.

Waterton Lakes National Park and the Glacier National Park in Montana are linked historically and form the Glacier-Waterton International Peace Park. Waterton Lake, the deepest in the Rockies, is the water link between the two parks. The lake has always been a sacred place to Natives on both sides of the international boundary.

Waterton was the site of western Canada's first producing oil well. John George "Kootenai" Brown and other settlers used the bitumen oozing out of the ground as a lubricant for wagon wheels and medicine for their cattle. The Rocky Mountain Development Company, based in Calgary, began drilling here in 1901. The following year it struck oil and started a small oil boom. Although short lived, the boom lasted long enough to establish the town site of Waterton. In June 1911, the federal government established Waterton Lakes Dominion Park, largely in response to the active lobbying of Kootenai Brown and other guides concerned about saving the wildlife of the area.

The town of Waterton, headquarters for the national park, looks much the same as it did in the 1920s and 1930s. The **Waterton Heritage Centre** on Main Street occupies the former fire station. The centre has all the information you need to begin your heritage hunting of the park's human and natural history.

High above the town is the **Prince of Wales Hotel**, the largest wood constructed building in Alberta. The hotel, which first opened its doors in 1927, commands a magnificent view of Waterton Lake and the rugged mountains that surround it. For a very special adventure, you will want to board the excursion boat, *The International*. The 250-passenger motor vessel has been ferrying visitors from the Waterton townsite at Emerald Bay to the U.S. side, at Goat Haunt, Montana, since 1928. The USA's Northern Railway built and financed this floating historic treasure.

Prince of Wales Hotel, Waterton. (Courtesy of Alberta Historical Resources Foundation, Medicine Hat Museum and Art Gallery, and James Marshall)

"Kootenai" Brown

John George "Kootenai" Brown
(Glenbow Archives, Calgary, Alberta
NA-2654-1)

John George "Kootenai" Brown was one of the most colorful characters to settle in southern Alberta. Born and educated in Britain, he served in the British Army in India in the 1850s, before the lure of gold attracted him to British Columbia in 1861. There he worked as a miner and constable. Later he became a buffalo hunter in Manitoba and a pony express rider for the U.S. Army. After being captured by Sitting Bull's Sioux Indians, he escaped and moved to Montana where he met and married Olive Lyonais, a Métis woman. He was arrested for killing a fur trader at Fort Benton in 1877, but he was acquitted. The same year, he moved his family across the border to Waterton Lakes (originally called Kootenai Lakes) where he ran a trading post for many years and guided visitors to the area. During the Riel Rebellion in 1885, Brown served as Chief Scout with the Rocky Mountain Rangers for three months. Returning to Waterton, he became one of the chief advocates in having the area proclaimed a national park. In 1911, at 71 years of age, he became Waterton Dominion Park's first park warden and held the position until he died in 1916.

Leaving Waterton Park, go east on Highway 5 to Cardston. Here we enter ranching country, rolling hills of rich grassland and splendid vistas. Look for Yellow-bellied Marmots sunning on the rocks along the Waterton River in the early summer.

Mormons settled Cardston. They came from Utah in 1887 to escape religious persecution and antipolygamy laws. They formed the largest single group of Americans to settle in Alberta and were also the first successful farmers with their knowledge of irrigation.

Cardston is named after its founder, Charles Ora Card, who chose this area for its fertile soil and accessibility to water for irrigation and for timber and coal. Today's Cardston is part of the Alberta Main Street Programme. Many of the older buildings on Main Street have been restored and businesses revitalized under the programme.

Zina Young Card (1850 - 1931)

Zina Card, third wife of Charles Ora Card, represents the best of Alberta's pioneers. After travelling 800 miles by covered wagon, the Cards and ten other families established the first Mormon settlement in Alberta. Zina, a daughter of Brigham Young, provided support to her husband and family, spiritual and social leadership to the community, and hospitality to all who came to the log home, called "the Cotton Flannel Palace" by Charles because she had lined the walls with colored flannel fabric. She used the money she received from her father's estate to fund many of Cardston's building projects. To the community she was known affectionately as "Aunt Zina."

When you drive around Cardston, you will notice the streets, typical of communities founded by the Church of Jesus Christ of Latter-Day Saints (Mormons), designed to be wide enough to enable a horse team and wagon to make a 180° turn. At Cardston's highest point sits the **Alberta Temple**. Built in 1923, it was the first Mormon temple constructed outside the United States. Although the inner temple is accessible only to Mormons, the visitor's centre is open to the public.

A block off Main Street is the **Court House Museum**. Built of local sandstone in 1907, it was one of the first courthouses in Alberta. The museum features the pioneer history of the Cardston area. On the main street is a small log structure that seems out of place among its two-story brick neighbors. The **Card Pioneer Home** is a registered Provincial Historic Site. Built in 1887, it served as a community centre and stopping place for travellers before the first hotel was built in 1894.

Continuing south on Main Street, you will come to the **Remington-Alberta Carriage Centre**. This provincially run museum features a magnificent collection of 19th and early 20th century horse-drawn transportation and interprets the historical importance of horse-drawn carriages. Be sure to take a ride in one of the vintage carriages pulled by Clydesdales and other horses kept on the grounds.

Card Pioneer Home (R.A. Hursey)

Tracks and Traces: Fay Wray, star of Hollywood silent films, was born in 1907 on a ranch southwest of Cardston. Her most famous role was in *King Kong*, produced in 1933. Her career spanned 33 years, during which time she played in nearly 80 films.

MUSEUMS IN THE WATERTON PARK AREA

☞ **Oldman River Cultural Centre** at *Brocket*
Box 70, Brocket, AB T0K 0H0
Governing body: Oldman River Centre Board
Open Year round * *Phone:* 403-965-3939
Admission by donation * *Visiting time:* one half hour

The centre is located on the Peigan Reserve. Artifacts include Native tools, beadwork, clothing, paintings, and natural history specimens. The main activities of the cultural centre are to do research on the collection and make reproductions of the original artifacts.

☞ **Card Pioneer Home** at *Cardston*
Box 1830, Cardston, AB T0K 0K0 * Located on Main Street
Governing body: Cardston & District Historical Society
Open June through August * *Phone:* 403-653-4322
Admission by donation * *Visiting time:* one half hour

🍷 🍷 🚗 ⛨ 🍴 ▬

Built in 1887 by Cardston's founder, Charles Ora Card, this home served as a community centre and a stopping place for travellers before the first hotel was constructed in 1894. The Card Pioneer Home is a log structure and Registered Provincial Historic Site on its original location.

☞ **Court House Museum**
Box 1830, Cardston, AB T0K 0K0 * 89 - 3rd Avenue West
Governing body: Cardston & District Historical Society
Open June through August * *Phone:* 403-763-4322
Admission by donation * *Visiting time:* one half hour

🍷 🍷 🚗 ⛨ 🎁 🍴 ▬

The museum is located in Cardston's original courthouse, built in 1907. One of the first courthouses in Alberta, the building was constructed of sandstone quarried a few miles from Cardston. This designated Provincial Historic Site has the original judge's bench and witness stand. In the basement are jail cells, now used for exhibits. The collections pertain to the history of the area. A square grand piano c1876 is one of the feature artifacts. A National Film Board photo display shows the lifestyle of a local Hutterite community.

☞ **Remington-Alberta Carriage Centre**
Box 1649, Cardston, AB, T0K 0K0 * Located on Main Street
Governing body: Alberta Community Development,
Historic Sites & Archives Service
Open year round except Christmas, New Year's Day and Easter Sunday
Phone: 403-653-5139 * *Admission charge* * *Visiting time:* one and a half hours

🍷 🍷 🍷 ♿ ⛨ 🎁 🍴 ▬

The Remington-Alberta Carriage Centre houses a unique collection of horse-drawn vehicles. The core of the collection is 49 carriages donated by Donald Remington, a Cardston businessman who began collecting and restoring carriages in the 1950s. There are more than 200 carriages at the Centre, on display in the main gallery and in a large open storage area where the visitor can walk through and learn more about history of horse-drawn transportation. Rides are available on vintage carriages pulled by Clydesdales and other breeds.

☞ **Oldman River Antique Farm Equipment and Threshing Club**
at *Pincher Creek* * Box 2496, Pincher Creek, AB T0K 1W0
Governing body: Oldman River Antique Equipment and Threshing Club
Open June through August * *Phone:* 403-627-4130
Admission by donation * *Visiting time:* one half hour

The club collects and restores antique farm equipment and holds annual threshing, ploughing, and seeding demonstrations every July.

☞ **Pincher Creek & District Museum**
Box 1226, Pincher Creek, AB T0K 1W0 * Located at James Avenue
Governing body: Pincher Creek & District Historical Society
Open May 1 to September 15 * *Phone:* 403-627-3684
Admission fee charged * *Visiting time:* one half hour

The museum has a historical park. It includes an early NWMP detachment cabin, a log church associated with Father Lacombe, the log house of Kootenai Brown, and one from the Walron Ranch.

☞ **Waterton Heritage Centre**
Box 145, Waterton National Park, AB T0K 2M0 * 306 Waterton Avenue
Governing body: The Waterton Natural History Association and the
Canadian Parks Service
Open May through September * *Phone:* 403-859-2624
Admission by donation * *Visiting time:* one half hour

Located in the old fire hall, this museum provides displays on the natural and human history of Waterton National Park. Collections include natural history specimens, photographs, paintings, and artifacts. The centre offers heritage education programs. An excellent bookstore on the premises has a variety of historical and natural history publications. Families can rent Activikits that provide entertainment activities teaching children about the wildlife and plants of the area.

3

LETHBRIDGE & AREA

L ethbridge has so many stories to show and tell that you might want to spend a couple of days there heritage hunting. Lethbridge is the third largest city in the province, with a population of 60,000. If you come into town going east on Highway 3, you will get the most dramatic view of the city, which perches on top of a deep coulee overlooking the Oldman River. The river alone holds many fascinating stories.

The Native history of the area reaches back long before the founding of Lethbridge. About 1500 years ago, bison hunters, classified by archaeologists as Neo-Indians, sojourned here. Small, triangular arrow points with tiny side notches called Avonlea points, have been excavated near Lethbridge at a site along the Oldman River. On its banks, just below the downtown area, sits Indian Battle Park. The park commemorates a famous battle fought between the Blackfoot Confederacy (Siksika, Peigan, Blood, and Sarcee) and the Cree and their allies, the Assiniboine (Stony).

The Cree and Blackfoot were traditional enemies and continually tested the boundaries of each other's hunting territories. Sensing the weakness of the Blackfoot from the smallpox epidemic of 1868-69, a war party of about 800 Cree and Assiniboine planned a sneak attack on October 25, 1870, on a band of Bloods camped along the banks of the Oldman River within the present city limits of Lethbridge. Unknown to the Cree, a band of Peigans were camped on the other side of the river. Approximately 1000 warriors of the Blackfoot Confederacy crossed the river and surrounded the Cree and Assiniboine. About 350 Cree and Assiniboine and 50 to 60 Bloods and Peigans were killed.

Fort Whoop-Up, a replica of an infamous whisky trading post, is located at Indian Battle Park. The historic Fort Whoop-Up was located near the junction of the Oldman and St. Mary's Rivers. By the 1860s, buffalo hides were in demand in the eastern industrial areas to make belts to drive machinery. The bison herds on the Northern Plains had quickly begun to be exploited (as well as the Plains People who provided the hides). Two American traders, J. J. Healy and Alfred Hamilton, appeared from Fort Benton, Montana, in 1869 and opened Fort Hamilton, the first of several whisky-trading forts along the "Whoop-Up Trail." Their evil mixture of watered-down whisky, tea leaves, molasses, tobacco, and other noxious ingredients was traded for tens of thousands of dollars worth of buffalo hides. The whisky trade disastrously affected the Blackfoot in southern Alberta and contributed not only to the end of the bison herds but also to the end of the Blackfoot's traditional way of life.

The notorious Fort Whoop-Up, and other American incursions into southern Alberta, became a concern to the Canadian government. To locate Fort Whoop-Up, the NWMP hired Jeremy Potts, a Métis from Fort Benton, as a guide. The detachment arrived at Fort Whoop-Up in October after an arduous journey. But, having had advanced warning of the NWMP's arrival, the traders fled the fort.

Jerry Potts (c1840 - 1896)

Born to Scottish and Blood Indian parents, Jerry Potts was a Métis guide and plainsman who led the detachment of bedraggled and hungry North-West Mounted Police to their destination—Fort Whoop-Up. Unable to find this elusive fort and very close to the end of their food and supplies, the NWMP, under the command of Lieutenant-Colonel G. A. French, detoured south to Fort Benton for much needed supplies. While there, French hired Jerry Potts to guide them to Fort Whoop-Up. He was successful in leading the mounties to the notorious fort. He also picked the location of the first NWMP post, Fort Macleod, on the Oldman River. Potts worked with the NWMP for 22 years and was given a rank of special constable. Following his death in 1896, Potts was buried with full honors at Fort Macleod.

Lethbridge has been called other names throughout its history. The Blackfoot, Cree, and Sarcee Indians had their own names for this area, which roughly translated to "the place of the black rocks." The area later became Sheran's Ferry, after Nicholas Sheran, a former whisky trader, who first began mining the banks of the river in 1874 and selling the coal to the NWMP at Fort Macleod. When it became known that the CPR would be running its line through southern Alberta, it attracted the interest of entrepreneurs to provide the railway, a large potential market, with coal. Even before the CPR completed the line to Lethbridge in 1885, several British investors led by Sir Alexander Galt had formed the North Western Coal and Navigation Company. The company began operations in 1882 at Coalbanks (now Lethbridge). Galt unofficially named the mining community after his friend, William Lethbridge, a wealthy English lawyer and investor and president of the North Western Coal and Navigation Company. The name was officially changed to

Lethbridge in 1885. Lethbridge never actually visited the town that bore his name.

Elliott T. Galt (1850 - 1928)

Elliott T. Galt was the son of Sir Alexander Galt, one of the Fathers of Confederation. E.T. Galt was 30 years old and the Assistant Indian Commissioner at the time he first visited Sheran's coal mine and realized the potential of the rich coal deposits in the area. In 1881, the opportunity to use the coal deposits arose when the Canadian Pacific Railway decided to cross the southern plains instead of the Yellowhead route to the Pacific Coast. Sir Alexander Galt organized British investors and financiers and in April 1882 formed the North West Coal and Navigation Company (NWC & NCo).

Elliott Galt and his family moved to Coalbanks in 1883 and lived in Lethbridge until 1905, when ill health forced him to give up active management of the family companies. The NWC & NCo's original plan was to ship coal by steamboats down the Oldman and the South Saskatchewan Rivers. The Galts built *The Baroness,* a 53-metre sternwheeler, and the 36.5-metre *Alberta,* as well as a small fleet of barges. River transportation never proved very successful due to problems with low water. In the fall of 1884, the Galts began construction of a narrow gauge railway from Coalbanks to Dunmore on the CPR mainline near Medicine Hat. The first train arrived on August 25, 1885, three months before the town's name officially changed to Lethbridge. For many years the NWC&NCo was the largest producers of coal in the Northwest Territories.

After his father's death in 1896, Elliott Galt became the general manager of the all family-owned companies. In 1905, ill health forced him to give up active management, and the Galts moved from Lethbridge. Elliott Galt left many legacies to the community he built, including the Galt Hospital, which is now the **Sir Alexander Galt Museum.** Shortly before his death in 1928, Elliott Galt donated the Galt Gardens to the city of Lethbridge.

Lethbridge enjoys a rich ethnic history. Coal mining and construction of the CPR brought in workers from Great Britain, Italy, and eastern Europe. A small group of Chinese immigrants arrived in southern Alberta around 1885 to build the railway line. Many remained in Lethbridge to open restaurants and laundries—the few businesses allowed them by the predominantly white Anglo-Protestant society. For many years Lethbridge had the second largest Chinatown in Alberta (the largest was in Calgary). The remains of the original Chinatown in Lethbridge is now a historic site. Italian immigrants who had worked with the CPR remained in Lethbridge to work in the coal mine. Most of the miners came from Great Britain, but in the 1920s, Slovaks and other Eastern Europeans came to work in the over 40 mining shafts along the banks of the river at Lethbridge, Coalhurst, and Taber.

Galt Hospital, Lethbridge. c1901 (Provincial Archives of Alberta A7633)

Ranches flourished in the Lethbridge area beginning in the mid-1880s. After the turn of the century, crop farming surpassed ranching as the primary agricultural industry. The federal government, the North Western Coal and Navigation Company and the Mormon Church launched one of the earliest and largest irrigation projects in 1898. Elliott Galt had become the sponsor for the large-scale irrigation project in 1893 after Charles Ora Card convinced him that irrigation would open up the soil-rich but drought-ridden land for farming. Card had bought land from the NWC & NCo near the St. Mary and Waterton rivers in 1887. Galt entered into an agreement with the Mormon church and formed the Alberta Railway Irrigation Company (AR&I). The Church provided labourers for the construction of the irrigation ditches. In August 1896, the first furrow was excavated and by 1900, 153 kilometres of canals were completed.

Irrigation brought Mormon settlers from the U.S. to farm irrigated crops, mostly sugar beets, in the areas south of Lethbridge and around Magrath and Raymond. A few Japanese came to Lethbridge to work on the railway and farm the irrigated sugar beet fields. By the 1920s Lethbridge had surpassed Medicine Hat as the largest community in southern Alberta, with a population of 21,000 and thriving businesses that served the mining and farming communities.

More recently, Lethbridge experienced a large influx of Japanese-Canadians during the Second World War, when the federal government forced them to leave the Vancouver area and relocate in other parts of Canada. Many families were sent to work for sugar beet farmers in the Lethbridge area. Lethbridge also housed a German POW camp during the war. POW Camp No. 133, completed in November 1942, was designed to hold 12,500 prisoners on 638 acres of land, now within the Lethbridge city limits. Many of first prisoners who arrived on November 28 had been captured in North Africa. The POWs eased the shortage of farm labour and were employed in the 1943 and 1944 harvests. Some 6000 POWs worked on southern Alberta farms until June 1946.

You can learn more about the history of Lethbridge by visiting **Sir Alexander Galt Museum**, one of the finest museums in southern Alberta. Located in the former Galt Hospital, which is now a Provincial Historic Resource, the Galt Museum focuses on the mining, railway, and history of Lethbridge and area. **Fort Whoop-Up Interpretive Centre,** a history museum, brings to life the area's Native and NWMP history. To learn about the agricultural history of the region, drive north on Highway 25 to Picture Butte and the **Prairie Acres Heritage Village & Farm Equipment Museum.** The natural history of the area is told by the **Helen Schuler Coulee Centre & Nature Reserve.** Two art museums attest to the importance of Lethbridge as a visual arts centre in southern Alberta—the **University of Lethbridge Art Gallery** and the **Southern Alberta Art Gallery.**

The **Nikka Yuko Japanese Garden** should be one of your main stops in Lethbridge. Housed on four acres, the garden opened in 1967 as a joint centennial project by the City of Lethbridge and the Japanese-Canadian community. It features a Japanese pavilion with a tea ceremony room where hostesses are dressed in traditional kimonos. Walking around the garden left a lasting impression on my scout and me. It is a place you will want to revisit each season of the year. Don't miss this extraordinarily beautiful garden for a relaxing break in your heritage travels.

Nikka Yuko Japanese Garden. (RLHursey)

Tracks and Traces: The "Old Man" in Oldman River derives from the Cree *wi-suk-i-ushak*, who is a mythical character with supernatural powers. In Blackfoot, his name is *napia-otzi-kagh-tzipi*, or *Napi.*

MUSEUMS IN LETHBRIDGE AND AREA

☞ **Alberta Birds of Prey Centre**
Box 1494, Coaldale, AB T0K 0L0 * Coaldale, Alberta
Governing body: Alberta Birds of Prey Foundation
Open May to October * ☎ (403) 345-4262
Admission fee charged *Visiting time:* one hour

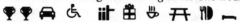

The Alberta Birds of Prey Centre is a living history museum featuring eagles, hawks, falcons, owls, and vultures from Alberta and around the world. This centre has about 200 birds of prey, of which about 50 are on display to the public. The centre is dedicated to public education, the breeding, rehabilitation, and release of raptors (birds of prey).

☞ **Fort Whoop-Up Interpretive Centre**
Mailing address: Box 1047, Indian Battle Park, Lethbridge, AB T1J 4A2
Governing body: Fort Whoop-Up Interpretive Society
Open Mid-May to Labour Day. daily; winter, closed Monday and Saturday
☎ (403) 329-0444 * *Admission fee charged* *Visiting time:* one hour

Located in a beautiful valley setting, Fort Whoop-Up is an authentic replica of the original whisky trading fort in the late 1860s and early 1870s. The Interpretive Centre's exhibits and programs give the visitor an excellent background of this notorious fort, and the interpretive programs bring to life its fascinating history. Children will enjoy the "hands-on" experiences, live performances, and storytelling. Demonstrations in the blacksmith and carpenter's shop are presented in the summer. Collections include a wide range of furs, trading goods, tools, and native artifacts.

☞ **Sir Alexander Galt Museum**
910 4th Avenue S, Lethbridge, AB T1J 0P6 * West end of 5th Avenue South
Governing Body: City of Lethbridge * Open Year round, daily
☎ (403) 320-3898 * Admission by donation * *Visiting time:* One hour

Located in the former Galt hospital, now a Provincial Historic Resource, the Galt Museum focuses on the history and development of Lethbridge and area. It has a wide range of excellent collections related to the coal mining, railroad, commercial and social history of Lethbridge. A unique display features a replica of a drift coal mine. There is also an excellent viewing gallery overlooking the Oldman River Valley and the CPR high level bridge. The museum successfully interprets the rich heritage of Lethbridge.

☞ **Helen Schuler Coulee Centre**
Mailing address: 910 4th Avenue S, Lethbridge, AB T1J 0P6
Indian Battle Park, 3rd Avenue and Scenic Drive S.
Governing body: City of Lethbridge
Open June to August, daily; September to May, closed on Mondays.
☎ (403) 320-3064 * Admission by donation * *Visiting time:* one hour

Located north of the CPR high level bridge at Indian Battle Park, this 196-acre urban nature centre interprets the natural history of the area. The reserve has many desert-like species including the Prickly Pear Cactus, Rock Wren and the Prairie Rattlesnake. Learn about the natural history of the area through its hands-on exhibits, organized group tours, and self-guided walking tours.

☞ **Nikka Yuko Japanese Garden**
Mailing address: Box 751, Lethbridge, AB T1J 3Z6
Mayor Magrath Drive (Highway 5), between 7th and 10th Avenues S.
Governing body: Lethbridge & District Japanese Garden Society
Open mid-May to end of September, daily * ☎ (403) 328-3511
*Admission fee charged *Visiting time:* One hour

"Nikka Yuko" means Japan-Canadian friendship. Built in 1967 as a centennial project by the City of Lethbridge and the Lethbridge & District Japanese Garden Society, the garden covers four acres and primarily features native species of plants. The pavilion provides the main focal point of the four-acre garden, which includes a "dry garden" and tea ceremony room. Hostesses, dressed in traditional kimonos, welcome visitors into the pavilion and explain its purpose and traditions. Walk through the garden slowly; contemplate its many surprises at each turn of the path. The bell tower and five-tiered pagoda, the many lanterns and ponds, streams, and waterfalls create a miniature world of perfection and a feast for the senses.

☞ **Southern Alberta Art Gallery**
Mailing address: 601 - 3rd Avenue S, Lethbridge, AB, T1J 0H4
Downtown Lethbridge in Galt Gardens, 601 - 3rd Avenue S.
Governing body: SAAG Association
Open June to August, daily; September to May, closed on Mondays
☎ (403) 327-8770 * *Admission by donation *Visiting time:* one half hour

---

Located in the former Lethbridge Public Library, the SAAG has three galleries that show mainly contemporary exhibits of local, regional, and national artists. The museum houses the City of Lethbridge art collection including the Buchanan bequest. When my scout and I visited this art gallery, we were a bit disappointed that the main gallery featured works from the UL Art Gallery collections rather than from its own collections.

☞ **University of Lethbridge Art Gallery**
4401 University Drive, Lethbridge, AB T1K 3M4
Governing body: UL Board of Governors * Open Year round
☎ (403) 329-2690 **Admission by donation *Visiting time:* one half hour

---

This art gallery has a large collection of 19th and 20th century Canadian, American, and European art, as well as Inuit and Amerindian art and crafts from all over North America. Its annual gallery exhibitions feature selections from the permanent collection. The gallery also hosts local, provincial, and national travelling exhibits; has an applied studies program; and includes a study collection centre and a loan program.

☞ **Prairie Acres Heritage Village and Farm Equipment Museum**
at Picture Butte
Box 768, Picture Butte, AB T0K 1V0
2.4 kilometers south of the village of Picture Butte, SR 843.
Governing body: Prairie Tractor & Engine Society * Open on request
☎ (403) 732-4067 * Admission by donation, except for special shows
Visiting time: one hour

🍷🍷 🚗 👫 ⛩

As this museum does not yet have regular opening hours, you will need to make advance arrangements for your visit, but it is well worth the trouble. Don't be put off by the "back forty" collection of old rusted machinery awaiting restoration. It overlooks a deep coulee and an old wagon road. This museum has a unique collection of sugar beet planting and harvesting equipment. Members will give you a personal tour and tell you the history of sugar beet farming in the area. Many of the steam and early diesel tractors are restored and fully operational. The beginnings of a heritage village include a CPR station, the earliest Christian Reformed Church in Alberta, and a 1930s auto shop, complete with the old-style gravity gasoline pumps.

☞ **Taber & District Museum**
Box 2734, Taber, AB T0K 2G0 * Taber Civic Centre Complex
Governing body: Taber & District Historical Society
Open Year round Monday to Friday * ☎ (403) 223-5708
Admission by donation *Visiting time:* one half hour

🍷 🚗 ♿ ⛩ ⛺ 🍴 —

The museum has artifacts reflecting the history of the Taber area.

4

MACLEOD TRAIL—HIGHWAY 2

D riving along the Macleod Trail (Highway 2) between Fort Macleod and Calgary, you will encounter long vistas of golden grasslands and rolling hills that join the great grey wall of the Canadian Rockies. The drive is worth a leisurely journey with many stops along the way. Imagine this stretch of prairie without highways, powerlines, and barbed wire fences, and you can visualize what this foothills country looked like 100 years ago. The buffalo were gone by then. The Blackfoot people had signed Treaty 7 and moved onto reserves. In their place came entrepreneurs from eastern Canada and the British Isles to establish large cattle ranches. It is still ranch country, but now most stockmen ride the range in pickups and on all-terrain vehicles instead of horses.

The foothills country is rich in wildlife, especially ducks and geese in the low-lying marshy areas along the route. Throughout the summer you can hear the hauntingly beautiful song of the Western Meadowlark. During the month of June you can see Richardson's ground squirrels surfacing from their burrows after their long hibernation. At this time of year they are easy prey for coyotes and hawks. On rare occasions you may see Golden Eagles riding the thermals. On one memorable trip through this area, I watched the courtship display of a pair of hawks flying in circles and joining together, talons clasped in a climactic spin.

The first stop along the way will be a journey back in time to **Head-Smashed-In Buffalo Jump,** about 13 kilometres west of Fort Macleod. Designated a World Heritage Site by UNESCO, Queen Elizabeth II formally opened it in the summer of 1987. After leaving Highway 2 going west on Highway 765, you may begin to wonder if such a place actually exists, because you won't see the Interpretive Centre until you are almost on top of it. The building is so unobtrusive that it seems to sink into the rock itself. If you take the upper trail to the top of the cliff, you have a magnificent view of the plains and the distant river valley. To your left, however, is an unsightly shed that interrupts your view of the best part of the jump site.

Head-Smashed-In is one of many buffalo jump sites found around Alberta that Indians used to kill buffalo. A buffalo jump was just one way that Native people hunted bison. Before the Blackfoot acquired horses and guns in the mid-1700s, their hunting methods depended largely upon the cooperation of many individuals and a thorough understanding of the bison's behavior. This archaeological site reveals a continuous, if intermittent, use by Native people for running herds of bison to their deaths for over 5000 years. The last time they used it for this purpose was about 180 years ago. The Interpretive Centre not only explains the use of the site but examines the traditional lifestyle of prehistoric Plains Indian culture and the changes in this lifestyle after the arrival of the Europeans. One display shows how archeologists work to uncover the past. During the summer you can also observe archeologists at work. There are local Native interpreters who will answer your questions or conduct group tours.

Tracks and Traces: How Head-Smashed-In got its name.

According to one legend, a young brave about 150 years ago wanted to observe the buffalo cascading over the cliff. During the hunt he positioned himself just under the sandstone cliff. So many buffalo plunged to their deaths that their bodies piled up, trapping the brave between the dead animals and the cliff. When he was discovered later by those who came to do the butchering, his skull was crushed by the weight of the buffalo. From then on the site was known as "Head-Smashed-In."

Head-Smashed-In Buffalo Jump
(R.A. Hursey)

After leaving Head-Smashed-In, you will want to return to Fort Macleod for some more heritage hunting. After dealing with the problem of Fort Whoop-Up, Colonel James Macleod and his detachment headed north to build a fort on the Oldman River. Built in 1847, it became the first North West Mounted Police fort established in Alberta. Macleod had taken the advice of Jerry Potts, their Métis guide, and chose the location on an island in the river where there was plenty of pasture for their horses and trees to build the fort.

Today, Fort Macleod is a thriving community of about 3000 people. The **Fort Museum** on the west end of Fort Macleod is a replica of the original fort. You will definitely want to spend some time here taking in all there is to see and do. Behind the wooden palisades a rustic village brings to life the history of the NWMP and the RCMP. Its many buildings house artifacts dealing with Native culture, mounted police history, and ranching. One of the main features includes the daily performances of the Fort Museum Mounted Musical Ride. Riders wearing replica NWMP uniforms take the dark bay quarter horses through their paces. It is hard to determine who enjoys it most—riders, horses, or spectators. The Fort Museum, built in 1956-57, is one of the oldest historical villages in western Canada.

Fort Museum and Macleod's main street (R.A. Hursey)

Fort Macleod is designated a Provincial Historic Area, the first of this type of designation. In the early 1980s, Fort Macleod was part of the Main Street Canada Programme, which guided the community in the restoration and revitalization of its downtown. If you are looking for a place that is the quintessential southern Alberta community, Fort Macleod comes very close, as it has been touched by most of the major historical events in southern Alberta. A self-guided "Walking Tour of Fort Macleod" will introduce you to a number of restored historical buildings like the old Empress Theatre, the American Hotel and the Silver Grill. Each building has its own special story to tell. My scout and I were very impressed by the town's friendly, helpful people.

> **Tracks and Traces:** Fort Macleod's Silver Grill on Main Street has a large mirror behind an ornate turn-of-the-century bar. Local legend has it that around 1912 the mirror was shattered by a bullet during a skirmish in the cafe.

Leaving Fort Macleod, go north on Highway 2 to Claresholm. This foothills community is in the heart of ranching and crop farming country. The **Claresholm Museum** is one of many local history museums housed in a former CPR railway station. The **Appaloosa Horse Club of Canada Museum** is dedicated to the history and promotion of the Appaloosa. Unfortunately, neither museum was open during its posted hours when we toured this area. It is best to check locally for any changes in hours of operation.

Louise Crummy McKinney (1868 - 1931)

Born in Ontario, Louise McKinney moved to the Claresholm area with her family in 1903. Founder and president of the Women's Christian Temperance Movement, she fought for prohibition, social reform, women's suffrage, and an end to illiteracy. She was also against non-Anglo-Saxon immigration. In 1917, McKinney ran for the agrarian Non-Partisan League in the Claresholm constituency, and became the first woman legislator in Canada, a position she held until 1921. She is perhaps best remembered as one of the "Famous Five" Alberta women who lobbied to get women declared as "persons" (along with lunatics) under the British North America Act in 1928, thus allowing women to be appointed to the Senate.

> **Tracks and Traces:** The name "Claresholm" has uncertain origins. It may have been named after the wife of CPR superintendent Niblock. It was more likely named after a woman named Clare, who ran a boarding house at this place where the railway line between Calgary and Fort Macleod was being constructed.

About 40 kilometres north of Claresholm on Highway 2 is the town of Nanton, home of the **Nanton Lancaster Society Air Museum.** For those who salivate over historic aircraft, this museum will definitely satisfy those cravings. On display you will find a restored Lancaster, the most successful four-engine bomber used by the RAF Bomber Command in World War II. This Lancaster is one of the 430 built in Canada. The museum relates the history and importance of the Lancaster and displays other aircraft awaiting restoration, like the Avro Anson and a Fairchild Cornell.

Lancaster bomber, Nanton Air Museum (R.A. Hursey)

Continuing north on Hwy 2 towards Calgary, you will want to stop at High River. Near this town was one of the early whisky trading forts—Spitzee Post. Also, west of town is a ranch once owned by the Prince of Wales. Although these sites are not available to the public, they are historically important to the High River area.

High River has several murals painted by Canadian artists on the walls of buildings throughout the town. These murals reflect the Native and ranching history of the area.

The **Museum of the Highwood**, located in a converted CPR railway station, has many interesting displays that interpret the history of the area. The museum houses one of the best collections of artifacts related to ranching history in the province. Alongside the museum are displayed a number of railway cars and locomotives in various stages of restoration; most appear to be rusting away. Beside the museum is a restored dining car where you can buy lunch. A caboose serves as a gift shop for train souvenirs.

Bar U Ranch

Near the foothills west of High River and Claresholm is some of the best ranching country in the province and home to some of the earliest ranches in the area. The Bar U Ranch, operated by the North-West Cattle Company from 1882 to 1902, became one of the most successful. The North-West Cattle Company began operations in 1882, with a lease of 59,000 acres of range. By 1884, the company controlled over 150,000 acres owned and leased.

Unlike many other early ranches in Alberta, the Bar U had adequate financial backing and good management under Fred Stimson and foreman George Lane. Many cowboys earned their spurs under the tutelage of Herb Millar, a stockman who worked for the Bar U for 53 years. Some went on to become successful ranchers themselves. One cowboy achieved a different notoriety:

Harry Longbaugh, a "top-notch" cowhand, came to Canada from Montana and worked for the Bar U briefly. When he returned to Montana, he joined the Currie gang. They blew up an express car and got away with $60,000. Longbaugh, who became known as "The Sundance Kid," and his companion-in-crime, Butch Cassidy, went on to more daring heists until their violent end in a shoot-out in South America.

The North-West Cattle Company sold out to the company organized by George Lane in 1902. Lane managed the ranch until he died in 1925, and Pat Burns took over the land leases in 1926. The range was finally broken up into smaller parcels in 1950. The site of the original Bar U headquarters is now a designated Provincial Historic Site, and there are plans to open it to the public within the next few years.

For a scenic drive, you may want to take a short detour along Highway 2A from High River through Okotoks, which takes you along the Highwood River and through some lovely farmland. About five miles west of town is the largest glacial erratic in North America, a very special rock to the Blackfoot, who called it "Okatok" meaning big rock. The town of Okotoks derives its name from this rock. Erratics are boulders that originated in the Rockies, were carried by advancing glaciers, and deposited far from their origin as the glaciers receded. Check at Okotoks for directions to the "Big Rock."

MUSEUMS ALONG THE MACLEOD TRAIL

> ☞ **Fort Museum**
> Box 776, Fort Macleod, AB T0L 0Z0 * 219 - 25th Street
> *Governing body:* Fort Macleod Historical Society
> Open May 1 to October 31 * ☎ (403) 553-4703
> Admission fee charged *Visiting time:* one and a half hours
> 🍷🍷🍷🍷 ⛴ ⚶ 🎁 ⛩ ⛰ 🍴 ⎯

The Fort Museum is a living history museum and historical village that features the history of the NWMP and RCMP, Native and early European settlers. The historical and replica buildings inside the fort resemble several small museums, with period rooms furnished with artifacts of exceptional quality. Exhibits include the history of the NWMP and a Native history diorama. In the summer there are daily performances of the museum's Mounted Patrol Musical Ride.

> ☞ **Head-Smashed-In Buffalo Jump Provincial Historic Site**
> Box 1977, Fort Macleod, AB T0L 0Z0
> 18 kilometres northwest of Fort Macleod on Secondary Highway 785.
> *Governing body:* Alberta Community Development
> Open Year round, daily * ☎ (403) 553-2731
> Admission fee charged *Visiting time:* one to two hours
> 🍷🍷🍷🍷🍷 🚗 ⛴ 🎁 ⛩

The interpretive centre at the site has a variety of exhibits with artifacts, replicas, and mounted specimens that depict the history of the jump site, the ecology of the area, hunting techniques, and lifestyle of the Plains People. Blackfoot-speaking guides provide interpretive tours. Special features include walking trails at the top and bottom of the actual kill site and on-site archeologists at work during the summer.

> ☞ **Appaloosa Horse Club of Canada Museum**
> *Mailing address:* Box 940, Claresholm, AB T0L 0T0 * 4189 - 3rd Street
> *Governing body:* Appaloosa Horse Club of Canada
> Open year round, weekdays. Other times by prior arrangement.
> ☎ (403) 625-3326 * Admission by donation *Visiting time:* one half hour
> 🍷 🚗⛴ ⚶ 🍴 ⎯

A museum dedicated to the history and promotion of the Appaloosa, it has artifacts, photographs, trophies, and records dealing with the activities and breeding of the Appaloosa.

☞ **Claresholm Museum**
Box 1000, Claresholm, AB T0L 0T0
5126 - 1st Street (Highway 2, in historic CPR station).
Governing body: Town of Claresholm
Open Victoria Day to Labour Day * ☎ (403) 625-3131
Admission by donation *Visiting time:* one half hour

🏆 🚗 🚻 🎁 🍽 ⊷

Claresholm Museum, housed in the historic sandstone CPR station, has many artifacts related to the area's history and settlement. A pioneer log cabin and Claresholm's first school sits on the site.

☞ **Museum of the Highwood**
129 - 3rd Avenue W, High River, AB T1V 1M9 * 406 1st Street, High River
Governing body: Museum of the Highwood
Open all year round * ☎ 403-652-7156
Admission by donation *Visiting time:* one half hour

🏆🏆 🚗♿🎁 🪑 ⛺ 🍽 ⊷

The Museum of the Highwood is in one of the original CPR sandstone railway stations. The museum tells the story of the town and the agricultural heritage of the area. Collections include fossils, Native artifacts, and objects related to early trading, ranching, farming, and domestic and commercial history. On site are several historical trains being restored by the High River Historical Railway Association. Guided tours are available to see the rolling stock.

☞ **Nanton Lancaster Air Museum**
Box 1051, Nanton, AB T0L 1R0 * Adjacent to southbound Highway 2
Governing body: The Nanton Lancaster Society
Open May to October, daily; November to April, weekends
☎ (403) 646-2270 * Admission by donation *Visiting time:* one hour

🏆🏆🏆 🚗 ♿ 🚻 🍽 ⊷

The museum honors all those associated with the Bomber Command during World War II. A restored Canadian-built Lancaster Bomber is the centre piece and pride of this museum's collection. Guided tours take you up into the cockpit of this four engine bomber. Other aircraft awaiting restoration include a Fleet Fawn, a Fairchild Cornell, and an Avro Anson. Take some time to look at the displays, which give a concise history of the British Commonwealth Air Training Programme and the men and women who served. A special tribute is shown to Ian Bazalgette, the only Albertan awarded the Victoria Cross during WWII.

☞ **Stavely & District Museum**
Box 389, Stavely, AB T0L 2L0 * 4819 - 52 Street
Governing body: Museum Society of Stavely and District
Open May to Labour Day weekend, Wednesday & Saturday
☎ (403)549-2460/3761 * Admission by donation
Visiting time: one half hour
🏆 🚗 🍽 🔺

The museum features a pre-1920 pioneer kitchen, a beauty parlor and farm tools. A large rock called the "Indian Rock" has pictographs including a lizard and a cross etched into its surface. The museum's archives contain records of the Stavely Tobacco Club (1939 - 1945). Its purpose was to send cigarettes and parcels to Canadian Forces personnel.

Red River Cart, Fort Museum, Fort Macleod (R.A. Hursey)

5

THE RED COAT TRAIL—
HIGHWAYS 4, 61, and 41 South

The Plains People called the North West Mounted Police the "Red Coats," distinguishing them from the "Blue Coats" of the U.S. Army. The long, hazardous trek of the NWMP across the Canadian West has become known as the **Red Coat Trail**. Today it is a tourist designation that spans three provinces. The trail begins in south central Manitoba and proceeds across southern Saskatchewan and Alberta. This chapter covers the southeastern portion of Alberta's Red Coat Trail.

The Red Coat Trail closely parallels the original trail of the North American Boundary Commission of 1872-75. The joint Canadian and American commission ordered a land survey be done of the disputed and unprotected border between the two countries from Lake-of-the-Woods, Manitoba, to the Rocky Mountains. The Plains People called this international boundary "the Medicine Line," as it proved "good medicine" for those seeking a haven from one country or the other. Sitting Bull and the Sioux crossed the line to Canada in 1867 seeking refuge from the U.S. Army after the Battle of Little Big Horn. Louis Riel fled south across the line following the Red River Rebellion in 1870. After evading the U.S. Army for weeks, Chief Joseph and his band of Nez Percé Indians tried to cross the Medicine Line into Canada in 1877 but were captured in Montana about 65 kilometres south of the border. The border country was also a haven for cattle rustlers, whisky traders, "wolfers," and smugglers.

In Alberta, the Red Coat Trail begins at the Saskatchewan border just south of the Cypress Hills and ends at the British Columbia border. You will want to take a few side trips off the trail to enjoy some of the area's fascinating history. If you are entering the province from Saskatchewan, make your first stop at Cypress Hills. This island of hills rising 762 metres (2500 feet) above the surrounding sea of shortgrass prairie reaches a maximum elevation of 1463 metres (4800 feet), the highest spot between Labrador and the Rocky Mountains. In the Cypress Hills are two parks: Fort Walsh National Park and Cypress Hills Provincial Park which span both Alberta and Saskatchewan. Each province governs its half of Cypress Hills Provincial Park.

Photographer's Camp by the Corp of Royal Engineers, 1873.
(Glenbow Archives, Calgary, Alberta NA 249-24.)

Long before the arrival of the NWMP in 1874, the Cypress Hills had been occupied by Amerindian cultures for thousands of years. The hills have had many names. The Blackfoot called it "the Pine Hills." French-Canadians explorers, mistaking the lodgepole pine as eastern jackpine *(cyprés),* named the hills "*Montagne de Cyprés.*" Bypassed during the last glaciation period, Cypress Hills has a unique ecosystem more commonly found much farther south. Here you will encounter desert species of flora and fauna, like Yucca grass, scorpions, and horned toads, and 14 species of wild orchids. The **Cypress Hills Interpretive Centre,** overlooking beautiful Elkwater Lake, has displays featuring the human and natural history of the area. The centre also offers interpretive programs and guided nature hikes.

Blackfoot and Assiniboine People viewed the Cypress Hills as a sacred place. They wintered here, sheltered from bitter winds and where game was plentiful. Although traditional enemies, these tribes considered the hills a "No Man's Land," and disputes over territories did not extend here. The Cypress Hills was one of the areas where Métis assembled to begin their massive spring and fall buffalo hunts. Captain John Palliser, who headed the first official exploration of western Canada in the 1850s, passed through here with geologist-physicist Dr. James Hector, who studied the geology of the Cypress Hills. It was also the site of a massacre that brought about the formation of the North West Mounted Police.

The Cypress Hills Massacre

The Canadian West in the mid-19th century was a breeding ground for scoundrels. The Hudson's Bay Company once held tight control over the area, but for a few years following the its sale of Rupert's Land to the Dominion Government in 1869, the southern border of western Canada was left unguarded and open to exploitation. A particularly noxious breed of Canadian and American exploiters, known as "wolfers" poisoned buffalo carcasses to bait wolves. They angered the Natives because the poison often killed their dogs. In the spring of 1873, a group (probably Blackfoot) raided one of the wolfers' camps and stole a number of horses. In retaliation, the wolfers attacked a party of Assiniboine camped in the Cypress Hills. With their repeating rifles, the wolfers killed and wounded about thirty men, women and children. The incident caused the Dominion Government to pass an act creating the North West Mounted Police.

In 1875 the NWMP built an outpost in the Cypress Hills. It was called Fort Walsh after its leader Superintendent J. M. Walsh. The following year, the Cypress Hills became a sanctuary for the Sioux after the Battle of Little Bighorn, which resulted in the massacre of General Custer and his 265 soldiers. Fearing reprisals, Sitting Bull led a party of Sioux to the Cypress Hills to seek refuge. By the end of the year, several thousand more Sioux had joined him. Superintendent Walsh and his command of 102 Mounted Police suddenly had to deal with keeping law and order, feeding 4000 Sioux at their doorstep, and preventing hostilities from breaking out between the Sioux and the Blackfoot Confederacy. Three years after the Battle of Little Big Horn, when Walsh's replacement refused to provide food for them, the Sioux were finally persuaded to leave Cypress Hills and return to the United States.

Today you can relive the history of this early post by visiting **Fort Walsh National Historic Park.** Located a few miles east of the Alberta-Saskatchewan border, Fort Walsh is a reconstruction of this NWMP outpost. Don't miss visiting the nearby cemetery. Many Mounties who served and died at Fort Walsh are buried there.

After leaving the Cypress Hills, you will want to explore the relatively remote corner of southeastern Alberta, where coulees, badlands, and cattail marshes provide relief from the vast stretches of grass and grain. This arid region gets about 10 inches of rainfall a year. In the uplands, ranches and farms are large and towns are few. In the coulees, migratory birds and other wildlife abound. My scout and I had the pleasure of watching a Great Blue Heron make a low pass in front of our van. We spotted deer and pronghorn, coyotes, a rare kit fox, and Yellowbelly marmots.

> *Tracks and traces:* Coulees are wide valleys carved by ancient glaciers. Badlands are hills and cliffs formed by wind and water erosion.

One town you won't want to miss is Etzikom, southwest of Cypress Hills on Secondary Highway 61. Etzikom means "valley or coulee" in Blackfoot. This hamlet may look like a ghost town, but it is home to one of the most unusual heritage collections in Alberta. The **National Historic Windpower Centre** features windmills from all over North America, including a very large wooden structure that was transported all the way from Martha's Vineyard, Connecticut. Each year more windmills will be added to this site, as these skeletal prairie landmarks pass into disuse.

Beside the National Historic Windpower Centre is the **Heritage Museum of South-East Alberta**, a cool place to be on a hot day. Not only will you want to see the attractive displays, but you will want to order a double-dip cone at the long counter of the 1950s style ice cream parlor. We spent an enjoyable hour wandering through this museum, which is housed in a former school. One of the galleries features a scaled-down version of the main street of Etzikom, with storefronts of some of the businesses that once thrived in this community. The stage of the former school has the original drop cloth from the old movie house, showing advertisements of early businesses. The wood used in the construction of this indoor village was salvaged from some of Etzikom's buildings that were demolished.

Leaving Etzikom head west on Highway 61 to Foremost and then south on SR 879 and west on the 501 turnoff to **Writing-on-Stone Provincial Park**, a unique natural, historical, and archeological preserve. Nestled along the Milk River in the shadow of the Sweet Grass Hills, Writing-On-Stone is a popular place for naturalists and heritage hunters alike. If you are on a camping holiday, you will definitely want to stay a few days at the campground of this lush green oasis, as there is much to see and do here.

National Historic Windpower Centre, Etzikom (R.A. Hursey)

Writing-On-Stone has one of the greatest concentrations of rock art in North America. The pictographs (rock paintings) and petroglyths (rock carvings) appear on the hoodoos and cliff faces along the river. The earliest rock art dates back at least 3000 years. Writing-On-Stone is a sacred place to the Blackfoot People, who have occupied this area for hundreds of years. They used the site for spiritual purposes and added their own pictographs of horses, guns, and human figures. If you follow the self-guided trail, you will see battle scenes, depictions of bison and bear, animal tracks, and ceremonial designs. As these works of art are fragile, it is important not to touch them. Be sure to wear sturdy shoes and carry water, as it can be a very hot walk.

The more adventurous hiker may want to take a walk in the past to the **Writing-On-Stone Police Post**, a reconstructed North West Mounted Police Post on the original site. Built in 1889 as a part of the boundary patrol system, this outpost was first used by the NWMP and RNWMP until the Alberta Provincial Police took over patrolling the Alberta-U.S. border in 1916-17. At the height of activity, in 1897, the post was home to five Mounties, two hired range riders and 12 horses. It closed in 1918 and was later burned down by persons unknown.

Writing-on-Stone Provincial Park (R.L. Hursey)

From Writing-On-Stone, head west on SR 501 to the town of Milk River and north on Highway 4 then west on 52 to the town of Raymond. Mormon farmers and ranchers settled here in 1902. The wide streets are a testament to its Mormon beginnings. These settlers from the U.S. laid out their towns so that a wagon and team of horses could easily turn around in the middle of the street. Raymond, a community of about 3000, has a lot to boast about. The stampede originated here long before it appeared in Calgary. Raymond's high school basketball team has won more provincial championships than any other high school in Alberta. It was the site of the first sugar beet factory, founded by Jesse Knight in 1903. The town has never had a liquor establishment.

Be sure to see the **Raymond Community Centre**, located in the former Church of the Latter Day Saints. This brick building reveals a unique architecture, with four wings branching off a central rotunda. There are supposedly only two of its type in North America.

Next to the Community Centre is the **Japanese Buddhist Temple**, built by the local Japanese-Canadian community in 1929. Japanese workers were brought in to work the sugar beet fields around Raymond in 1908. Many of them stayed to become an integral part of the town. The temple is now a registered Provincial Historic Site.

The Community Centre houses the **Raymond & District Museum** on its upper floor. This small museum has period rooms showing the story of the community.

MUSEUMS ALONG THE RED COAT TRAIL

☞ **Cypress Hills Interpretive Centre**
Box 12, Elkwater, AB T0J 1C0 * Elkwater, Cypress Hills Provincial Park
Governing body: Alberta Environment, Provincial Parks Service
Open May long weekend to September long weekend, daily
☎ (403) 893-3777 * Admission by donation *Visiting time:* one half hour

🍷🏆🚐 ♿ 👫 👫 🏕 ⛽ ▲

The Cypress Hills Interpretive Centre overlooks the beautiful Elkwater Lake in the heart of the Cypress Hills. It encompasses two provincial parks and a national historic site. The interpretive centre features exhibits and programs on the natural history, geology, and cultural history of the Cypress Hills area. Audio-visual presentations and exhibits depict the Native history, the arrival of the NWMP, and the early ranching industry. Park naturalists and interpreters provide a series of programs throughout the summer. Four nature walks originate from Elkwater. Inquire at the centre for brochures on geology, birds, and orchid species found at Cypress Hills.

☞ **Fort Walsh National Historic Park**
Box 278, Maple Creek, SK S0N 1N0
54 kilometres southwest of Maple Creek, SK in the Cypress Hills.
Governing body: Parks Canada * Open May to October
☎ (306) 667-2645 * Admission by donation
Visiting time: One and a half hours

🍷🍷🍷🏆 🚐 ♿ 👫 🏛 🏕 ▲

In 1875, Fort Walsh was the first North West Mounted Police fort built in the Cypress Hills. The present Fort Walsh is an authentic reconstruction as it appeared around 1880. This living history museum consists of the stockade, barracks, horse stable, workshops, guardroom, and officer's quarters. Staff in period dress bring to life the fascinating history of this NWMP post, which served as headquarters for NWMP operations from 1878 to 1883, when it was abandoned. The nearby cemetery tells another chapter in the saga of the NWMP, with its early graves of mounties and civilians who died at Fort Walsh.

☞ **Heritage Museum of Southeast Alberta** at Etzikom
Box 585, Etzikom, AB T0K 0W0 * Etzikom's former school building
Governing body: Museum Society of Etzikom
Victoria Day to Labour Day * ☎ 403-666-3737
Admission by donation * *Visiting time:* One hour
♥ ♥ ♥ 🚗 ♿ ⛩ ☕

This museum features a reconstruction of Main Street and contains period rooms displaying the museum's extensive collection of
domestic artifacts. The attractive Natural history displays, featuring
the wildlife of the area, are of a quality rarely found in community
history museums. Special collections include fashions of yesteryear,
musical instruments, and phonographs. A 1950s style ice cream
parlour serves ice cream cones at the soda fountain.

☞ **National Historic Windpower Centre**
Box 585, Etzikom, AB T0K 0W0
In the field next to the Heritage Museum of South-East Alberta
Governing body: Museum Society of Etzikom
Open Victoria Day to Labour Day * ☎ 403-666-3737
Admission by donation * *Visiting time:* one-half hour
♥ ♥ 🚗 ♿ 🚶 ⛩

This new centre displays a large collection of windmills from all
over North America. A winding path leads the visitor through the
history of these disappearing landmarks of the prairie. A windpower
interpretive centre, telling of the importance of windpower in
Canadian history, is planned for the near future.

☞ **Raymond & District Museum**
Box 1151, Raymond, AB T0K 2S0
Raymond Community Centre on Broadway Street
Governing body: Raymond & District Historical Society
Open July and August * ☎ 403-752-3496
Admission by donation * *Visiting time:* one half hour
♥ 🚗   👫   🍴 —

This community history museum has a sports hall of fame and
period rooms featuring the religious, social, and commercial history
of the area. It is best to call before visiting. We found the museum
closed when we got there, but the manager came to give us a tour.

☞ **Writing-On-Stone Provincial Park**
Box 297, Milk River, AB T0K 1M0
32 kilometres east of Milk River on SR 501, then south at signage to park
Governing body: Government of Alberta
Open mid-May to mid-September * ☎ (403) 647-2364
Free parking; charge for camping
Visiting time: Guided walk of rock art, two hours

Located on a 1,780 hectare site (4400 acres), Writing-On-Stone Provincial Park has the greatest concentration of rock art in the North American plains, with over 50 sites featuring pre-historic and historic petroglyths and pictographs. There are numerous archeological sites and a reconstructed NWMP outpost. The park provides excellent camping facilities and a wide variety of interpretive programs and guided hikes. Inquire at the Visitor Service Office for self-guiding trail brochures and other information.

Main Street Gallery, Etzikom Museum (R.A. Hursey)

6

MEDICINE HAT & AREA

Medicine Hat is located in an area known as the Palliser's Triangle, one of the driest regions of Canada. Captain John Palliser of the British-sponsored Palliser Expedition of 1857 to 1860 reported that the semi-arid area, which stretched across the American border, was unsuitable for farming. In 1857-58, the government of the Canadas sponsored a scientific expedition led by Henry Youle Hind. Hind was more optimistic in his report, claiming that farming in the region was marginal, but it had potential.

Two prominent geographic features dominate the land around Medicine Hat: Cypress Hills, 30 kilometres to the south, and the South Saskatchewan River valley. The rest of the land consists of gently rolling prairie grasslands. Many species of grass grow here: native fescues, wheat grasses, wild rye, and grama. Intermixed with the grasses grow rich varieties of wildflowers like the prairie crocus, yellow evening primrose, wild gaillardia and lupine, prairie cone-flower, wild sunflowers, and moss phlox. Where there is more moisture around sloughs, coulees and river bottoms, you will see cottonwood poplars, willows and trembling aspen. The wildlife found here is equally rich: pronghorn, white-tailed and mule deer, red fox, and coyotes. Swainson's hawks, waterfowl, and shorebirds are common. Golden eagles are not so common, but are occasionally seen riding the thermals.

Tracks and Traces: "Medicine Hat" in Blackfoot is *saamis,* meaning "headdress of a medicine man." One explanation is that the Cree and Blackfoot were engaged in battle along the South Saskatchewan River. When their medicine man lost his medicine hat, the Cree took this as a bad omen and lost the battle. The spot became known as the place-where-the-medicine-man-lost-his-hat.

The area around Medicine Hat has a long history of human occupation. On the Trans-Canada Highway adjacent to the **Saamis Teepee** (the world's largest) is the **Saamis Archaeological Site.** A local resident discovered this archaeological site along Seven Persons Creek in 1970. Extensive excavations by Medicine Hat College and the Archaeological Survey of Canada in the 1970s unearthed bison bones, ceramics and stone points, the earliest points dating from about 500 years ago. The Saamis site appears to have been a centre for buffalo processing and stone tool making.

Although there are older archaeological sites just north of Medicine Hat, the Saamis site is within city limits and accessible to tourists.

About the time that the Canadian Pacific Railway arrived in 1883, several small cattle ranches were established by former NWMP officers around Maple Creek, Saskatchewan in 1882 and 1883. The first ranch in the Medicine Hat area was the Pyrennes Ranch, established in 1883 by N. Oxarart. Both the NWMP and the ranchers discouraged farming, but the Canadian Government and the CPR promoted settlement and homesteading of the area. Consistently, efforts to farm this region on a large scale proved Palliser's claims. The good years provided bumper crops of grain, but the inevitable years of drought and severe winters drove many homesteaders to seek more arable land farther north.

The NWMP arrival in Medicine Hat coincided with the arrival of the CPR and brought law and order to the instant frontier town that grew up around the railway. In 1883, the Mounties built barracks at Police Point, on the north side of the South Saskatchewan River. **Police Point Park and Interpretive Centre,** with its network of nature trails, portrays the history and natural history of the 300-acre park.

By 1885 buildings and houses replaced the tent city, and steamships travelled up and down the river carrying coal from the Galt mines in Lethbridge. Medicine Hat instantly became an important railway centre in southern Alberta.

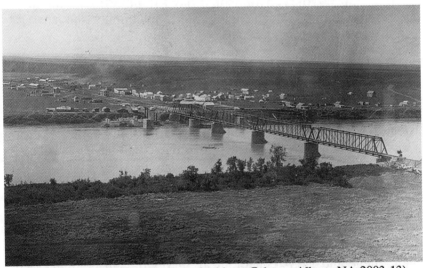

Medicine Hat, Alberta. (Glenbow Archives, Calgary, Alberta NA-2003-13)

The Rocky Mountain Rangers

In the spring of 1885, the people of Medicine Hat were experiencing much anxiety, as news of the North-West Rebellion in Saskatchewan came by railway and telegraph. When the rumor spread that the Blackfoot were planning to attack Medicine Hat, the Rocky Mountain Rangers, mostly cowboys and ranchers led by "Kootenai" Brown (see Chapter 1 for brief biography), were hastily formed to fend off the attack by fortifying the town. The attack never happened, owing to the statesmanship of Crowfoot, who convinced other chiefs not to join the rebellion. After patrolling the area between Medicine Hat and High River for three months, the Rocky Mountain Rangers were disbanded.

The discovery of abundant natural gas in 1892 turned Medicine Hat into a thriving industrial centre. By 1909, gas-powered lamps lit the town's streets. Today, turn-of-the century gas lamps are a feature of historic downtown Medicine Hat. This source of cheap and plentiful energy led to the development of brick works and pottery industry. Medalta, the Medicine Hat Pottery Company, founded in 1912, is a household word to most Albertans and Canadians who grew up before the 1960s. Medalta produced a variety of ceramic products, from utilitarian items like crocks and toilets, to fine china that graced the CPR's dining cars. In 1915 the company became known as Medalta Stoneware Ltd. By 1920, about three-fourths of the china and stoneware in Canada was manufactured at Medalta. The company closed in 1954.

In 1937, the Yuill family, owners of Alta Clay Products Co. began construction of Medicine Hat Potteries. The company was sold and became known as Hycroft Ltd. Several other potteries were established in Medicine Hat and Redcliff during the 1950s, including the Gas City Pottery Ltd., Sunburst Ceramics and Canada Potter. Medalta Potteries (1966) Ltd. opened in Redcliff in 1966.

Today many of the Medalta products have become valuable collectors' items. The pottery plants may no longer operate, but you can see some of the massive machinery—moulds and kilns—used to make the clay products at the **Medalta Potteries Historic Site**. The Friends of Medalta Society have ambitious plans to preserve, restore and interpret Medalta Potteries, a designated provincial and national historic site, into a major tourist attraction. In the meantime, you can learn about how the clay products were made by visiting the **Clay Products Interpretive Centre** next to the original Medalta

Potteries Plant. Another feature that brings alive Medicine Hat's pottery history is "the Great Wall of China," located at the old Hycroft building. The display shows an impressive array of Medalta and Hycroft products.

Medalta Potteries Plant, 1924. (Provincial Archives of Alberta A6210)

To learn more about the fascinating history of Medicine Hat and region, you will want to visit the **Medicine Hat Museum & Art Gallery.** The museum maintains a substantial ethnology collection of archaeological artifacts and fur trade items. One of the special exhibits features a log cabin—the original Medicine Hat museum in 1951. This museum-in-a-museum displays artifacts reflecting the importance of ranching in the area. The art gallery hosts exhibits of works by local and national talent. Its permanent collections reflect the importance of Medicine Hat as a visual arts centre.

One of the best ways to enjoy the heritage of Medicine Hat is to go on the **Historical Walking Tour** of downtown. In the 1980s, Medicine Hat was part of the Main Street Canada Programme, which helped the community restore its downtown area. The self-guided brochure, available at a number of places in town, highlights some of the distinctive architecture of the city, including St. Patrick's Church. Built in 1913, it is one of the finest examples of Gothic Revival architecture in North America.

If you plan to combine camping with heritage hunting, you may want to stay at Echo Dale Regional Park, about eight kilometres west of Medicine Hat. This beautiful park by the South Saskatchewan River includes a restored farm site. **Echo Dale Historical Farm** is a living farm museum.

The Woolfrey farm was built in the late 1880s, when the land was established as a "model farm." The large barn holds chickens, geese, a cow, horse, pig, and sheep—livestock reflecting subsistence farming of the settlement period. You can watch interpreters milk the cow, tend to the livestock, and work in the historically authentic vegetable garden. While we were there, a very large gray goose, obviously the farm's security guard, followed us. On site you can also visit the restored **Woolfrey farmhouse,** built in 1902. Take a hike on the trail that leads from Echo Dale Farm to the **Ajax Coal Mine**. It operated from 1884 to 1967. Along the way you will pass the remains of an old boarding house and a barn used to house the ponies that worked in the mine. Coal from the mine was used primarily by local people for heating their homes and businesses.

Photograph: Echo Dale Historical Farm. (R.L. Hursey)

As you drive north out of the river valley on the Trans-Canada Highway, the community of Redcliff comes into view at the top of a hill. Redcliff was once an important pottery centre and glassworks. There you can see the skeletons of deserted factories and imagine what this important industrial centre must have been like in the 1950s, when Medalta relocated here. Today cheap, abundant natural gas is used to heat over 35 acres of greenhouses on the west end of town. Redcliff is the "Greenhouse Capital of the Prairies," and the greenhouses are open all year round.

MUSEUMS IN THE MEDICINE HAT AREA

☞ **Ajax Coal Mine**
580 1st Street, Medicine Hat, AB T1A 8E6 * Echo Dale Regional Park
Governing body: Echo Dale Farm Historical Society
Open June through August * ☎ (4030 529-6225
Admission by donation * *Visiting time:* one half hour

This mine is under restoration. The self-guided trail leading from Echo Dale Historical Farm to the mine site has outdoor signage providing the early history of the sites.

☞ **Clay Products Interpretive Centre**
521 - 12th Street SW, Medicine Hat, AB T1A 4T9
Location: 820 Industrial Avenue SE.
Governing body: Friends of Medalta Society
Open Year round * ☎ 403-529-1070
Admission by donation * *Visiting time:* one half hour

Collections include ceramic pieces of Medalta pottery as well as products made by Alberta Clay Products, Hi-Croft China, National Porcelain, IXL Brick, and Plainsman Clay. Next to the centre are some of the massive kilns and molds used in production of clay products. Interpretive displays tell the story of the clay products industry of Medicine Hat. A variety of ceramic gifts are available in the gift shop.

☞ **Echo Dale Historical Farm**
580 1st Street, Medicine Hat, AB T1A 8E6 * Echo Dale Regional Park.
Governing body: Echo Dale Farm Historical Society
Open June through August * ☎ (403) 529-6225
Admission by donation * *Visiting time:* one half hour

A living farm museum, Echo Dale Farm has farm livestock of the subsistence era, an authentic vegetable garden, large restored barn and farmhouse, and historic farm equipment. Interpretive programs and demonstrations bring to life small subsistence farming in the Medicine Hat area.

☞ **Medicine Hat Museum, Archives & Art Gallery**
1302 Bomford Crescent, Medicine Hat, AB T1A 5E6
Governing body: City of Medicine Hat * Open Year round
☎ (403 527-6266 * Admission by donation * *Visiting time:* one hour

Medicine Hat Museum is a comprehensive museum, with a large collection of palaeontological material, Plains Indian textiles, tools and beadwork, fur trade and ranching artifacts and objects related to the development of Medicine Hat. Exhibit galleries feature the history and natural history of the Medicine Hat region. The Art Gallery features exhibits of local, national and international visual artists.

☞ **Police Point Park and Interpretive Centre**
580 1st Street SW, Medicine Hat, AB T1A 4T9 * Police Point Park
Governing body: City of Medicine Hat * Open year round
☎ 403-529-6225 * Admission by donation * *Visiting time:* one half hour

This nature centre, located in a beautiful park on the peninsula, features a variety of insects, fossils, and literature pertaining to the shortgrass prairie. Featured is a working beehive and a wildflowers collection. Interpretive programs and guided tours are available.

☞ **Saamis Teepee and Saamis Archaeological Site**
101, 266 - 4th Street, Medicine Hat, AB T1A 4E5
Trans-Canada Highway, southwest end of town.
Governing body: Saamis Teepee Association
Open May to September * ☎ (403) 527-6773
Admission fee charged* *Visiting time:* one half hour

The most visible landmark in Medicine Hat and the world's tallest teepee, the Saamis Teepee, stands approximately 20 stories high and is made of steel and concrete. The two main columns of the teepee were built for the 1988 Calgary Olympics and later bought by Medicine Hat as a basis for a monument to the Native people of North America. The teepee overlooks Seven Persons Creek Coulee, where the Saamis archaeological site is located. There are walking trails down to the site. Future plans include a permanent centre and archaeological interpretation.

☞ **Redcliff Museum**
Box 758, Redcliff, AB T0J 2P0 * #2, 3rd Street NE
Governing body: Redcliff Historical & Museum Society
Open year round * ☎ 403-548-6260 * *Admission by donation*
🏆 🚗 🍽 ⚊

The museum's collections pertain to the industrial and social history of Redcliff. Exhibits feature industries such as Medalta Potteries and Domglas, as well as farming, ranching, and commercial industries.

7

TRANS-CANADA HIGHWAY 1

The original Trans-Canada highways were waterways—rivers, lakes and portages—first used by Natives and then by fur traders who transported furs in freight canoes and York boats from western Canada to Montreal or the Hudson's Bay. Wagon roads, Red River cart trails, and railways formed 19th and early 20th century highways.

Today's Trans-Canada Highway spans the width of Canada from St. John's, Newfoundland, to Victoria, B.C. In Alberta, Highway 1 parallels the original route of the Canadian Pacific Railway, west from the Alberta-Saskatchewan border through Medicine Hat, northwest toward Calgary, and west again through the Rocky Mountains by way of Banff and Lake Louise. This chapter focuses on the region from Medicine Hat to Calgary, where the Trans-Canada Highway goes through some of the flattest and most sparsely populated areas in Alberta. It is an area rich in wildlife, where you may spot dozens of pronghorn right from the highway almost any time of the year.

The pronghorn may look like an antelope, but it is not related to the African antelope species. A distant relative of mountain sheep, the pronghorn exists in the wild nowhere else but in North America and is the only species of its kind. The pronghorn has unique horns worn by both sexes. They consist of a bony core and a sheath that is shed each year. Another distinctive feature is the large white rump. Pronghorn were not hunted to extinction like its range partner the buffalo. These remarkable mammals can outrun most of their predators at speeds up to 65 kilometres per hour.

The Canadian Forces Base at Suffield was established as a military reserve in 1941. Its primary purpose during the Second World War was for chemical warfare experimentation. It employed hundreds of people who conducted research on toxic chemicals, flame warfare, and ballistics. Today stockpiles of chemical weapons are being dismantled, and research and training of safety equipment to protect infantry from exposure to chemical warfare is the mandate.

Your first stop will be the town of Brooks, a green oasis full of interesting sites for the heritage hunter. Incorporated in 1910, Brooks was named after Noell Edgell Brooks, a divisional engineer for the CPR who actually lived in Calgary. Even before Brooks became a town, John Ware, a former black slave, had a ranch in the district around the turn of the century.

John Ware (c1850 - 1906)

John Ware and family (Glenbow Archives, Calgary, AB NA-263-12)

One of the myths perpetuated by Hollywood is that the early cowboys in the West were all white men. In truth, one-fourth were blacks. Many immigrated to western Canada in the 1880s. One was the legendary John Ware, born into slavery on a cotton plantation in South Carolina sometime between 1845 and 1850. When the American Civil War ended, he moved to Texas and learned horsemanship. Joining a cattle drive, Ware helped to move herds of Texas longhorns to Montana. In 1882 he came to Canada with his trail buddy Bill Moodie after Tom Lynch persuaded them to come and work for the Bar U Ranche near the Highwood River.

At the Bar U, John Ware earned a reputation as a horseman when he rode the worst bucker in the remuda (a herd of horses kept during roundups). He achieved further fame when he tracked down a couple of rustlers who had stolen some of the Bar U's cattle and brought them back single-handedly to the ranch, leading them by a rope tied to his saddle horn. After working for other ranches in southern Alberta, he started his own on Sheep Creek, near Millarville. In 1892 he married the daughter of a black farmer from Ontario. In 1903, he and his family acquired land on the Red Deer River north of Brooks, near the town of Dutchess. Tragedy struck the Ware family within a few years. His wife died in 1905, and shortly after, Ware died after he fell from his horse and the horse rolled over him. Throughout his life in Alberta, Ware was known for his warm personality, his sense of humor, and horsemanship. His cabin is preserved at Dinosaur Provincial Park.

There are several worthwhile sites in and near Brooks to give you a good idea how important agriculture and irrigation is to the region. The **Brooks Aqueduct Provincial Historic Site**, about three kilometers from town, is an unusual concrete structure built between 1912 and 1914 by the CPR to carry water from the Bassano Dam, the first irrigation project in Alberta. The 2.5 kilometres of aqueduct was replaced in 1983 by the earthen irrigation canal that runs beside it. The **Brooks and District Museum** portrays the cultural heritage of the area around Brooks from the Red Deer River to the Bow River. The **Brooks Pheasant Hatchery**, open on weekdays, is one of the largest pheasant hatcheries in Canada. The ring-necked pheasant is an introduced species, and it has thrived in Alberta. The hatchery releases about 40,000 pheasants into the wild each year. Nearby the **Alberta Special Crops and Horticultural Research Centre** offers tours to visitors during weekdays. For bird lovers, nearby **Kinbrook Island Provincial Park** at Lake Newell offers one of the best places in southern Alberta to view migrating waterfowl and shorebirds. A colony of double-crested cormorants and white pelicans nest on the islands in the lake.

Brooks Aqueduct Provincial Historic Site. (R.L. Hursey)

About 50 kilometers north of Brooks is **Dinosaur Provincial Park.** This fascinating park was declared a World Heritage Site by UNESCO for the significant dinosaur finds that have been excavated since palaeontologist Joseph B. Tyrrell began working there in 1884. Under the direction of the Royal Tyrrell Museum of Palaeontology, professional and amateur palaentologists come here to continue the work of learning about our geologic past in the cliffs along the Red Deer River. The **Royal Tyrrell Museum of Palaeontology Field Station**, a satellite of the main museum at Drumheller, is the place to go to learn about the research being done here. A variety of exhibits reveal Alberta's rich fossil heritage of more than 70 million years ago. The Tyrrell Field Station offers bus tours and guided hikes. While at Dinosaur Provincial Park, be sure to visit **John Ware's Cabin.**

To get to Dinosaur Provincial Park, go north from Brooks on SR 550, east on 544 to the town of Patricia, then north again on 876 for about 10 kilometres. If you are on a camping holiday, you will find this a magical place, rich in history and scenic beauty. The best time to visit the park is in May or September as it is cooler and relatively free of mosquitoes.

Father Lacombe & Chief Crowfoot (Provincial Archives of Alberta P200)

After returning to Brooks and then travelling northwest on the Trans-Canada Highway, you will be entering the reserve of the Siksika Nation, which spans the Bow River from Bassano to Gleichen. The Siksika nation is a tribe belonging to the Blackfoot Confederacy, previously known as Blackfoot Proper. "Blackfoot" is a translation of the tribe's own name, *siksikauwa,* referring to the moccasins they wore, which became blackened from the ashes of forest fires.

Chief Crowfoot

One of the greatest statesmen of the Canadian West was Chief Crowfoot, a Blackfoot (Siksika) Indian of extraordinary vision and diplomacy. Born in southern Alberta around 1830, he was known by several names, including Shot Close, Bear Ghost, and Packs a Knife. As a young warrior, he showed great courage and was made a chief of one of the bands. In 1870, he became one of the three head chiefs of the Blackfoot Confederacy. It was a difficult time for the Blackfoot. They faced starvation and extinction from the scourge of smallpox, whisky, and the disappearance of the buffalo. Their options were running out.

Chief Crowfoot became a friend of Father Albert Lacombe, and Colonel James Macleod of the NWMP. He trusted Macleod, one of the treaty commissioners who took part in the negotiations leading to the signing of a treaty that would set aside reserves for the Blackfoot, Blood, and Peigan tribes. Chief Crowfoot's diplomacy helped influence the Blackfoot Confederacy to sign Treaty No. Seven at Blackfoot Crossing (Cluny) in 1877.

Disease and starvation continued to haunt the Confederacy once they moved onto the reserves. By 1880 Macleod had retired and the responsibility of the reserves transferred from the NWMP to the newly organized Department of Indian Affairs, run by political appointees with little knowledge of Indians. During the Riel Rebellion of 1885, Crowfoot persuaded his people not to join. He had visited Winnipeg the year before and had seen first hand its burgeoning population of 15,000. He understood that rebellion would be futile for his people in the light of this growing power.

He died of tuberculosis at Blackfoot Crossing on April 25, 1890.

The Siksika Nation is planning to build a park and interpretive centre at Blackfoot Crossing on the Bow River in the next few years. Meanwhile you can visit the **Siksika Nation Museum of Natural History** at the Old Sun College in Gleichen. The museum depicts the four transition periods in the lives of the Blackfoot Nation. Make arrangements in advance. When I was there, I was unable to visit the museum because the curator was not available.

> **_Tracks and Traces:_** Originally the 12th Siding of the Canadian Pacific Railway, Gleichen was named after German Count Albert Edward Wilfred Gleichen, a financial backer of the CPR. He, however, never actually visited the town.

From Gleichen, a short drive south on SR 547 takes you to the village of Arrowwood and to the **Arrowwood Restoration Society Museum,** a restored general store.

MUSEUMS ALONG THE TRANS-CANADA HIGHWAY

> ☞ **Arrowwood Restoration Society Museum**
> Box 238, Arrowwood, AB T0L 0B0 * Main Street
> *Governing body:* Arrowwood Restoration Society
> ☎ (403) 534-3325 * Opening hours vary. Check locally.
> Admission by donation * *Visiting time:* one half hour

The museum is a restored general store, one of Arrowwood's original buildings. Displays include irrigation history, the Doukhobor Colony and the Brethren Church.

> ☞ **Brooks Aqueduct Provincial Historic Site**
> Alberta Community Development, Box 1522, Cochrane, AB T0L 0W0
> 8 km southeast of Brooks, 3 km south of the Trans-Canada Highway.
> *Governing body:* Historic Sites & Archives Service
> Open May 15 to Labour Day * ☎ (403)932-2902
> Admission by donation * *Visiting time:* one half hour

The Brooks Aqueduct was built by the CPR in 1914. Now a national and provincial historic site, it was once the longest concrete and steel structure of its kind in the world. This 2.4 kilometres aqueduct carried water from Bassano Dam to irrigated farmlands.

> ☞ **Brooks & District Museum**
> Box 2078, Brooks, AB T1R 1C7 * 568 Sutherland Drive
> *Governing body:* Brooks and District Historical Society
> Open May through August * ☎ (403) 362-7053
> Admission fee charged * *Visiting time:* one half hour

This museum portrays the history of Brooks and the area from the Red Deer River south to the Bow River. Displays and artifacts pertain to the RCMP history, irrigated farming, and the Canadian Pacific Railway.

☞ **Siksika Nation Museum of Natural History** at Gleichen
Box 249, Gleichen, AB T0J 1M0 * Third floor, Old Sun College
Governing body: Siksika Nation Chief and Council
Open year round, Monday to Friday * ☎ (403) 734-3862
Admission by donation * *Visiting time:* one half hour
🍷 🚗 👥

The museum features artifacts from stone age specimens; horse culture; fur trade and contemporary arts and crafts. When I arrived there, no one was available to give me a tour. It is best to make prior arrangements before visiting.

☞ **Royal Tyrrell Museum of Palaontology Field Station** at Patricia
Box 60, Patricia, AB T0J 2K0
In Dinosaur Provincial Park, 48 kilometres northeast of Brooks.
Governing body: Jointly operated by Alberta Community Development and the Provincial Parks Service
Open Victoria Day to Labour Day * ☎ (403)378-4342
Admission by donation * *Visiting time:* one hour
🍷🍷🍷🍷 🚗 ♿ ⊞ 🚻 ⛺

Located in the heart of the Red Deer River badlands, the field station is a satellite of the Royal Tyrrell Museum in Drumheller. The summer is an active time for research teams to come and excavate new finds. The interpretive centre presents a number of displays featuring fossils excavated from the area. The centre reveals the palaeontological history and research done at this World Heritage Site. You will want to spend some time hiking the trails around the centre, but the trails can be very slippery in wet weather. Guided and bus tours are also available to sites around the park.

☞ **Eastern Irrigation District (EID) Historical Park** at Scandia
General Delivery, Scandia, AB T0J 0Z0
32 kilometres south of Brooks on Highway 36.
Governing body: Board of Directors
Open May 1 to September 30 * ☎ (403)362-5010
Admission by donation * *Visiting time:* one half hour
🍷 🚗 🚻 ⛺

The museum's collection includes a threshing machine, ditchers, plows, wagons, haying and harvesting equipment, and potato equipment. In addition, there are musical instruments, rocks, and wild birds on display.

Royal Tyrrell Field Station, Dinosaur Provincial Park (R.L. Hursey)

8

DRUMHELLER & AREA

Alberta's landscape is full of surprises. Nowhere is this more evident than in the badlands of Drumheller Valley. It is a land of many moods, awe-inspiring on a sunny day, gloomily forbidding on a rainy one, and brutal in the heat of mid-summer. At any season it is breathtaking in its beauty. The first time I came upon the badlands of Drumheller, I was struck by how similar it appears to parts of the southwestern United States. The deep corrugated canyons and sculptured hoodoos are reminiscent of Bryce Canyon in Utah. Even some of the plants and wildlife, like prickly pear and pin cushion cacti, horned lizard, scorpion and rattlesnake, are more commonly associated with Arizona and New Mexico than Alberta.

The geology of the Red Deer River valley is equally fascinating. The Red Deer Badlands extends from Nevis, just west of Stettler, to almost the eastern border of Alberta. The river cuts a winding furrow through millions of years of sediments, rocks, and fossils. Alberta's badlands originated at a time when decayed volcanic ash blew over Alberta from erupting volcanoes in B.C. and deposited in the bottom of Cretaceous lakes and river deltas, forming bentonite. Bentonite seals off rock underneath so that moisture cannot enter or escape. The rock layers do not erode in a normal manner; instead they are formed into steep, fluted cliffs and hoodoos. The river carves through as much as 400 feet of multicolored sediments— black coal, gray to white clays and shale, brown ironstone, and yellow gravel. All roads entering Drumheller offer dramatic views of the badlands, but my favorite view overlooks Horseshoe Canyon on Highway 9, about 19 kilometres southwest of Drumheller.

Tracks & Traces: Hoodoos got their name from early Natives who claimed that these strange conical hills with mushroom-shaped hats were petrified giants that came alive at night and hurled rocks at intruders.

Using Drumheller as the hub, you will want to venture into the outlying communities like Rosebud, Wayne, East Coulee, Rosedale, and Munson. If you have time, plan to spend at least two or three days in the Drumheller area. You will be richly rewarded with some of the best palaeontological heritage hunting in the province. Let's start at Drumheller.

The Royal Tyrrell Museum of Palaeontology is located 6 kilometres from Drumheller. Each year nearly a half million people from all over the world come to see the extraordinary fossil collection of Alberta's dinosaurs and other ancient life. International palaeontologists come to study specimens. Another museum you shouldn't miss is the **Drumheller Dinosaur and Fossil Museum.** It maintains an impressive collection of prehistoric fossils, Indian artifacts, and rocks and minerals.

Drumheller's economic history is rooted in coal mining. The town was named after coal mining pioneer Samuel Drumheller. Alberta's railway expansion period in the 1910s and 1920s created the need for ready sources of coal, vital to the running of the steam locomotives. Coal was first mined in the Drumheller Valley in 1910. By the 1920s there were about 2000 miners working at 29 coal mines in the Drumheller Valley and as many as 10,000 people living in the surrounding communities. After the Canadian Northern Railway built a branch line through the Drumheller Valley in 1911, Drumheller became a commercial centre for the new coal mines at Nacime, Wayne, Rosedale, Midlandville and Newcastle.

Drumheller Miner's Strike

While coal mining brought prosperity to mining companies and businesses, the miners worked for low wages in unsafe conditions and lived in poverty. Ninety percent of Alberta's 12,000 miners were immigrants, mostly from Europe, where labour movements had met with some success in improving working conditions. Frustrated with the conservative United Mine Workers of America (UMWA), which sided with the government in crushing the Winnipeg General Strike in May 1919, many Alberta miners joined the new western Canadian labour union, the One Big Union (OBU).

Violence erupted in Drumheller when miners went on strike in support of the OBU and attempted to stop strikebreakers from entering the mines. The strikebreakers, mostly veterans, armed themselves, attacked the miners, and destroyed some of their homes. Management, the federal and provincial governments, and the UMWA quickly squelched the strike. The miners had no choice but to go back to work. OBU leaders were rounded up and forced out of town. The incident did, however, bring about a strong political representation of the Labour Party in Alberta's provincial and municipal governments during the 1920s. Wages and working conditions improved for many labourers but not for the miners.

Considered undesirable aliens by much of society, the predominantly immigrant coal miners remained voiceless and experienced little change in their lives for another generation.

Immigrant miners on strike, Drumheller, 1919.
(Glenbow Archives, Calgary, Alberta NA-2513-1)

One of the best places to learn about the coal mining history of the region is the **Atlas Coal Mine**, a registered provincial historic site. The mine closed in 1984. Atlas Coal Mine boasts the last standing ore-sorting tipple (a building where coal is sorted and then loaded for shipping in boxcars or wagons) of its type in Canada. You will also want to visit the rebuilt **Rosedale Suspension Bridge**, where miners once crossed the Red Deer River to work in the Star Coal Mine. In the town of Wayne is the famous **Last Chance Saloon** in the restored Rosedeer Hotel. The **East Coulee School Museum and Cultural Centre** features many displays of the community life in mining towns. There is also an excellent tea room to enjoy a light lunch.

Before leaving the area, we recommend two side trips. The first is Rosebud, about 50 kilometres southwest of Drumheller on SR 840. The Blackfoot named Rosebud Creek, *akokiniskway,* "many rosebuds." Peter Fidler, the famous explorer for the Hudson's Bay Company, crossed Rosebud Creek in 1792 and saw his first buffalo jump. The hamlet, now home of the Rosebud School of the Arts, hosts the **Rosebud Dinner Theatre.** The whole community is a walk in the past, with its opera house, art gallery and museum.

The second is a drive along the Dinosaur Trail, which starts and ends at Drumheller. You cross the river at Munson on the **Bleriot**

Ferry, one of the last cable-operated ferries in the province. It is 27 kilometres northwest of Drumheller. In 1919 there were 77 such ferries in Alberta, when few bridges spanned its mighty rivers; today the province of Alberta continues to operate seven.

MUSEUMS IN THE DRUMHELLER AREA

☞ **Drumheller Dinosaur and Fossil Museum**
Box 2135, Drumheller, AB T0J 0Y0 * 335 - 1st Street East, Drumheller
Governing body: Drumheller and District Museum Society
Open May 1 to October 15 * ☎ (403)823-2593
Admission fee charged * *Visiting time: one half hour*

This museum has excellent collections of smaller fossils as well as minerals, lapidary and coal mining paraphernalia. The museum offers a good overview of the geology and mining industry of the area. The exhibits are arranged by collection and displayed by private collectors. There are good historical photographs of the Sternberg party (one of the earliest dinosaur hunting expeditions to the Red Deer Valley).

☞ **Homestead Antique Museum**
Box 3154, Drumheller, AB T0J 0Y0 * 901 Dinosaur Trail
Governing body: Homestead Antique Museum Society
Open Daily, May 15 - September 30 * ☎ (403)823-2600
Admission fee charged * *Visiting time:* one hour

This museum is located in a unique building that resembles a wooden igloo. A wide range of collections include native, domestic, medical, industrial, railroad, and agriculture artifacts. It is worth a visit to see the vast number of artifacts in the museum's collection, although labelling could certainly be improved.

☞ **Royal Tyrrell Museum of Palaeontology**
Box 7500, Drumheller, AB T0J 0Y0
Midland Provincial Park, North Dinosaur Trail (Highway 838)
Governing body: Alberta Community Development, Historic Sites & Archives
Service * Open year round; closed Mondays except holidays.
☎ (403)823-7707; *Fax:* (403)823-7131
Admission fee charged * *Visiting time:* three hours

This museum provides state-of-the-art exhibits depicting the theme "A Celebration of Life." The exhibits explore the origin and evolution of life on Earth and the astonishing diversity of life from earliest times. The *tour de force* is the large collection of dinosaur skeletons on display. The size and variety of marine life and invertebrate fossils will amaze you as well. One of the best features is being able to watch preparators working with saws, drills, brushes, and dental tools to scrape away the matrix rock from the fossils. Here you can witness palaeontology in action. Plan to get there in the morning because you might decide to spend the whole day at the museum and on the grounds, where there are walking tours of the badlands.

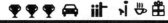

☞ **Atlas Coal Mine** at East Coulee
Box 203, Drumheller, AB T0J 0Y0 * East Coulee
Governing body: Atlas Coal Mine Historical Society
Open daily, Mid-May to Labour Day * ☎ (403) 823-2171
Admission fee charged * *Visiting time:* one hour

Atlas Coal Mine (Courtesy of Alberta Historical Resources Foundation, Medicine Hat Museum and Art Gallery, and James Marshall)

When this historic mine closed in 1984, the mine tipple and much of the equipment remained on the site, but the underground mine was sealed. You can take a guided or self-guided tour around the site on the walking trail. The visitor centre features exhibits, a simulated mine tunnel, audio-visual presentations and demonstrations. The mine tipple alone is worth the visit.

☞ **East Coulee School Museum & Cultural Centre**
Box 539, East Coulee, AB T0J 1B0 * On Highway 10 in East Coulee
Governing body: Dinosaur Valley Heritage Society
Open Victoria Day to Labour Day * ☎ (403)822-3970
Admission by donation * *Visiting time:* one hour

The museum is located in a 1930s school building and features collections related to mining and town history. It has a 1930s classroom and a fully operational post office, with a special stamp for outgoing mail. The art gallery hosting local collections and a tea room serving light lunches are also located at the museum. The warm hospitality and helpfulness of the volunteers in making my visit a pleasurable one very much impressed me.

☞ **Rosebud Centennial Museum**
Box 601, Rosebud, AB T0J 2T0 * Main Street
Governing body: Rosebud Historical Society
Open March to December: mornings, Wednesday and Thursday; evenings,
Thursday to Saturday
☎ (403)677-2284/677-2208/ or 677-2256 * Admission fee charged

---

The museum is housed in an old Chinese laundry built about 1916. Collections include pioneer, domestic, and agricultural artifacts as well as war memorabilia. As the hours seem to vary from day to day, it is best to check locally or call before visiting. It appears to be open before and after performances of the Rosebud Dinner Theatre.

9

HANNA AND THE BUFFALO TRAIL
HIGHWAYS 9 and 41

Big sky, big valleys, vast fields of grain, strong winds. Everything is big in this part of Alberta, except the small, starved, wind-beaten hummocks of poplar trees trying to maintain a root-hold in an area where drought is a frequent visitor. Once grasslands and buffalo reigned supreme. Today wheat fields and cattle populate the uplands.

We begin northeast of Drumheller, in the Hand Hills near Delia on Highway 9, where we leave the transition between parkland and open prairie. The Hand Hills rise high above the prairie some 185 metres. According to one version, the hills were named by the Cree Indians, who called them *michichi ispatinan*, from the resemblance of the hills to outstretched fingers of a hand. According to early explorer Peter Erasmus, another version emerges: a Blackfoot chief, who had a little hand, was killed on the top of one of the hills. Whatever the origin of the name, the Hand Hills serve as a promontory above the surrounding prairie landscape.

Beneath the Hand Hills is the picturesque village of Delia, a green oasis with trees and gardens. Delia originated as a stopping house opened in 1910 by early settler, A. L. Davis, who named it after his wife. The **Delia & District Dawson Historical Museum** is located in the original two-room school built in 1913-14. The museum restored a classroom to this period. Delia plans soon to restore its grist mill—one of the oldest in Alberta.

Hutterite Colony near Fort Macleod 1938.
(Provincial Archives of Alberta A4509)

The Hutterites

The Hutterites, or Hutterite Brethren, are a religious group that are easily recognized by their distinctive dress. The men wear trimmed beards and wear black denim pants and jackets and broad brimmed black hats. Women wear long plaid or flowered skirts and polka-dot kerchiefs. As you drive down most highways in southern and central Alberta, you may notice large communal dwellings surrounded by farmland. The Hutterites live communally like the early Christians, whom they take as their model. They believe that salvation lies in communal living, according to Acts 2:44: "The faithful all lived together and owned everything in common." There are approximately 30,000 Hutterites living in 300 colonies throughout Alberta, Saskatchewan, British Columbia, Montana and Washington.

The Hutterites belong to the Anabaptist tradition that includes Mennonites and the Amish, who all share the belief that baptism into the religious community should take place when one enters adulthood. Hutterites differ from other Anabaptist groups in their adherence to communal living and common ownership of property. Unlike the Amish, the Hutterites do not eschew modern technology for large-scale farming. Hutterites in western Canada came originally from Moravia and speak a dialect of German. An entire group of 1,265 Hutterites immigrated to South Dakota between 1874 to 1879 to escape religious persecution; but when the First World War began, they were again persecuted. Many were imprisoned as conscientious objectors, and many left the United States in 1918 to form new colonies in western Canada. The earliest colonies in Alberta were established between 1918 and 1920.

From Delia we head east on Highway 9 toward Hanna. The elevation drops gently onto flat, open prairie where farms are large and far apart. Our next stop is Hanna, where a giant Canada Grey Goose welcomes you. Hanna began as an agricultural community in the marginal lands east of the fertile crescent, which later became known as the Special Areas. Until 1913, when the Canadian Northern Railway (CNoR) arrived, it had been the Cooperville Post Office. Renamed Hanna after David B. Hanna, former president of the CNoR, the town soon became one of the most important divisional points on the line.

The Special Areas—Land of Hope and Despair

Farmers are the world's most persistent optimists. Pioneers who settled and farmed around Hanna saw good years and bad. The region just east of the fertile crescent and north of the Palliser Triangle was considered by the Palliser's expedition as marginal for growing crops. By the turn of the century, improved wheat seed and dryland farming techniques made it possible to grow crops in these marginal areas during years of sufficient rainfall. However, droughts, hailstorms, wind damage, grasshopper infestations, early frosts or too much or too little rain at the wrong times caused frequent crop failures.

There were a few good years in the beginning, and the arrival of the Canadian Northern Railway in 1913 ensured that crops would get to markets. Then came the depression of 1914 and despair. For the homesteads around Hanna, 1914 was also a bad crop year. All that changed the next few years, when the First World War in Europe created a large demand for wheat, and prices were high. The years of unprecedented rainfall in 1915 and 1916 were good crop years and brought prosperity to the area. But again, despair! In the late 1920s and early 1930s, a long period of drought set in, proving again that Palliser was right all along. Farms around Castor and Hanna were the hardest hit in the province. About 6000 farms were abandoned to the wind and dust. The provincial government passed the Special Areas Act of 1934, took over the abandoned lands, and set up a board to administer them. The hundreds of thousands of abandoned acres became available for private and community grazing to help farmers make the transition to a more viable ranching-farming economy.

Hanna and the district's history are eloquently told by one of the province's most interesting historical villages. **The Hanna & District Historical Village and Pioneer Museum**, which maintains about a dozen restored historical buildings dating from 1912 to 1927. They include a CN railway station, an operational windmill, a blacksmith shop, and a jail cell. What makes this historical village different is that it *looks* like a real village. You'll also want to stop at **The Doll Palace**. It features over 1500 dolls in the tea room and gift shop. If you are camping, Fox Lake Park (4.8 kilometres north of Hanna) has good camping facilities and the fishing and bird watching are excellent.

Hanna & District Historical Village. (R.L. Hursey)

East from Hanna towards Oyen the land becomes table-flat. This is mostly ranching country. While driving between Hanna and Oyen, I had to stop for awhile to watch cattle being herded across the highway from one pasture to another. Having grown up on western novels by Zane Grey and Will James, I suffered a bit of culture shock when I realized there wasn't a horse in the whole outfit. The cowboys were herding the cattle with three pickups, a motorcycle, and two all-terrain vehicles!

Our next stop is Oyen, where Highway 9 and the Buffalo Trail (Highway 41) intersect. Perhaps its strategic location at the crossroads of two main highways has spared Oyen the fate of so many other communities in this area, which look as if they are on the brink of becoming ghost towns. Oyen is a prosperous-looking green oasis that supports the **Oyen Crossroads Museum**, another historical village on a smaller scale than Hanna's, but well worth the time to visit. I was delighted to explore the 1915 Callum Cook Car, a large wooden horse-drawn wagon with a fully equipped kitchen and dining room—a unique artifact. The restored two-story home, beautifully furnished with 1920 period artifacts, gives the visitor some idea of the lifestyle of the more affluent Alberta town dweller.

Tracks and Traces: Buffalo rubbing stones are large erratic boulders that were deposited over 12,000 years ago by receding glaciers. Many are worn smooth and shiny by millions of bison using them as scratching posts to rub off their mangy winter coats. Many museums along the Buffalo Trail display buffalo rubbing stones.

From Oyen we head south along the Buffalo Trail through gently rolling wheat and alfalfa fields, wide valleys, and a big blue sky that seems to go on forever. Imagine what this land must have looked like 150 years ago, with grazing bison and pronghorn scattered about and plains wolves lurking on the edges of the herds! Long before settlers arrived, it was favored hunting ground for the Blackfoot and Plains Cree nations, who often fought over control of the territory. The Métis mounted their semiannual buffalo hunts along this trail, which parallels the Alberta-Saskatchewan border from the North Saskatchewan River to the border of the United States.

About 25 kilometres south of Oyen is Acadia Valley, which isn't really a valley but more of a shallow depression in the ground. Settlers from Nova Scotia began homesteading here in 1911. One's first impression of Acadia Valley might be that it has lost the battle to maintain its service centre. Most of the businesses are boarded up. The hope and future of many small prairie towns will depend upon young, vigorous men and women to keep these communities alive. In Acadia Valley, that seems to be happening at the **Prairie Elevator Museum**. When the village's one grain elevator was closed in 1993, a few enterprising people formed the Prairie Elevator Society and talked the Alberta Wheat Pool into allowing them to convert the facility into a museum. During July and August, the Acadia Valley Grain Elevator Society offers guided tours and demonstrations of how the grain is weighed, tested, stored, and shipped. Having never seen the workings of a grain elevator before, I acquired an understanding and respect for these marvels of human ingenuity. It is gratifying that a few communities are preserving these fast disappearing landmarks.

MUSEUMS IN THE HANNA REGION AND BUFFALO TRAIL

☞ **Acadia Valley Prairie Elevator Museum**
The Prairie Elevator Society, Acadia Valley, AB
You can't miss it. It's the only grain elevator in the village.
Governing body: The Prairie Elevator Society
Open July and August *☎ (403) 972-2408
Admission by donation * *Visiting time:* one hour
♟ ♟ 🚗 ♿ ⊞ 🛆 ▲ ♨

This fairly new museum is dedicated to interpreting the historical importance of grain elevators on the prairies. Well-trained interpreters will show you an informative video and explain how grain is weighed, quality tested, stored, and unloaded into box cars for shipment. Samples of various grains grown in the area as well as tools and a large hay wagon are on display. Be sure to spend some time in the former office, where there is a tea room and gift shop.

Jamie, tour guide at Arcadia Valley Grain Elevator Museum (R.L. Hursey)

☞ **Prairie Pioneer Museum** at Cereal, AB
Box 131, Cereal, AB T0J 0N0 * Cereal CNR Station
Governing body: Cereal & District Historical Society
Open May 1 to August 31 * ☎ (403)326-3899
Admission by donation * *Visiting time:* one half hour

The museum has restored the CNR station living quarters including the downstairs kitchen and dining room and the bedrooms, sewing room, and sitting room upstairs. Collections include artifacts from the old hospital and a working windmill used to grind flour and pump water. On the grounds are a cook car, bunkhouse, caboose, former town office, and a jail house.

☞ **Delia & District Dawson Historical Museum**
☞ Box 93, Delia, AB T0J 0W0
307 Main Street, next to the United Church
Governing body: Delia Historical Society
Open May long weekend through Labour Day * ☎ (403)364-3848
Admission by donation * *Visiting time:* one half hour

The museum occupies the original two-room schoolhouse. One school room is a restored classroom of the 1910s, and the other room houses local artifacts and photographs.

☞ **Hanna Pioneer & Village Museum**
Box 1528, Hanna, AB T0J 1P0 * Pioneer Trail at 3rd Avenue East
Governing body: Hanna and District Historical Society
Open June to September * ☎ (403)854-4244
Admission fee charged * *Visiting time:* one and a half hours

🏆🏆🏆🚗♿ ⊞ 🎋▲

This museum has an amazing collection of historical buildings in a village setting, including a boardwalk. Buildings include a CNR station, church, store, hospital, ranch house, school, blacksmith shop, telephone office and many more. The quality of restoration is very good, and the wealth of artifacts collected from the area since 1966 could hold your interest for hours. An RV trailer park is located next to the museum.

☞ **Crossroads Museum** at Oyen
Box 477, Oyen, AB T0J 2J0 * 1st Avenue
Governing body: Oyen & District Historical Society
Open May 15 to August 31 * ☎ (403)664-3850
Admission by donation * *Visiting time:* one hour

🏆🏆🚗 🍴 ⎯

This community history museum displays a variety of local artifacts and fossil specimens in the community hall. A small pioneer village contains a very interesting 1915 Callum Cook Car with a fully restored kitchen and dining room, once used to feed the hired hands. There is also a blacksmith shop and a restored pioneer home.

10

THREE HILLS—TROCHU AREA
HIGHWAYS 9 AND 21

The Three Hills-Trochu area is located on the edge of Alberta's parkland, a transition zone between grassland prairie and the boreal forest. Here one begins to see more hummocks of trembling aspen, the dominant tree species. As more moisture falls in this region (457 mm to 500 mm per year), crops can be grown with reasonable assurance that they can be harvested. The upper Red Deer river valley, east of Trochu, provides a rich habitat for many forms of wildlife and plantlife.

The two famous explorers, Anthony Henday and Peter Fidler, were the first white men to provide a written record of the areas around Three Hills and Trochu. Anthony Henday travelled overland by foot from Hudson's Bay with a large group of Cree traders in 1754. He entered today's Alberta near Edgerton. His route took him near Delburne, where he crossed the Red Deer River downstream of Content Bridge. In 1791 Fidler travelled with some Peigan Indians from the Red Deer River to the Porcupine Hills. Although he was not the first white person to see the Canadian Rocky Mountains (Anthony Henday was in 1754), Fidler was the first to take compass bearings and describe the distinctive Devil's Head mountain near Banff and Chief Mountain in Waterton Lakes National Park. The following spring, on his return trip to Buckingham House, he returned near the area where Three Hills Creek joins the Red Deer River. There he recorded in his journal the first discovery of coal on the Canadian prairies.

Our heritage hunting begins at Irricana, on Highway 9, 35 kilometres north of the Trans-Canada Highway. In 1909, the CPR dug an irrigation canal within a few miles of this village. Although the canal was never used and it gradually filled in, the early settlers called their village Irricana, combining the words "irrigation" and "canal." The village is located near the site of the "Slaughter Camp" where Captain Palliser's expedition killed 17 buffalo in 1859. Irricana is home to the **Pioneer Acres of Alberta,** where the Plowmen's & Threshermen's Club of Alberta holds its annual show and reunion on the second weekend in August. You can relive the early days of agriculture watching demonstrations of horse-drawn and steam-powered plowing and threshing equipment.

Nine kilometres north of Irricana is the village of Beiseker, named after Thomas L. Beiseker, the leader of the first settlers who came in 1910. The **Beiseker Station Museum** occupies a former CPR station. The facility also houses the village office and library.

From Beiseker, you may want to go north on SR 806 to the village of Linden, originally settled by a branch of Mennonites called Holdamanites. They followed a traditional way of life that included social separateness and conservative dress. Linden has become a rural industrial centre and home of the woolen mill that still makes traditional custom wool blankets.

While driving on SR 806 toward Three Hills, I noticed many small bluebird boxes on the fence posts lining the road. This is one area where you will actually find bluebirds nesting in the boxes instead of sparrows, which manage to drive most blue birds from nests in other areas. The bluebird boxes, however, have helped these remarkable birds to make a comeback in the province.

In the distance appears the distinctive landmark of Three Hills. Long before European occupation, the hills were frequented by Cree and Blackfoot Indians. Three Hills is also near the site of one of the oldest trails in Alberta, predating the Calgary-Edmonton trail. The town of Three Hills developed from a post office that was established in 1904.

Three Hills is the home of the Prairie Bible Institute. This institute began as a small school in 1922. A local family hired Leslie Maxwell from Kansas to start a school for their children and their neighbor's children to teach them about the Bible. Under Maxwell's dynamic leadership and radio evangelism, the Prairie Bible Institute developed into one of the largest Bible schools in North America. For over 60 years it has provided training for missionaries to teach Christian fundamentalism in rural Alberta and in Third World countries.

Three Hills is an immaculate, orderly town. The motel I stayed in had received awards three years in a row for its cleanliness. The spotlessly clean restaurant where I had dinner was crowded with local customers saying grace before eating and reading the Bible at their tables. When I drove to the **Kneehill Historical Museum**, I was struck by how out of place these old buildings looked in such a modern, orderly town. I was also disappointed to discover that the museum was closed in July and August, the height of the heritage hunting season.

Trochu, some 15 kilometres north of Three Hills on Highway 21, provided more successful heritage hunting. A group of former French cavalry officers, under the leadership of Armand Trochu settled this community in 1903. Trochu established St. Ann Ranch in the coulee below the present townsite. Most of the officers returned to France at the beginning of World War I. Between 1904 and 1911,

Jewish families, assisted by the Jewish Colonization Association, began to farm around Trochu and Rumsey. In 1905, the Fathers of Tinchebray, a French Roman Catholic Order, accepted Bishop Legal's invitation to serve the people at Trochu. Eight Sisters of Evron joined the Fathers in 1909. Armand Trochu turned St. Ann Ranch over to the Sisters, who began to set up a temporary hospital on the ranch.

The Sisters of Charity of Notre Dame d'Evron

First Sisters of Evron in Alberta. 1909. (Glenbow Archives, Calgary, Alberta NA-2653-1)

In 1909, eight Sisters of Evron came to Canada in response to Bishop Legal's invitation to join the Priests of Tinchebray in the community founded by Mr. Armand Trochu. In Trochu, their first home was St. Ann Ranch, down in the coulee below the town. Imagine their delight when they discovered on the wall of each of their rooms, a paper crucifix that the women of Trochu had thoughtfully cut out of a religious journal. The Sisters went to work immediately, converting a granary next to the house into a hospital. Within two years the Sisters and the community built a permanent hospital, St. Mary's. In 1922, the Priests of Tinchebray left Alberta and returned to France after friction developed between the Order and the new Archbishop. The Sisters of Evron remained to serve the community to the present day.

Today you can visit **St. Ann Ranch,** now a provincial historic resource. The ranch includes a country bed and breakfast, a tea house, and a museum and interpretive centre.

St. Ann Ranch House. (R.L. Hursey)

In the town of Trochu enjoy visiting the **Trochu Valley Museum,** located in the old fire hall. Its small thematic displays portray the community's history. The **Trochu Arboretum** is a beautiful living museum, with over 100 species of native and exotic trees and shrubs as well as an astounding variety of flowers.

Continuing north on Highway 20, you will want to drive through the village of Delburne, just south of SR 595, known locally as "the Coal Trail." In Delburne The **Anthony Henday Museum** is named in honor of the famous explorer whose journey through central Alberta brought him very close to today's Delburne. The museum, located in the 1913 Grand Trunk Pacific railway station, interprets its agricultural, coal mining and railway history. One of the museum's unique features is a 1930 four-storey CN water tower.

MUSEUMS IN THE THREE HILLS-TROCHU AREA

☞ **Beiseker Station Museum**
Box 149, Beiseker, AB T0M 0G0 * Main Street
Governing body: Beiseker Museum Society
Open May 1 - September 31, Monday to Friday * ☎ (403) 947-3774
Admission by donation * *Visiting time:* one half hour
🍷 🚗 ⛩ 🍽 ⎯

The Beiseker Station Museum is located in the former CPR station. A kitchen and bedroom have been restored to reflect the lifestyle of the station agent's family. One room contains local history artifacts. The society is also setting up a music museum.

☞ **Anthony Henday Museum** at Delburne
Box 374, Delbourne, AB T0M 0V0 * Main Street
Governing body: Anthony Henday Historical Society
Open June, Wednesday to Sunday: July to Labour Day, daily
☎ (403) 749-2436 * *Admission by donation* * *Visiting time:* one-half hour
♥ 🚗 🎪 🍴 ━

The museum is housed in the 1913 GTP railway station and in the original four storey CNR water tower from the 1930s. Collections include coal mining, railway, and farming artifacts as well as household items. The collection interprets the history of Delburne, an area settled around the turn of the century.

☞ **Pioneer Acres of Alberta** at Irricana
Box 58, Irricana, AB T0M 1B0
Irricana, 45 kilometres northeast of Calgary, on Highway 9
Governing body: Pioneer Acres Plowmen and Threshermen's Club of Alberta
Open May long weekend to Labour Day,
Tuesday through Sunday and holiday weekends
☎ (403)953-4357 * Admission fee charged * *Visiting time:* two hours
♥ ♥ 🚗 🎪 ⛺

Pioneer Acres has collections of working farm machinery, including antique steam tractors, stationary engines, and threshing equipment. Tours are available. The best time to see demonstrations of the working collection in operation is the second weekend in August, when the museum holds its Annual show and Reunion. This is a good place to camp. There are RV facilities and treed campsites.

☞ **Kneehill Historical Museum** at Three Hills
Box 543, Three Hills, AB T0M 2A0 * Access road to Highway 21 east.
Governing body: Kneehill Historical Society
Open May, June, September and October
☎ (403)443-2092 or 443-5970 * Admission fee charged
♥ 🚗 🎪 ⛺

The museum has the original CNR station and domestic, farming, medical, and commercial artifacts that depict the pioneer era.

☞ **St. Ann Ranch** at Trochu
Box 249, Trochu, AB T0M 2C0
In the coulee below the town. From Highway 21, drive east on SR 585 through town and follow signs.
Governing body: Privately owned and operated by Lorene and Louis Frere
Open May 1 to September 30 * ☎ (403)442-3924
Visiting time: one hour for non-guests

St Ann Ranch has a Queen Anne style four-storey ranch house used as a bed and breakfast, with rooms furnished in antiques. Collections include domestic and ranching artifacts, a 1904 log cabin and a 1907 post office. A tea house serves luncheons and tea in the afternoons.

☞ **Trochu Valley Museum**
Box 538, Trochu, AB T0M 2C0 * In the old Fire Hall on Arena Avenue
Governing body: Trochu Valley Historical Society
Open May through August * ☎ (403)442-2334
Admission by donation * *Visiting time:* one half hour

This small museum features artifacts collected from the local area, including Indian artifacts and dinosaur fossils. A small collection of men's clothing and accessories is one of the most successful displays. It includes a suit once owned by Louis Bleriot, the famous French aviator. He gave it to his brother, who operated the Munson (Bleriot) ferry.

☞ **Trochu Arboretum**
Box 340, Trochu, AB T0M 2A0 * In Trochu, at North Road and School Road
Governing body: Trochu and District Arboretum Society
Open Victoria Day to Labour Day * ☎ (403)442-2111
Admission by donation * *Visiting time:* one hour

This arboretum maintains over 1000 trees and shrubs from over 100 native and non-native species for scientific, educational, and recreational purposes. Walking trails wind through the lovely, peaceful grounds, displaying the many varieties of flowers that can be grown in southern Alberta.

11

CALGARY

Sandstone City, Cowtown, Oil Capital of Canada, Home of the 1988 Winter Olympics, Gateway to the Canadian Rockies. Calgary, located at the junction of the Bow and Elbow rivers and within sight of the foothills of the Canadian Rockies, comprises many identities. Calgary and Edmonton are Alberta's largest cities, but which is larger is arguable. Within Calgary's city limits reside some 710,000 people; Edmonton's metropolitan area has about 840,000. Calgary prides itself on its ranching past and its cowtown image. In July of every year, thousands of Calgarians partake in strange rituals as they hang up their business suits, brush off big hats and put on outfits that would have given any self-respecting horseman of the 1890s cause to ponder. Calgarians have been doing this ever since the first Stampede, which was organized by four prominent ranchers in 1912.

Tom Three Persons, Blood Indian Cowboy and bronc rider. (Glenbow Archives, Calgary, AB, NA-584-1)

Tracks and Traces: A Stampede combines a rodeo, outdoor exhibition and "a damned good party." In 1912, Pat Burns, George Lane, A. E. Cross, and A. J. McLean organized Calgary's first Stampede. Since 1923, it has been a regular event each summer in Calgary.

The city of Calgary originated as a North West Mounted Police (NWMP) post in 1875. Like Fort Macleod, the first post built in 1874, Fort Calgary was established to discourage American whisky traders. Ironically the post was built by I. G. Baker Company of Fort Benton, Montana, the same company that outfitted many of the whisky traders whose operations the Mounties came to shut down. Inspector Ephrem Brisebois, the first commander of the post, wanted to name it after himself, but Colonel James Macleod chose the Scottish name "Calgary," believing that the Gaelic term meant "clear, running water."

Fort Calgary served as the centre of a growing community of businesses, churches and ranches until 1883, when the Canadian

Pacific Railway made a decision to place its line a mile or so west. Fort Calgary began to succumb to urban expansion and development before the turn of the century. By 1914, railway yards had obscured its existence. Recent archaeological excavations have uncovered the original foundations of the fort as well as many small artifacts, now on view at the **Fort Calgary Interpretive Centre.** The centre's displays and programs interpret the history of Fort Calgary and the NWMP.

Just west of Calgary is the Sarcee Nation reserve. Although the city of Calgary began as a NWMP post, the area around the city had been occupied by Native people for thousands of years. By the time the NWMP arrived in 1875, the Sarcee and Blackfoot Indians frequented the area. The word Sarcee is a Blackfoot term meaning "bold people." But the name the Sarcee call themselves is *Tsuu-T'ina* meaning "many people." The Sarcee, or Tsuu-T'ina, is an Athapaskan-speaking tribe, once an off-shoot of the Beaver Indians of northwestern Alberta. The group became a distinct tribe centuries ago when they chose to live a prairie and mountain lifestyle.

In the 1700s, the Sarcee lived near the Rocky Mountains around the headwaters of the North Saskatchewan River, about the time that the Cree, with their superior weapons, were displacing many of the Alberta tribes. By the 1800s, the Sarcee had become closely aligned with the Blackfoot Confederacy. Although culturally similar to the Blood and Peigan, the Sarcee retained their language and identity.

Chief Bull Head of the Sarcee. (Glenbow Archives NA-583-1)

When the Sarcee signed Treaty No. Seven in 1877, the tribe had been decimated to about 100 people, following smallpox epidemics and the loss of the buffalo herds that had sustained them. At first the Sarcee were given unsuitable agricultural land on the Blackfoot reserve, about 32 kilometres upstream on the Bow River. When food rations ran out, Head Chief Bull Head moved the hungry tribe to the outskirts of Fort Calgary, and the people resisted moving back to Blackfoot reserve, even after they were sent south on an arduous journey in winter to Fort Macleod where there was a better supply of rations. Bull Head was insistent that the reserve they wanted was the land around Fish Creek; and finally in June of 1883, he succeeded in getting a new treaty signed, giving the Sarcee people an area of about 259 square kilometres west of Calgary.

The best place to go to learn about the Sarcee People is the **Tsuu T'ina Museum and Archives** on the Sarcee Reserve. The museum has a series of exhibits that portray the lifestyle and history of the Sarcee People. A painted hide features Chief Bull Head's war history. The **Glenbow Museum** houses one of the most extensive historical collections of Plains Indian art and material culture in North America.

The arrival of the Canadian Pacific Railway changed the little village of Fort Calgary into a major railway centre. In 1881, the promise of the railroad attracted a fledgling business community with false-fronted frame buildings. By August of 1883, the Canadian Pacific Railway (CPR) line had reached Calgary, changing the sleepy village into a booming railway town. In 1886, after the American-owned Eau Claire Lumber Company built its sawmill on the Bow River, Calgary became an important lumber centre as well. In the spring there were log drives. Logs cut in the Kananaskis were floated down the Bow River to the millsite. Stockyards were added by 1890. Calgary became not only a major railway distribution centre but a commercial, industrial and service centre to surrounding ranches and homesteads.

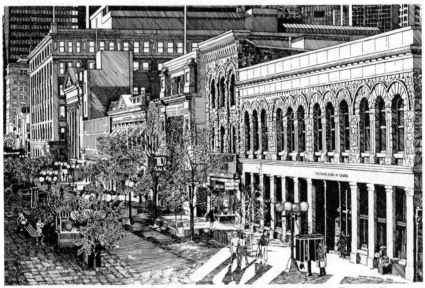

Stephen Avenue (Courtesy of Alberta Historical Resources Foundation, Medicine Hat Museum and Art Gallery, and James Marshall)

By the time rancher and meat packer Pat Burns had become Calgary's first millionaire in the early 1900s, the look of Calgary changed from a frontier town to an emerging metropolis. Buildings of sandstone from nearby quarries gave Calgary the name of "Sandstone City." During the first decade, hundreds of stone workers kept busy erecting the "fireproof" buildings along Stephen Avenue (today's 8th Avenue). Many of these early sandstone buildings have been preserved and restored. **The Stephen Avenue Tour** offers a self-guided walking tour of this area. A pamphlet contains a wealth of information about the history of these buildings and can be obtained at the Calgary Convention & Visitor's Bureau at 237 - 8th Avenue SE.

Bob Edwards—Philosopher of the Prairies

For years, Robert C. "Bob" Edwards, editor of the *Calgary Eye Opener*, poked fun at the pretensions and foibles of Calgary's social elite. Born in Scotland, he came to Alberta in 1895 and started his own newspaper. Not dependent upon his own printing facility, Bob established his newspaper wherever he moved, including Wetaskiwin, Strathcona, and High River before he settled in Calgary in 1904. He published his newspaper off and on until his death in 1922. Edwards' satirical wit, humorous anecdotes, and fictitious characters became so popular that his subscribers tolerated many late issues, sometimes weeks behind schedule, due to his life-long problem with drinking. A champion of the underdog, defender of the defenseless, and master of the one-liner, Bob Edwards became an institution unto himself and developed a devoted readership in western Canada and around the world.

"A good man who goes wrong is just a bad man who has been found out." (*Eye Opener*, September 22, 1917)

"There isn't a woman so bad in arithmetic that she cannot calculate how much her husband would save if he didn't smoke." (*Eye Opener*, July 20, 1918)

"The water wagon is certainly a more dangerous vehicle than the automobile. At least more people fall off of it." (*Eye Opener*, August 25, 1906)

"Had Moses been a Methodist, he would undoubtedly have had five hundred commandments instead of ten." (*Eye Opener*, May 6, 1916)

Several museums in Calgary feature collections that portray the early history. **Fort Calgary Historic Park** has collections and research material on Calgary's local history as well as historic buildings like the restored **Deane House Historic Site and Tea Room**. The **City of Calgary Archives** has archival material pertaining to the civic and social history of Calgary. **Glenbow Museum** has extensive collections reflecting the history of the Canadian Pacific Railway. Its archives contains one of the best photographic collections in western Canada. **Heritage Park Historical Village** features many of Calgary's restored historic homes and commercial buildings as well as locomotives and other rolling stock.

Heritage Park Historical Village (R.L. Hursey)

In 1891, Calgary had a population of 3,876, most of whom were British and American in origin. Many of the leaders had been ranchers, politically conservative and Victorian in tastes and attitudes. Polo and cricket were popular sports played among the men, as well as "fox" hunts (actually coyotes) imported by the British establishment. "At Homes," church socials, and afternoon teas were popular pastimes among the fashionable women. Further down the social ladder were the working class—railway workers, lumber men, meat packers and construction workers. Many stone masons found employment in Calgary during the years that it was converting to sandstone.

Near the bottom rung of the social ladder were the Chinese, who had come to build the CPR and settled in Calgary after the completion of the railway. Most originally came from the southern province of Guangdong, by way of the United States and British Columbia. The only occupations the prejudiced Anglo-British establishment allowed these men were domestic work, running laundries or working as cooks at nearby ranches. In 1885 the Dominion Government passed the Chinese Immigration Act and Head Tax, which restricted the entry of Chinese by requiring a head tax of $50; this escalated to $500 by 1903. No other ethnic group was subjected to this treatment. In 1921, of the 3,500 Chinese-Canadians who lived in the province, only 200 were women. The act was finally repealed in 1923. As immigration laws of the time also prohibited Chinese men from bringing their wives and families to Canada, those in Calgary lived very lonely lives. In spite of hardships, many Chinese acquired land and established successful market gardens and restaurants. Gradually, a core of small businesses formed Calgary's Chinatown, the largest in the province.

The Hing Wah family. Immigration laws prevented men from bringing their wives and families to Canada. (Glenbow Archives, Calgary, AB NC-26-27)

Today's Chinatown has few residents (most Chinese-Canadians live throughout the city), but it is still an important business centre. The focal point and showpiece of Calgary's Chinatown is the new **Calgary Chinese Cultural Centre**, a replica of the Temple of Heaven in Beijing. This extraordinary centre contains a library, classrooms, gymnasium, multi-purpose hall, gift shop, restaurant, auditorium, an acupuncture and holistic health clinic, a museum and art gallery. The **Calgary Chinese Cultural Centre Museum** features a magnificent collection of ancient ceramics and pottery, representing 6000 years of Chinese culture.

In 1914, oil was discovered in Turner Valley, southwest of Calgary, launching the first major oil boom in western Canada. Within months, more than 500 oil companies formed, but only 50 oil derricks actually pumped oil. By 1920, there were only nine wells. Though the total oil output of Turner Valley was modest compared to future oil strikes, it established Calgary as a major oil and gas centre. During the oil boom of the 1950s and 1960s, Calgary became the headquarters for many oil and gas companies.

Turner Valley, c1930. (Glenbow Archives, Calgary, Alberta NA-67-67)

Today Calgary's economy revolves around oil, agriculture, banking and energy. To learn more about Calgary's petroleum heritage, the **Canadian Western Natural Gas, Light, Heat and Power Museum** contains exhibits on the evolution of the natural gas industry. The **Energeum** is a science centre where its many hands-on exhibits tell the story of the formation of oil and gas and their recovery.

For the heritage hunter, Calgary offers much. If you were to spend a week doing nothing but visiting Calgary's 30-some museums, you would not have sufficient time to see them all. Many of Calgary's museums have a broad regional, national, and international scope, like the **Glenbow Museum** and the **Heritage Park Historical Village**. Others like the **Aero Space Museum of Calgary,** the **Grain Academy Museum,** and the **Calgary Police Museum** are more specialized and provide key pieces in Calgary's jigsaw puzzle of human and natural history. One of the newest and most impressive of the specialized museums is the **Museum of the Regiments.** Four Calgary military regiments have come together to establish one of the finest military museums in Canada. The life-like dioramas of battle scenes and military life are so realistically done that you feel as if you have stepped right into a moment in history. Another newer museum you won't want to miss is the **Olympic Hall of Fame and Museum**, the largest museum in the world that features the Olympic Games. Here you can relive Calgary's Winter Olympics of 1988 or experience the vicarious thrill of riding a bobsled.

For those interested in natural history, the **Calgary Zoo, Botanical Garden and Prehistoric Park** is one of the finest and most respected zoological parks in the world. The zoo has more than 1000 animals, many of which are rare and among the endangered species. Currently the Calgary Zoo is developing spacious exhibits that feature five distinct Canadian ecosystems.

Museum of the Regiments
(R.L. Hursey)

MUSEUMS IN CALGARY

☞ **Aero Space Museum of Calgary**
Hangar #10, 64 McTavish Place, NE, Calgary, AB T2E 7H1
Hangar #10, southeast corner of Calgary International Airport,
Governing body: Aero Space Museum Association
Open year round, daily * ☎ (403)250-3752
Admission fee charged * *Visiting time:* one hour
🏆🏆🏆🚗♿🎁🍴 ⎯

Located in a World War II hangar originally used as part of the British Commonwealth Air Training Programme, the museum exhibits vintage bush pilot planes, military planes, commercial and recreational aircraft, helicopters, and aviation art. A very good display introduces the history of aviation in Canada. One of the best features about this museum is that the visitor can actually see restoration of old aircraft taking place and interact with the volunteers. If you are looking for books on Canadian aviation history, the museum has an excellent bookshop.

☞ **Alberta Science Centre/Centennial Planetarium**
Box 2100, Station M, Calgary, AB T2P 2M5
701 - 11th Street SW
Governing body: Alberta Science Centre Society
Open year round, daily * ☎ (403) 221-3700
Admission fee charged * *Visiting time:* one and a half hours

This museum has changing exhibits that focus on scientific themes and programs. The centre aims at providing science activities to schools, families, and other children's groups. The planetarium features a 360-degree Star Theatre, which presents a variety of star and laser shows.

☞ **Arctic Institute of North America**
2500 University Drive, NW, Calgary, AB T2N 1N4
University of Calgary * *Governing body:* University of Calgary
Open year round, Monday to Friday * ☎ (403) 220-7515
Admission by donation * *Visiting time:* one-half hour

This art museum contains collections of early explorer drawings, painting, prints and photographs. This is primarily a museum for research purposes.

☞ **Beth Tzedec Heritage Collection**
1325 Glenmore Trail, SW, Calgary, AB T2V 4Y8
In the Beth Tzedec Synagogue
Governing body: Beth Tzedec Congregation
Open year round, Monday to Friday * ☎ (403) 255-8688
Admission by donation * *Visiting time:* one-half hour

This museum comprises collections of Calgary's early Jewish Community. Artifacts include books, textiles, archival documents, photographs, art work and religious objects from two synagogue congregations that merged in 1989.

☞ **Calgary Chinese Cultural Centre Collection**
197 First Street, SW, Calgary, AB T2P 4MA
Across the street from the Eau Claire Market
Governing body: Calgary Chinese Cultural Centre Association
Open year round * ☎ (403) 262-5071
Admission fee charged *Visiting time:* one hour
🍷🍷🍷🍷🚗 ♿ 🎁 🍴 ⎯

The Calgary Chinese Cultural Centre is an architectural masterpiece—a replica of the Temple of Heaven set in the heart of Calgary's Chinatown. A multifaceted building, it includes a lending library (the largest outside of China), a museum, classrooms, an auditorium, a restaurant, an acupuncture and holistic health centre, a gift shop, and many more attractions. The museum showcases the artistic and technological achievements of the Chinese culture. Collections include a variety of Shiwan clay figures and Chinese pottery dating as early as the Neolithic period of Chinese history (4000 to 6000 BP). Of interest are the full-sized replicas of the terra cotta soldiers unearthed in 1980 from Emperor Shihuang's tomb. Children will enjoy the singing fish basin, which sprays water up when you rub its sides. A mixture of ancient and contemporary Chinese brush paintings and calligraphy scrolls adorns its walls.

☞ **Calgary Police Service Interpretive Centre and Museum**
133 - 6th Avenue, SE, Calgary, AB T2G 4Z1 * 2nd floor, 316 - 7th Avenue
Governing body: Calgary Police Service Museum Society
☎ (403) 268-4565 * Admission fee charged
🍷🍷 ♿ 🚻 🍴 ⎯

The museum has approximately 4000 catalogued artifacts including uniforms, communications and photographic equipment, weapons and crime scene evidence and archival records that include hundreds of finger prints and mug shots.

☞ **Calgary Zoo, Botanical Gardens and Prehistoric Park**
Box 3036, Station B, Calgary, AB T2M 4R8 * 1300 Zoo Road, SE *
Governing body: Calgary Zoological Society * Open year round, daily
* Admission fee charged * *Visiting time:* three hours
🍷🍷🍷🍷🚗 🚻 🎁 🍴 ⎯

The Calgary Zoo has more than 1000 live species of mammals, birds, reptiles and amphibians from all over the world. Many are rare and endangered species. Generally I find most zoos depressing, but this one is spacious and designed primarily for the animals' welfare rather than for optimum visitor viewing. It changed my attitude. Reconstructed natural habitats provide spacious environments for many species. The newly opened "Canadian Wilds" displays cover 25 acres (10 hectares) and recreates five distinct Canadian ecosystems. The Prehistoric Park contains realistic dinosaur models placed within authentic settings of rock formations and vegetation. It has walking trails that lead the visitor on an imaginary trip through Alberta's prehistoric past. The Botanical Garden has changing garden displays and features a tropical rain forest and a butterfly garden. In the spring, 20,000 blooming tulips provide a feast for the eyes.

☞ City of Calgary Archives
Box 2100, Station M, Calgary, AB T2P 2M5
Main floor, Administration Building, 313 - 7th Avenue, SE
Governing body: City of Calgary
Open year round, Monday to Friday * ☎ (403) 268-8180
No admission fee
♥ 🚗 ⛪ 🍴 ⎯

The City of Calgary Archives houses all valuable civic records, personal papers of elected City officials, records of community groups and organizations, and records relating to the XV Olympic Winter Games. Exhibits and displays feature archival material of interest to the public.

☞ Energeum
640 - 5th Avenue, SW, Calgary, AB T2P 3G4
Governing body: Energy Resources Conservation Board
Open year round, Monday to Friday * ☎ (403) 297-4293
No admission fee * *Visiting time:* one half hour
♥♥ 🚗 ⛪ 🍴 ⎯

The Energeum has hands-on displays that explore Alberta's energy resources, including coal, oil, oil sands, natural gas and hydroelectricity. Working models, computer programs and static displays are aimed at visitors of all age groups, but especially school-aged children.

☞ Fort Calgary Historic Park
Box 2100, Station M, Calgary, AB T2P 2M5 * 750 - 9th Avenue, SE
Governing body: Fort Calgary Society and the City of Calgary
Open year round, daily * ☎ (403)290-1875
Admission by donation * *Visiting time:* one hour
♥♥🚗♿🛈⊞🎋🍴➖

Fort Calgary is located on the original site of the NWMP post established in 1875. The 40-acre historic park includes an interpretive centre, an archaeological site, the Deane House Historic Site and Tea Room, and the Hunt House Historic Site. Collections cover the history of the North West Mounted Police and Calgary's human and natural history. The newly renovated interpretive exhibits bring to life the archaeological site and give a human perspective to Fort Calgary's role in the early history of Calgary and southern Alberta.

☞ Glenbow Museum
130 - 9th Avenue, SE, Calgary, AB T2G 0P3
Adjacent to the Calgary Convention Centre and Calgary Tower
Governing body: Board of Governors, Glenbow-Alberta Institute
Open year round, Tuesday to Sunday * ☎ (403) 268-4100
Admission fee charged * *Visiting time:* two hours
♥♥♥♥♥♿⊞🍴➖

Glenbow Museum is a multi-disciplinary museum with a Western North American focus. Glenbow's extensive artifact collections cover a variety of subjects, from ethnology, cultural history and military history to mineralogy and numismatics. Works of art features Canadian and Western North American historical and contemporary paintings, drawings, prints and illustrations. The newly renovated permanent galleries provide an opportunity for visitors to see the museum's significant collections in a thematic context. Glenbow has a major research library and archives that specializes in Western Canadian development. It opened its newly renovated permanent galleries in 1995, so if you haven't been there for a while you will want to be sure to see the new exhibits. Parking is a bit of a problem for visitors with RV's, but there is an open lot a couple of blocks east of the museum.

☞ **Grain Academy Museum**
Box 2700, Calgary, AB T2P 2P5
Plus 15 Level, Roundup Centre, Stampede Park
Governing body: Alberta Wheat Pool Grain Museum Society
Open year round, Monday to Friday * ☎ (403) 263-4594
No admission fee * *Visiting time:* one half hour

Alberta Wheat Pool's Grain Academy Museum features the history of grains, transportation and end products. The museum's exhibits and programs feature the economic importance of grain in Alberta and its impact on our daily lives. Historical farm tools, dioramas, a working model grain elevator, a scale model steam tractor and model trains showing transportation of grain, and an award winning film, *The Way it Was*, provide an educational and entertaining visit.

☞ **Heritage Park Historical Village**
1900 Heritage Drive, SW, Calgary, AB T2V 2X3
Adjacent to the Glenmore Reservoir
Governing body: Heritage Park Society
Open Mid-May to Mid-October * ☎ (403) 255-1182
Admission fee charged * *Visiting time:* three hours

Heritage Park Historical Village is located on a peninsula overlooking the Glenmore Reservoir. It is the largest living historical village of its type in Canada, with over 100 original and replica buildings and exhibits. Historical buildings from all over Alberta have been relocated, restored, and furnished to three time periods— 1886, 1910 and 1930. Its collections include the Laggan Railway Station; the home of Sam Livingstone, an early rancher; an original wooden oil rig from Turner Valley; and an early amusement park, with a carousel, swings, and a small Ferris wheel. Visitors can take rides on a steam-powered train, horse-drawn wagons, a streetcar, a 1920s bus, or a paddle wheel steamboat that cruises the perimeter of the park. Costumed communicators are found throughout the park to answer visitors' questions. One can have an old fashioned dinner at the Wainwright Hotel or purchase bakery products at an old fashioned bakery. There is so much to see and do here that you will want to come back for many repeat visits.

☞ **Museum of the Regiments**
CFB Calgary, Calgary, AB T3E 1T8
4520 Crowchild Trail, SW (at Flanders Avenue)
Governing body: Calgary Military Museums Society
Open year round, Monday to Sunday; closed Wednesdays
☎ (403) 240-7674 * Admission by donation * *Visiting time:* one hour

♥ ♥ ♥ ♥ 🚗 ♿ 🎁 🍴 ⎯

The Museum of the Regiments was opened by Her Majesty, Queen Elizabeth II, in 1990. The museum collects, preserves, and exhibits the historical collections of four regiments and CFB Calgary. Separate exhibit galleries focus on the history of the four regiments: Princess Patricia's Canadian Light Infantry Regiment, Lord Strathcona's (Royal Canadian) Regiment, King's Own Calgary Regiment, and The Calgary Highlanders. Collections include uniforms, weapons, medals, equipment, trophies of war, vehicles and many other military artifacts. I have rarely seen better full scale dioramas than those at the Museum of the Regiments. Life-like mannequins are displayed in battle scenes, a prisoner of war camp, and a bombed European village. This is a destination museum for anyone interested in military history. For families it is a good place to share memories with younger members and for all to learn about the contributions of these Canadian regiments.

☞ **Naval Museum of Alberta**
1820 - 24th Street, SW, Calgary, AB T2T 0G6
Governing body: Tecumseh Historical Society
Open year round, Tuesday to Sunday * ☎ (403) 242-0002
Admission by donation * *Visiting time:* one half hour

♥ ♥ 🚗 🍴 ⎯

The Naval Museum of Alberta is located at the HMS Tecumseh, referred to as "stone frigate," a land-based naval station. Three large naval aircraft dominate the museum's gallery: *The Banshee, The Sea Fury* and *The Sea Fire.* Some very well-crafted scale models of ships are on display. I was disappointed, however, that there was no evident storyline to the exhibits nor labels to inform the visitor about the history of the navy in Alberta. This museum will be of interest to active and retired naval personnel and aviation enthusiasts.

☞ **Nickle Arts Museum**
The University of Calgary, 2500 University Drive, NW, Calgary, AB T2N 1N4
434 Collegiate Boulevard off 32 Avenue
Governing body: The University of Calgary
Open year round, Tuesday to Sunday; closed Mondays
☎ (403) 220-7234 *Admission fee charged * *Visiting time:* one hour

---

This art museum collects primarily contemporary works of art including sculpture, paintings, decorative arts, ancient coins and African and Inuit collections. Its program of changing exhibits of its permanent collection and travelling exhibits offers visitors plenty of opportunities to make return visits. Those interested in coins will not want to miss the excellent numismatics collection.

☞ **Olympic Hall of Fame and Museum**
Canada Olympic Park, Calgary, AB T2M 4N3, 8880 Canada Olympic Drive
Governing body: Calgary Olympic Development Association
Open year round, Tuesday to Sunday * ☎ (403) 286-2632
Admission fee charged * *Visiting time:* one hour

The Olympic Hall of Fame and Museum is the largest museum in the world dedicated to the Olympic Games. It opened in February 1988 in conjunction with the XV Olympic Winter Games in Calgary. The Hall of Fame pays tribute to the achievements of Canada's Winter Olympians. The museum exhibits artifacts related to the XV Olympic Winter Games. Its collections include uniforms, costumes, sports equipment, pins, medals, posters, awards and Nag Arnold sculptures. Be sure to see the introductory video production and take a simulated ride on the bobsled. You actually get the feeling of being in one. This is the best museum I have seen in Canada that is dedicated to sports.

☞ **Tsuu T'ina Museum (Sarcee People's Museum)**
Box 135, 3700 Anderson Road, SW, Calgary, AB T2W 3C4
In the arena on the Sarcee Nation reserve
Governing body: Sarcee People's Museum Society under the jurisdiction of the
Tsuu T'ina Chief and Council
Open year round, Monday to Friday
☎ (403) 251-5871; for tours, 238-2677 * Admission by donation
Visiting time: one half hour

This modest museum is one of the best first people's museum in the province and one of the most accessible to non-native visitors. The exhibits of ethnographic artifacts and replicas each portray a separate theme—the origin of the Tsuu T'ina, Sarcee legends, hunting practices, and women's and men's roles. Collections include clothing, beadwork, hand tools, games, artwork and replicas. Many artifacts are on loan from other museums, like the Glenbow and the Royal Ontario Museum. Of special interest is a replica of Chief Bullhead's War History, painted on a hide. The original resides at the Royal Ontario Museum. The Sarcee Nation is planning to build a larger facility with environmental controls. Perhaps someday, many of their artifacts housed in other museums can be returned and displayed. It is best to call ahead for a guided tour.

☞ **Ukrainian Museum of Canada**
404 Meredith Road, NE, Calgary, AB T2E 5A6
Governing body: Ukrainian Women's Association of Canada, Calgary Branch
Open year round, Tuesday, and by appointment. * ☎ (403) 264-3437
Admission by donation * *Visiting time:* one half hour

🏆 🚗 ⛪ 🏛 🍴 ➖

This museum is located in St. Vladimir Basilica, a Ukrainian Orthodox church. It has limited visiting hours, so it is best to call to arrange a tour. Collections include artifacts dating back to the 1890s, including Ukrainian traditional folk dress from different regions of the Ukraine, ceremonial cloths, kilims (rugs), embroidery, ceramics, pysanky (Easter eggs), weavings and religious icons. This museum is a branch of the Ukrainian Museum of Canada, with its main branch at Saskatoon, Saskatchewan.

12

BANFF—CALGARY TRAIL

B anff National Park. The name is famous all over the world. Hundreds of thousands of visitors come each year from around the globe to visit this gem of the Canadian Rockies. Its craggy mountain peaks, glacial lakes and valleys, foaming rivers and teeming wildlife have made it the best known and most visited national park in Canada. It was Alberta's earliest tourist destination.

Alberta's first "tourists" were aboriginal people who left their traces in today's Banff National Park over 10,000 years ago. They were nomadic hunters after big game, and they left projectile points and other stone material near Vermilion Lakes, Lake Minnewanka and other locations within the park.

Tourism, in a sense, predates the settlement of the prairies. Tourists have been coming to Banff since 1885, when Canadian Pacific Railway (CPR) General Manager William Cornelius Van Horne persuaded Prime Minister William Pearce to establish a mountain park along the railway right of way. Van Horne wanted to generate revenue for the railroad by attracting wealthy tourists from eastern Canada, the United States and Europe to the Canadian Rockies to enjoy the spectacular scenery and bask in the warm waters of the Cave and Basin Hot Springs, rediscovered by three CPR construction workers. Local natives had used the springs long before the arrival of the CPR.

Cave & Basin Hot Springs, 1912. (Provincial Archives of Alberta A3179)

Tom Wilson, Outfitter and Guide (1860 - 1933)

The CPR hired Major A. B. Rogers to lead a party through the Canadian Rockies and the Columbia Mountains to survey the route for the railway line. He was a highly competent surveyor but had a reputation for being "hell on men and horses." As the survey parties neared the Continental Divide, 22-year-old Tom Wilson was the only volunteer to accompany the major to explore Kicking Horse Pass and to try to find Roger's nephew, Albert, who had gotten lost. Rogers and Wilson left their Bow Valley camp in July of 1881 and ascended Kicking Horse Valley to the pass originally explored by Sir John Hector in 1858. It was the beginning of Wilson's fame when he found Albert four days later. He is credited for having discovered Lake Louise and Emerald Lake and Marble Canyon and for having taken the first trip into Yoho Valley. Wilson stayed on in Banff and began operating an outfitting business in 1885. For 25 years he remained there, guiding tourists and mountaineers and passing on his knowledge of the mountains to guides and outfitters.

Tracks and Traces: Kicking Horse Pass on the Alberta-B.C. border was so named in 1858 when Dr. James Hector, geologist with the Palliser Expedition, was kicked by his horse and knocked senseless in the pass.

In November of 1885, the Dominion Government set aside ten square miles as Canada's first forest park reserve. The area was expanded to 2,600 acres when the Rocky Mountains Park Act of 1887 established Banff as Canada's first national park. By then development had already begun and plans were in place to build a large resort hotel. Van Horne himself chose the location and hired an architect to design the CPR hotel to look like a 16th century French Château. The Banff Springs Hotel opened in the spring of 1888. Wealthy visitors and mountaineers came by train each summer and invaded the small mountain village of Banff.

The first Canadian national parks were not intended to be nature reserves. Rocky Mountains Park (as Banff was called before 1930) hired its first three fire and game wardens in 1909, headed by Howard E. Sibbald. Although conservation of wildlife was a factor, the parks permitted extractive industries, like coal mining and logging. It was not until after the National Park Act of 1930 that these industries were excluded from the park.

Around the turn of the century, the Banff townsite began to expand around the CPR railway station below the Banff Springs Hotel and the Cave and Basin Hot Springs. Outfitting and packing businesses, stables with horses for trail riding and pack trips into the mountains, tea rooms, hotels, rooming houses and a sanitarium sprang up. In 1904, Byron Harmon, Banff's first and best known photographer, began his life-long work, photographing every major peak and glacier in the Rocky and Selkirk Mountains.

Byron Harmon, Mountain Photographer (1876 - 1942)

Born in Tacoma, Washington in 1876, Byron Harmon first visited the Canadian Rockies in 1903, and it was love at first sight. There being no permanent photographer in Banff, he returned the following year to set up shop. He soon became an Alpinist and a member of the Alpine Club of Canada (ACC), becoming the club's official photographer and photographing mountaineering expeditions with his glass plate view cameras. In 1910 he joined A.O. Wheeler, president of the ACC, on a three-week trip into the Purcell Range and the following year a three-month expedition with Wheeler and a team of scientists from the Smithsonian into the Jasper and Mt. Robson area. His early black and white photographs are some of the finest anyone has ever taken of the Canadian Rockies.

There are several museums in Banff for the heritage hunter. The **Banff Park Museum** is western Canada's oldest natural history museum, with specimens dating back to 1895. The present facility was built in 1903. In 1992, it was declared a National Historic Site. Norman Bethune Sanson became its first curator. Many of the existing collections were originally acquired by this avid naturalist, who remained at the museum until his retirement in 1932. The **Luxton Museum,** established in 1951, contains exhibits and artifacts related to the native history of the area, as well as natural history displays. The **Whyte Museum of the Canadian Rockies** has recently completed a new heritage gallery that interprets the human history of Banff National Park and the Rockies. The museum's archives have an extensive collection of historical photographs in the library and archives of the Alpine Club of Canada. The **Walter Phillips Art Gallery** at the Banff Centre has a significant collection of over 1500 works of contemporary artists. The **Cave & Basin National Historic Site** has displays that interpret the park and the importance of the Cave and Basin Springs. You can explore the original cave that brought about the formation of a national park.

From Banff, you will want to spend some time exploring the route between the park and Calgary. This route approximates the original trail taken by a group of American gold miners in 1864 or 1865. This party became lost while trying to find the Old Stony Trail to Rocky Mountain House; instead, they followed the Bow River to its confluence with the Elbow River, the future site of the Calgary's North West Mounted Police post. Among the party were Sam Livingston and John Healy, two names that are carved deeply in Alberta's history. Livingston started a small trading post near Cochrane. Healy established the infamous Fort Whoop-Up. By 1871, the trail through the foothills corridor was well-used by American whisky traders.

Canmore railway station, c1900. (Provincial Archives of Alberta A1345)

Gold miners and whisky traders were not the first to explore the area along the corridor between Banff and Calgary. Stoney Indians occupied the region for more than two centuries. The Stoneys, or Assiniboines (the term means "stone people"), were once part of the Sioux tribe living near the headwaters of the Mississippi River. Sometime in the 1650s, they separated from the Sioux, journeyed north and became aligned with the Cree. The Stoneys and Cree were two of the earliest tribes to acquire guns and metal goods when the Hudson's Bay Company began fur trading operations in Canada in 1670. They began to move into central Alberta in the 1700s, displacing other tribes, particularly the Blackfoot and the Beaver. By the 1800s, the Stoney People had explored and occupied the foothills and upper regions of the North Saskatchewan River.

The Trans-Canada Highway parallels the original coach road that was built between Banff and Calgary. Canmore, a coal mining town with beginnings in the 1880s, lies about 20 kilometres east of Banff National Park. The mines in the area and around the ghost towns of Bankhead and Anthracite provided coal to fire the engines of CPR's steam locomotives. The **Canmore Centennial Museum** contains artifacts that depict the coal mining history of the area. The museum also can arrange historic mine walks.

From Canmore we leave the Trans-Canada Highway and follow Highway 1A through Dead Man's Flats and on to Exshaw. In 1906 the Western Canada Cement and Coal Company mined limestone to make cement using a dry process. Within a year the company folded and the Canada Cement Company took it over. Exshaw continues to operate as a cement plant.

Morley, some 20 kilometres east of Exshaw, is the main tribal centre of the Stoney Nation. Morley began as a Methodist mission established in 1873 by John McDougall at the Stoney Indians' traditional winter camp ground. Soon there was a trading post run by his brother David, a post operated by the Hudson's Bay Company, and a frame church, which still stands. In 1877, the area became a reserve for the Stoneys following their signing of Treaty No. 7. Today, the multi-purpose **Nakoda Institute** provides a research facility, archives and library where one can do research into the history of the Stoney People or arrange a cultural tour.

Cochrane is our final stop along Highway 1A. The town is named after its founder, Senator Matthew Cochrane, a cattleman from Compton, Quebec. In 1881, Cochrane established the first large-scale cattle ranch in Alberta. It was named after him. Taking advantage of the amendments to the Dominion Lands Act to permit the leasing of land for grazing, Senator Cochrane acquired 360,000 acres (144,000 hectares) mostly bordering the Bow River. The Cochrane Ranche was not successful because of management problems, underfinancing, and a couple of severe winters that devastated the cattle herds. The Cochrane family sold the ranch along the Bow River to the British American Company and moved operations to their holdings near Fort Macleod.

The **Cochrane Ranche Provincial Historic Site** located in the coulee northwest of the townsite on Highway 1A encompasses the original ranch headquarters. The site is not as well developed as other provincially run sites, but it is a pleasant spot for a picnic. The future home of the **Western Heritage Centre**, a major museum devoted to the history of livestock and rodeo in western Canada, sits on a ridge overlooking Cochrane Ranche Historic Site. The museum is expected to open sometime in 1996 or 1997. Meanwhile, the **Stockmen's Memorial Foundation Museum & Rodeo Hall of Fame** is open to visitors. The exhibits are rather mundane, but the facility has an extensive library and archives dedicated to the history of ranching in Alberta.

MUSEUMS IN BANFF AND AREA

☞ Banff Park Museum
Box 160, Banff, AB T0L 0C0 * 93 Banff Avenue
Governing body: Canadian Parks Service
Open year-round daily (closed Wednesdays and Thursdays in winter)
☎ (403) 762-1558 * Admission by donation * *Visiting time:* one hour
♔ ♔ ♔ 🚗 ♿ 🧍 🍴 ━

Banff Park Museum (R.L. Hursey)

Declared a National Historic Site in 1992, the Banff Park Museum is the oldest natural history museum in western Canada, with collections dating back to 1895. Called a "museum of museums," the Banff Park Museum has displays of mounted wildlife specimens reflecting the style of exhibitry that was done in the Victorian era. One can use the references in the Brewster Reading

Room, a learning centre pertaining to Banff's natural history. The present building, originally constructed in 1903, was extensively restored in 1985 as part of the 100th Anniversary of the establishment of Banff National Park. Even the former Curator's office appears as if he just stepped out to go fishing. It presents a fascinating look at Victorian attitudes toward nature and what museums used to look like.

☞ Cave & Basin National Historic Site
Box 900, Banff, AB T0L 0C0 * 311 Cave Avenue
Governing body: Canadian Parks Service
Open Victoria Day to Labour Day, daily * ☎ (403) 762-1557
No admission fee * *Visiting time:* one hour

The Cave & Basin Hot Springs became the birthplace of Banff National Park when it was developed as a resort spa for wealthy tourists in 1885. Natives used the site long before CPR engineers discovered it in 1883. The building, constructed in 1914, is made of local field stone. An interpretive centre presents exhibits and a slide show depicting the history of this famous place. It is well worth your while to spend some time there before touring the Cave and the 1914 hot springs pool. Guided tours are available. You can visit the cave where the original pool was located. You can smell the sulphur and feel the warm spring waters. The 1914 pool was closed for repairs at the time of my visit.

☞ Luxton Museum
Box 850, Banff, AB T0L 0C0 * One Birch Avenue
Governing body: Buffalo Nations Cultural Society
Open mid-May to mid-October, daily * ☎ (403) 762-2388
Admission fee charged * *Visiting time:* one hour

The Luxton Museum presents the heritage of the Indians of the Northern Plains and Canadian Rockies. Its collections include native costumes, teepees, travois, tools and weapons and native crafts. To enter the Luxton Museum, you virtually walk into the past through the log palisades. The dioramas are most impressive, especially the Treaty No. 7 and teepee diorama, and the quality of the artifacts is exceptional. The natural history specimens, however, are in tough shape and need to be replaced. I hope that the Buffalo Nations Cultural Society will find the funding to redevelop or revitalize this important museum so that it reflects more contemporary views and attitudes about Native culture.

☞ **Walter Phillips Art Gallery**
Box 1020, Banff, AB T0L 0C0 * The Banff Centre for the Arts, St. Julian
Road, ground level of Glyde Hall
Governing body: The Banff Centre for the Arts
Open year-round, daily *☎ (403) 762-6281
No admission fee charged * *Visiting time:* one hour

♈ ♈ 🚗 ♿ ⛺ ⛩ ⛺ 🛖 ─

The Walter Phillips Art Gallery has over 1500 artworks by contemporary artists in a variety of media including photography and video collections. Many of the works have been produced by artists who have attended the Banff Centre. The gallery maintains an ongoing exhibit program of artworks from the collection and travelling exhibitions from other museums and galleries.

☞ **Whyte Museum of the Canadian Rockies**
Box 160, Banff, AB T0L 0C0 * 111 Bear Street
Governing body: Peter and Catherine Whyte Foundation
Open year-round, daily; closed Mondays, November to May
☎ (403) 762-2291 * Admission fee charged * *Visiting time:* one hour

♈ ♈ ♈ 🚗 ♿ ⛩ 🎁 ♿ 🛖 ─

The Whyte Museum of the Canadian Rockies has an eclectic collection of artwork, memorabilia, artifacts and archival collections. Special collections include Catherine and Peter Whyte paintings, the photographic collections of Byron Harmon and Mary Schaeffer, and the library and archives of the Alpine Club of Canada. The new Heritage Gallery presents the best overview of Banff's unique history, from fur trade days to the present. Attractive displays feature historical vignettes on the CPR, early tourists, mountaineers, alpine guides, the park warden service, and packers and outfitters. There is a small tea room and a well-equipped gift shop providing a wide selection of art, handicrafts and reproductions of photographs from the museum's extensive collections.

☞ **Canmore Centennial Museum**
Box 2131, Canmore, AB T0L 0M0 * 801 - 7th Avenue
Governing body: Centennial Museum Society of Canmore
Open year-round, daily * ☎ (403) 678-2462
Admission by donation * *Visiting time:* one half hour

♈ 🚗 ⛺ ⛺ 🛖 ─

This community museum maintains collections featuring coal mining, ethnic and historical artifacts, and memorabilia on the 1988 Winter Olympics. A special feature is the historical doll collection of 1250 pieces, of which 460 are on display. The museum is in the process of restoring the original 1905 NWMP barracks. Inquire here about historical mine walks.

☞ **Cochrane Ranche Provincial Historic Site**
Box 1522, Cochrane, AB T0L 0W0
A half kilometer west of town, on Highway 1A
Governing body: Alberta Community Development, Historic Sites & Archives
Service * Open mid-May to Labour Day *☎ (403) 932-2902
Admission by donation * *Visiting time:* one half hour
🏆 🏆 🚗 ♿ 🐴 ⛩

The historic site covers 150 acres (61 hectares) of land that once was the first large-scale ranching operation in Alberta. Established in 1881, the Cochrane Ranche operated as a cattle ranch for two years until the company moved its stock to southern Alberta. The small visitor centre provides a map of the grounds, showing the locations of the original buildings. I was disappointed that this site is so under developed. It is a better place to have a picnic and enjoy the natural beauty of the coulee than it is to learn about the history of ranching.

☞ **Stockmen's Memorial Foundation Museum**
& Rodeo Hall of Fame
Box 459, Cochrane, AB T0l 0W0 * 105 River Avenue
Governing body: Stockmen's Memorial Foundation
Open year-round, weekdays * ☎ (403) 934-5803
Admission by donation * *Visiting time:* one half hour
🏆 🚗 ⛩ 🍴 —

This is the temporary headquarters of the Western Heritage Centre until their new centre opens within the next few years. Rather unimaginative displays feature collections of ranching paraphernalia (saddles, branding irons, barbed wire), western paintings, and sculpture. Of interest to researchers are the extensive library and archives, with collections of *Cattleman* magazine, an almost complete collection of the books of registered brands going back to the early 1910s, and oral histories on video tape.

☞ **Nakoda Institute** at Morley
Box 120, Morley, AB T0L 1N0 * On Highway 1A at Chief Hector Lake on the
Stoney Indian Reserve
Governing body: Board of Directors, Nakoda Learning Centre of the Goodstoney
Band Council, Stoney Tribe
Open year-round, weekdays * ☎ (403) 881-4949/881-3951
Admission by donation * *Visiting time:* one half hour
🍷 🚗 🍴 ⎯

The Nakoda Institute is a multi-faceted cultural centre that includes a library, archives, art gallery, audio-visual centre, and a research and publications program. The library has approximately 50 films on the Indian and a living history collection of 30 videotapes. Artifact collections include historical and anthropological objects related to the Stoney People, their Assiniboine relatives and the Northern Plains Indians. In the planning is a tribal museum that will present the history and culture of the Stoney and their Siouan relations. Those interested in doing research at the Nakoda Institute can arrange to stay at the Nakoda Lodge.

Byron Harmon, Banff's first photographer
(Whyte Museum of the Canadian Rockies V263 NAH 2400)

13

CALGARY-EDMONTON TRAIL SOUTH—HIGHWAY 2

Time and distance are relative when it comes to travel. When I drive between Calgary and Edmonton along Highway 2, which parallels the old Calgary-Edmonton Trail (C&E Trail), I try to imagine what it must have been like for pioneers to travel this route in the early days. In Alberta, where distances are great, we tend to measure travel in terms of time rather than distance. We say that the drive between Edmonton and Calgary is about three hours. We rarely say that the trip is 186 miles or 300 kilometres.

Before the Canadian Pacific Railway completed the line between Calgary and South Edmonton in 1891, the trip had to be made by horse-drawn wagons or ox carts, which could take up to two weeks along the C&E Trail. In 1879, there were only about a dozen people living along this trail. Now, most of the people in the province live in the cities, towns, and villages dotting Highway 2.

Bullwackers and freight wagons. (Provincial Archives of Alberta A415)

The C&E Trail, which linked with early Native and fur trade trails, wound through rolling hills, muskeg swamps, and valleys thick with willows and aspen. It saw just about every kind of conveyance—hikers, horses, covered wagons, Red River carts, ox trains, and stagecoaches. All had to ford countless creeks along the way and the river at Red Deer Crossing, the major stopping place on the C&E Trail. In the spring and summer, the trail was a sea of mud, manure and ruts made from countless wagons. In the fall, the holes and deep ruts froze solid, wearing down horses' hooves and breaking wagon wheels.

The trail was little used until the Riel Rebellion, when General Thomas Bland Strange was sent to command the Alberta Field Force. With 800 troops and 175 wagons, Strange's force travelled north along the trail, reassuring the settlers along the way, who feared attacks from the Cree and Blackfoot following the Frog Lake massacre. In the wake of the Alberta Field Force, freight wagons pulled by teams of oxen and scheduled stage coaches made frequent use of the trail.

When managers of the Canadian Pacific Railway observed the number of freighters and new settlers using the C&E Trail, they decided to run a railway line between Calgary and Edmonton. Work began in July 1890. New villages and towns sprang up along the Calgary-Edmonton Railway (C&E) and names of British origin like Airdrie, Crossfield, Carstairs, Didsbury, Olds, and Bowden were bestowed upon these new rural communities by the CPR. The first train arrived at South Edmonton on August 10, 1891. The trip by train between Calgary and South Edmonton took a mere couple of days compared to two weeks by wagon. The C&E line opened up new agricultural areas and brought in a flood of American and European homesteaders to break up some of the most recalcitrant land in Alberta—uprooting trees and brush and plowing and harrowing the checkerboard fields of wheat, oats, and barley.

Let us take a historic journey along Highway 2, which more or less parallels the routes of the C&E Trail and C&E Railway. Starting at Calgary, the highway rises in elevation, paralleling the Nose Creek Valley to Airdrie, about 22 kilometres north. In 1886, John M. Dickson ran the Dickson Stopping House, a day's journey from Calgary. The establishment provided water, feed and meals for tired animals and people.

The Benevolent Highwaymen

By 1883, weekly mail service became a reality. Mail was delivered by stagecoach along the C&E Trail. Robberies occasionally occurred along the trail. About two miles from Dickson's Stopping House, two masked men waited for the stage to appear. As it came around a bend, the robbers, armed with carbines, jumped out and held up the stage. They forced five passengers to turn over their money. But these were not totally heartless highwaymen. They gave back a few dollars to each of the victims to ensure that none were left destitute. Nor did they steal personal effects, like watches. Then the robbers rummaged through the mail bags, unhitched the horses, and rode off. Their total take was $435. The robbers were eventually caught by the NWMP.

By 1901, the CPR railway station established the town of Airdrie. The first inhabitants were railway workers who lived in the section house and maintained the line. Today Airdrie is a bustling town of over 12,000 people. Most have jobs in Calgary and commute to work in less than a half hour. The **Nose Creek Valley Museum**, a regional museum, features the history of the valley and the communities of Airdrie, Crossfield, and Carstairs. It is well worth a stop to see its extensive collection of pre-historic and Native history.

Crossfield, 10 kilometres north of Airdrie, was originally another stop along the C&E trail when a Mrs. Hannington opened a stopping house in 1890. Then in 1892 it became a siding of the CPR. The company named it Crossfield after an engineer with the survey crew. By 1903 Crossfield had a post office, lumber and hardware store, a blacksmith shop, livery, and a one-room school.

Farther north on Highway 2, Carstairs, named after a town in Scotland, comes into view. The first settlers in the area were of Scottish descent. In 1890, the CPR built a small station house. It also served as a mail drop-off, a church, and a general meeting place. Mr. E.W. Stone, the first businessman in Carstairs, built a general store in 1901, and later the Albion Hotel. Carstairs' local history museum, the **Roulston Museum,** has collections from the settlement period to the present.

Didsbury, our next stop, was originally another stopping place along the C&E Trail. Named after a town in Manchester, England, Didsbury's first settlers were descendants of Dutch Mennonites, Empire Loyalists from Pennsylvania, who resettled in Ontario. In 1893, Jacob Y. Shantz constructed an immigration hall, a barn, and and dug wells for the 34 new settlers who came the following year to acquire homesteads. By 1905, Didsbury incorporated as a village. **Didsbury and District Museum** features the local history of the area.

Our trek continues to the town of Olds. About 6.5 kilometres northeast of the town, there used to be a very popular stopping house. Lone Pine Stopping House was where the Morley Trail branched off the C&E Trail. John McDougall cut the Morley Trail to run his cattle south to the Methodist Mission at Morley. Lone Pine Stopping House was popular among the freighters for its food and company. Its origin is a bit confusing. One account states that it was run by a Chinese man and a "colored" woman named "Steamboat," who regaled her guests with stories about steamboats on the Mississippi. Another account claims that Jean-Baptiste Langlais, a French Canadian, and his half-breed wife built it in 1886. The Lone Pine Stopping House continued to operate until the C&E Railway bypassed it. Olds, named after George Olds, a CPR traffic manager, became the Sixth Siding out of Calgary in 1891. Within a year a large group of Scandinavian immigrants settled the area. Olds is now home to one of the finest agricultural colleges in Alberta.

The **Mountain View Museum,** located in the former Alberta Telephone Exchange building in Olds, brings to life the history of the area with its interesting and well-crafted displays.

Farther along this southern stretch of the old C&E Trail appears the town of Bowden. Here we are well out of the prairies and into parkland, with rolling hills of aspen and fertile farmland. In 1887, the Brewster family took out a homestead in the area. James Brewster got his start freighting from Winnipeg to Edmonton in the 1870s. His sons and their descendants have made their mark in the hotel and transportation industries all over the province. In 1892, CPR's Seventh Siding was named Bowden, after Bowden, Manchester, England. The community's first school classes were held in the blacksmith shop in 1894.

Robert Hoare (1878 - 1964)

One of Bowden's most famous residents was Gerald Robin O'Bryan Hoare, a remittance man who came to the Bowden area to homestead. He opened a photographic studio, which he operated until 1914. His excellent photographic portraits and landscapes give us a glimpse of life around Bowden. He had an eye for portraying people in natural poses in their own setting. Following his death in 1964, the Bowden Historical Society deposited the collection of some 823 negatives on permanent loan at the Provincial Archives. It represents one of the finest collections of photographs of rural Alberta in the early part of the century.

Innisfail is our last stop along the southern stretch of the old C&E Trail. Anthony Henday, the first white man to travel in Alberta in 1754, camped at Mud Lake, near Innisfail, with a party of Crees.

The area was first settled in 1883 by the Brown family. Innisfail had its beginnings as a stopping house on the C&E Trail. "The Spruces" was a cabin built by Napolean Remillard and used as a stopping house for freighters and stagecoaches. In 1891, the CPR siding became Innisfail, named by an early resident after a place in Ireland. By 1897, Innisfail had three churches, a creamery, a school, two hotels, three general stores, a resident lawyer, and Dr. George.

Dr. Henry George

Dr. Henry George established a medical practice in Innisfail in 1892. He was a former NWMP physician and had been in attendance at Chief Crowfoot's death. His home served as a medical office, and occasionally a hospital. It also served as the first museum of its kind in the Northwest Territories. Dr. George was an inveterate collector, and he started the "Innisfail Museum," charging 25 cents admission to see his natural and human history collections. When he moved to Red Deer a few years later, he took his collections with him. In 1977 his home was registered as a Provincial Historic Resource.

To learn more about the history of Innisfail and area, you should visit two museums. **Dr. George House** has many of the doctor's collections gathered in one room in commemoration of his original museum. **Innisfail Historical Village** has an impressive collection of 13 pioneer buildings and farm machinery from the settlement period. Its centre piece is the cabin that was at "The Spruces" stopping place.

MUSEUMS ALONG THE CALGARY-EDMONTON TRAIL AND REGION

☞ **Nose Creek Valley Museum** at Airdrie
Box 3351, Airdrie, AB T4V 2B6 * 1701 Main Street, South
Governing body: Nose Creek Valley Museum Society
Open year-round, daily * ☎ (403) 948-6685
Admission fee charged * *Visiting time:* one hour
🏆🏆🚗 ♿ ⛩ 🍴 ━

The museum has an extensive collection of archaeological artifacts and Native history collections. The stone-aged tools represent thousands of years of aboriginal occupation of the area. There are also exhibits on agriculture, transportation, and the petroleum industry.

☞ **Bowden Pioneer Museum**
Box 576, Bowden, AB T0M 0K0 * 2011 - 20th Avenue
Governing body: Bowden Historical Society
Open year-round: July and August, daily; September to June, Monday,
Wednesday, and Friday afternoons * ☎ (403) 224-2122
Admission by donation * *Visiting time:* one half hour
♥ 🚗 ⛺ 🍴

The Bowden Museum has a large collection of cameras and photographs from the turn of the century, military artifacts from both world wars, Native and pioneer artifacts, and fossil specimens. Special artifacts include the doorknob to John A. MacDonald's office and the last Union Jack to fly on Capitol Hill on Ottawa's Parliament Buildings.

☞ **Roulston Museum** at Carstairs
Box 1067, Carstairs, AB T0M 0N0 * 1138 - Nanton Street
Governing body: The Carstairs & District Historical Society
Open September to June, Wednesday and Thursday; July and August, Thursday
to Saturday * ☎ (403) 337-371 * Admission by donation
Visiting time: one half hour
♥ 🚗 ⛺ 🍴

This museum has collections depicting the history of Carstairs and the Didsbury district, from early settlement to recent times. The historical society has restored and furnished the McCaig House from the homesteading period.

☞ **Didsbury & District Museum**
Box 1175, Didsbury, AB T0M 0W0 * 2118 - 21st Avenue
Governing body: Didsbury & District Historical Society
Opens July and August, Wednesday to Saturday;
September to June, Wednesday and Friday * ☎ (403) 335-9295
Admission by donation * *Visiting time:* one half hour
♥ 🚗 ⛱ 🍴 🚌

The museum keeps artifacts pertaining to the local history of the area. Special collections include Native and military artifacts.

☞ **Dr. George House** at Innisfail
5713 - 51 Avenue, Innisfail, AB T4G 1R4
Governing body: Dr. George House Preservation Society
Open May 15 to Labour Day, daily; winter, Tuesday to Sunday.
☎ (403) 227-1920/227-5447 *Admission by donation
Visiting time: one half hour
♟♟🚗 ⛩ ☕ 🍴 ⎯

Dr. George House, Innisfail (R.L. Hursey)

Dr. George House was the residence and medical office of Dr. Henry George, Innisfail's first medical doctor. The home has recently been restored. One room is set aside as a Natural History Museum in a tribute to Dr. George, who had opened the first museum of its type in the Northwest Territories. Many of the George family's personal items have been reunited and are on display.

☞ **Innisfail Historical Village**
Box 642, Innisfail, AB T0M 1A0
On 42 Street between 51 and 52 Avenues
Governing body: Innisfail & District Historical Society
Open May 15 to Labour Day; closed Mondays
☎ (403) 227- 2906 (summer); 227-1177 (rest of year)
Admission fee charged * *Visiting time:* one hour
♟♟🚗🎁⛩☕🍴⎯

This historical village maintains 13 pioneer buildings interpreting the history of the area from the pioneer era to 1930. There is also a large collection of early farm machinery. Tea is served every Friday afternoon at the Tea Room.

☞ **Mountain View Museum** at Olds
Box 63, Olds, AB T0M 1P0 * 5038- 50 Street
Governing body: Olds Historical Society
Open year-round, July to August, Monday to Friday; September to June, Tuesday and Thursday * ☎ (403) 556-8464
Admission by donation * *Visiting time:* one half hour

🍷 🚗 ♿ 🎁 🍴 ➖

Housed in the former AGT exchange building, the museum contains exhibits with artifacts reflecting the history of Olds and District. Thematic displays depict life during the pioneer era. Special collections include some historical AGT telephones and telecommunications equipment.

☞ **Sundre Pioneer Village Museum**
Box 314, Sundre, AB T0M 1X0 * 130 Centre Street South
Governing body: Sundre & District Historical Society
Open year-round, Wednesday to Sunday * ☎ (403) 638-3233
Admission by donation * *Visiting time:* one half hour

🍷 🚗 ⛺ ⛩ 🍴 ➖

The museum's collections include local artifacts of the pioneer era, historic buildings and farm equipment.

14

RED DEER & AREA

Red Deer occupies the hub of central Alberta, as most roads seem to lead there. Nestled in the beautiful parkland valley of the Red Deer river, the city is surrounded by some of the richest agricultural land in the province. Here the river and valley appear more gentle than farther downstream near Drumheller. White spruce, poplars and willows clothe the contours of the cliffs, and the valley abounds with wildlife. The Cree called the area *Wawaskasoo Seepee* (*wawaskasoo* = elk; *seepee* = river). The early fur traders called it Red Deer River, thinking that the large herds of elk along its banks were the same species as the European red deer. Today, Red Deer takes pride in its **Waskasoo Park**, which preserves undisturbed areas for birds and mammals, such as migratory water fowl, deer, beaver, muskrat and other small mammals.

The area's written history goes back to the journals of Anthony Henday, the first white man to venture into today's Alberta. With a party of Cree, he crossed the river west of today's Nevis in 1754 and visited the Blackfoot camped near the Red Deer River. Peter Fidler sojourned in the region in 1792, and just west of today's Red Deer, he took compass bearings on the Rocky Mountains. In 1787, David Thompson, the famous explorer-surveyor, came upon the area after following an old Indian trail leading south from Fort Edmonton. The trail became the main north-south land route for traders after Rocky Mountain House was established in 1799.

The Pine Lake Massacre

During the early 19th century, the Red Deer River valley became disputed territory between the Blackfoot and Cree. With superior weapons, the Cree drove the Blackfoot south of the river around 1800. In 1812, the Blackfoot launched a surprise attack on a Cree party camped at Pine Lake, southeast of Red Deer. All but one Cree warrior were massacred. Enraged by the loss of his family and friends, the warrior stalked the Blackfoot party and attacked and killed six of them before he himself was killed. The lake was known as Ghostpine Lake for many years, as Indians believed it was haunted by the murdered Cree.

Several old trails intersected in the area around Red Deer Crossing, a few kilometers west of today's Red Deer. These trails included the Calgary-Edmonton Trail, a trail from Buffalo Lake, and one that ran west to Rocky Mountain House. Today's highways generally follow the routes of these early trails. Red Deer Crossing became an important stopping place for traders, freighters, and settlers after Addison McPherson built the first building in 1873 where the Calgary-Edmonton Trail crossed the Red Deer River. During the Riel Rebellion of 1885, the Alberta Field Forces led by General Strange built three posts along the C&E trail. One of these was Fort Normandeau, established at the Crossing to protect white settlers from attack by Indians supporting Riel. No doubt the presence of the Alberta Field Forces in the area acted as a deterrent to any potential attack.

The Gaetz Family

One of the first families to settle in the area of Red Deer Crossing in 1884 was Dr. Leonard Gaetz, a Methodist preacher, and his wife and family of 10 children who came from Ontario. The Gaetz family have remained prominent members of the community throughout Red Deer's history. His son, Raymond Gaetz, ran a store and post office at the Crossing. When word got out that a railway line from Calgary to Edmonton would pass through the area, Gaetz offered the CPR one half interest in his 640-acre farm, downstream of the Crossing. Thus the Red Deer Crossing was bypassed by the CPR in 1891, in favor of the location of today's downtown Red Deer. R. L. Gaetz became the first mayor of Red Deer in 1901 when the town incorporated.

Once the Blackfoot buried their dead in trees on top of North Hill, where North Red Deer now stands. The community was founded in 1894, when Halley Hamilton Gaetz purchased and subdivided a tract of land as an industrial area. The Great West Lumber Company bought out two smaller sawmills (one owned by Gaetz) and started operations around the turn of the century. In 1908, the Daughters of Wisdom, a women's religious order from France, came to begin their mission to Roman Catholics in Red Deer. North Hill became known as Convent Hill, when the Sisters founded St. Joseph's Convent in 1908.

Today Red Deer is the fourth largest city in Alberta, with a population of 60,000. It is an important centre for conventions and conferences, attracting over 25,000 delegates a year.

There is so much to see and do in Red Deer that you may want to spend at least a couple of days of heritage hunting here. To learn about the local history, the **Red Deer & District Museum and Archives** is the best place to start. This multi-purpose museum features exhibits that highlight its Native and settlement history. The museum also features art exhibitions of local, regional, and national artists. **Heritage Square**, located just south of the Red Deer & District Museum, features many historical structures: a large steeple in need of a church; the library of Dr. Gaetz; the Alberta Genealogical Society; and Aspelund Laft Hus, a replica of a 17th century Norwegian log house. Several Historical Walking Tours start from Heritage Square. The **Red Deer Cemetery Walking Tour,** a unique self-guided tour, reveals personal histories engraved upon the tombstones. **Fort Normandeau Historic Site & Interpretive Centre** is a replica of the original fort that was constructed at Red Deer Crossing in 1885. For those interested in the natural history of the area, the **Kerry Wood Nature Centre,** located in Waskasoo Park, offers informative exhibits, programs, and nature trails. Be sure to visit the Gaetz Lakes Sanctuary, where you can observe wildlife in this wet marshland environment.

Kerry Wood Nature Centre (R.L. Hursey)

Large numbers of Scandinavian immigrants settled the area west of Red Deer in the late 1880s. Groups of Norwegians, Swedes, Danes, and Icelanders, many of whom had originally settled in the United States, came to Canada in search of farming areas. Although the land west of Red Deer is not the best for growing crops, there was plenty of wood, good water, and land suitable for dairy farming, growing hay, and planting vegetables. Today, as you drive along winding gravel roads through wood lots, fields of grazing dairy cattle, and quiet villages with their steepled churches, you may feel as if you are caught up in a time warp.

Our unique tour of Alberta's Scandinavian-Canadian heritage begins a few miles south of Red Deer. Take Highway 2 south to Penhold, then turn west on SR 592. Beyond the intersection with SR 781, the pavement ends and you continue on a good gravel surface toward the hamlet of Markerville. Icelanders who originally immigrated to the United States came up from North Dakota to settle Markerville in 1888. One of the settlers, Stephan G. Stephansson, would become, within his lifetime, Iceland's greatest 20th century poet.

Stephansson House Provincial Historic Site (R.L. Hursey)

Stephan G. Stephansson (1853 - 1927)

Stephan Stephansson was born in Iceland and emigrated to Wisconsin with his wife. They settled there in an Icelandic community where they lived for seventeen years. In 1889, the family came to Markerville, where Stephan became a dairy farmer and, for several years, tried to grow wheat with little success until the introduction of the hardy Marquis wheat. Although he had little formal education, his mother taught him to read and write in Icelandic. In the evenings after farm chores, he would write poetry in Icelandic. Stephansson was a "free thinker," a pacifist, and socialist; and often his ideas got him into trouble. Nevertheless, he was highly respected in his community and venerated in Iceland, where he is credited for having done much to revive the use of the Icelandic language. Five volumes of poetry and papers in Icelandic have been published. In recent years, many of his poems have been translated into English and set to music.

Stephansson Provincial Historic Site is located on the property that Stephansson spent so many years writing his poetry. The Stephansson house, perched on top of a wooded hill, overlooks the peaceful valley of the Medicine River. The home has been meticulously restored to the 1920s and furnished with many of the original objects that had been scattered about the community. I found this modest house and surroundings a compelling place, where the spirit of this great man, so little known outside Icelandic communities, lives on.

Six miles south of Stephansson House is Markerville. This hamlet of less than 100 residents has changed very little since the early Twenties. You will definitely not want to miss the **Markerville Creamery.** All the equipment for processing cream into butter was left in place when the creamery closed in 1972. The museum staff gives an excellent tour; and the **Kaffistofa,** the coffee house cafe at the Markerville Creamery, serves delicious Icelandic lunches and pastries. A woodworking shop nearby caters to visitors. Take some time to see the unique architecture of the homes and the Lutheran Church, built in 1904.

From Markerville, drive south on SR 592 to Highway 54 and west to Spruce View and Dickson, two communities that five Danish families settled in 1903. Dickson will eventually become the home of the **Danish Canadian National Museum.** Just south of Spruce View, Dickson today has a very different type of museum, **The Dickson Store Museum.** It was once the general store and post office for Dickson.

MUSEUMS IN RED DEER & AREA

> ☞ **The Dickson Store Museum** at Dickson
> Box 54, Spruce View, AB T0M 1V0 * Hamlet of Dickson
> *Governing body:* Danish Heritage Society of Dickson
> Open daily during summer months. * *Phone* (403) 728-3355/728-3331
> Admission by donation * *Visiting time:* one half hour

The museum is located in the original Dickson general store and post office. On display are goods commonly sold in general stores in the 1930s. Original and replica packages conjure up a nostalgic feeling in many older people. The upstairs living quarters, restored to the 1930s, include a living room, dining room, bedroom, kitchen, pantry, and utility room. The Dickson Store Museum was officially opened by Her Royal Highness, Queen Margrethe II of Denmark, on October 14, 1992.

> ☞ **Historic Markerville Creamery Museum** at Markerville
> General Delivery, Markerville, AB T0M 1M0
> Beside the Medicine River, across the bridge from the public parking lot.
> *Governing body:* Stephan G. Stephansson Icelandic Society
> Open Victoria Day to Labour Day, daily * ☎ (403) 728-3006
> Admission by donation * *Visiting time:* one hour

The Markerville Creamery has been restored to the 1930s. Collections include churns, pasteurizers, a stationary steam engine, and testing equipment. The coffee shop on the premises, "Kaffistofa," features traditional Icelandic lunches and desserts.

> ☞ **Stephansson House Provincial Historic Site**
> Reynolds-Alberta Museum, Box 6360, Wetaskiwin, AB T9A 2G1
> 7 kilometres north of Markerville
> *Governing body:* Alberta Community Development, Historic Sites & Archives
> Services * Open May 15 to Labour Day, daily
> ☎ Summer: (403) 728-3929; Year-round: 361-1351/352-5855
> Admission by donation * *Visiting time:* one hour

This is the pioneer home of Stephan G. Stephansson, Iceland's greatest 20th century poet. It has been restored to its 1927 appearance. Stephansson wrote most of his poetry in this home at night by lamplight. Many of the family's original furnishings and objects are featured. An outdoor interpretive display tells the story of Stephansson, his family, and the Icelandic settlement of the Markerville community. Interpreters in period costumes provide guided tours.

☞ **Cronquist House Multicultural Centre** at Red Deer
Box 224, Red Deer, AB T4N 5E8 * Bower Ponds, off Kerry Wood Drive
Governing body: Red Deer Cultural Heritage Society
Open year round, Tuesday to Friday and Sunday
☎ (403) 346-0055 or 347-9440
Admission by donation * *Visiting time:* one half hour

Cronquist House, a designated Municipal Historic Resource, is a three-story Victorian style brick farmhouse that a prominent Red Deer family built in 1911. The house was moved to Bower Ponds from its original location and restored in 1976. It serves as a multicultural centre where ethnic arts and crafts are displayed.

☞ **Fort Normandeau Historic Site & Interpretive Centre**
#1, 6300-45 Avenue, Red Deer, AB T4N 3M4
West of Highway 2 on the Red Deer River;
take the 32nd Street exit and follow the signs.
Governing body: Normandeau Cultural and Natural History Society
Open May to September, daily * ☎ (403) 347-7550
Admission by donation * *Visiting time:* one hour

This reconstructed fort sits on the site of the original fort built during the Riel Rebellion of 1885 at Red Deer Crossing, the first permanent settlement in the area. Interpretive programs and events bring to life the history of this fascinating area. You will want to spend time enjoying the beauty of this location. The setting provides the perfect spot to have a picnic. There is also a canoe launch.

☞ **Kerry Wood Nature Centre**
#1, 6300 - 45th Avenue, Red Deer, AB T4N 3M4
At entrance to the Gaetz Lakes Sanctuary, Waskasoo Park
Governing body: Normandeau Cultural and Natural History Society
Open year-round, daily * ☎ (403) 346-2010
Admission by donation * *Visiting time:* one hour

This nature centre has excellent exhibits showing the formation of the Red Deer Valley, its wildlife and habitats. A hands-on discovery room provides families with young children opportunities to share in learning about Red Deer's natural history. The centre offers programs, guided tours, and lectures. Be sure to spend time walking along the well-marked nature trails that cover the Gaetz Lakes Sanctuary. This beautiful and interesting spot can be visited any time of the year.

☞ **Red Deer & District Museum**
Box 800, Red Deer, AB T4N 5H2 * 4525 - 47 A Avenue
Governing body: Normandeau Cultural and Natural History Society
Open year-round, daily * ☎ (504) 343-6844
Admission by donation * *Visiting time:* one and one half hours

The Red Deer & District Museum's broad collections include palaeontological, archaeological, and historical artifacts related to the human and natural history of the area. Its textiles and clothing collection is one of the finest in the province. The permanent exhibits portray the Native, settlement, agricultural, and urban history of the area. One of its newest and most interesting galleries, titled "Where the Old Man Slept," interprets the Native History of the area. Red Deer Museum is also the home of "the world's most boring postcard."

15

CALGARY-EDMONTON TRAIL NORTH
HIGHWAY 2A

Imagine what it was like along the old Calgary-Edmonton Trail before the CPR put a railway line paralleling this route in 1891. The trip from Red Deer to Leduc could have taken a week; today you can make the trip in less than 1 1/2 hours! There were no hotels, just stopping houses that were hardly more than log cabins, with no electricity, running water or adequate heating. Guests commonly suffered from bed bugs and fleas. Meals consisted of plain food— whatever the cook had on hand for the day. The C&E Trail could be hot and dusty in the summer, a sea of gumbo whenever it rained, and in winter, deep frozen ruts could break a horse's leg and often did.

Highway 2 does not follow the same route as the old C&E Trail, so you will have to venture along Highway 2A, which did. This is a more scenic and less travelled route. Our first stop will be the town of Lacombe.

The first settler in the Lacombe area was Ed Barnett, of the North-West Mounted Police, who served at Fort Walsh before being discharged in 1881. Barnett moved north in 1883 and took up squatters' rights at the present site of Lacombe. He started a ranch and stopping house on the C&E Trail. When the CPR built a rail line from Calgary to Edmonton, the Lacombe area became Siding 12, commonly known as Barnett Siding. William Van Horne, president of the CPR, renamed it in honor of Father Albert Lacombe, who had travelled many times through the area with the Cree as early as 1850.

In 1893, only 25 people lived in Lacombe. By 1901, the village had become an important agricultural and business centre with a population of 500. In 1907, the federal government established an agricultural station at Lacombe to develop and distribute new varieties of seed and animal stock. The stately Edwardian homes that border the western entrance to Lacombe attest to the town's affluence based on agriculture. By 1912 the town had replaced many of its false-fronted commercial buildings with more fire-proof brick structures. The most distinctive construction of this period is the flatiron building, one of only two in Alberta. In the 1980s, Lacombe received assistance from the Alberta's Main Street Programme to revitalize its downtown area. Since 1988, Lacombe has restored over twenty historic buildings. Heritage Canada recognized

Lacombe as having the best collection of Edwardian-era buildings in Alberta.

You will want to spend some time strolling along Main Street to fully appreciate the historic buildings and vintage homes. The **Michener House Museum**, a block off Main Street, is the birthplace of the Rt. Hon. Roland Michener, Governor-General of Canada from 1967 to 1974. His father, Reverend E. Michener came to Lacombe in 1894 and served as minister at the Grace Methodist Church until 1901. A block away is the **Lacombe Blacksmith Shop**, which opened its doors on May 1994. Here the art and craft of blacksmithing is being revived.

Father Albert Lacombe (1827 - 1916)

During the last half of the 19th century, Father Albert Lacombe took part in practically every major event in western Canada's history. Born in St. Sulpice, Quebec, to a devout family of farmers, he was ordained in 1849. That year he arrived in the Canadian West to answer the call of Bishop Provencher at St. Boniface for men to minister to the free-spirited and devout Métis People. For the first few years, Father Lacombe spent time travelling by horseback and Red River cart with the Métis on their annual buffalo hunts. In 1852 he was assigned to Lac Ste. Anne to replace Father Thibault who had founded the mission in 1844.

Father Lacombe travelled all over, camping in teepees with Cree and Blackfoot, founding new missions at St. Albert, St. Paul des Cris, St. Paul des Métis, Calgary, Dunbar, Pincher Creek, and Midnapore. He became a friend to some of the most famous people in western Canadian history. They included Bishops Provencher and Taché, Chief Factor John Rowand of Fort Edmonton, Chief Crowfoot of the Blackfoot, Sir John Hector of the Palliser expedition, and William Van Horne and Donald Smith of the Canadian Pacific Railway. He was as much at home in aristocratic mansions as in humble Blackfoot teepees. His most compelling mission was to try to prepare the Plains Indians for the inevitable time when the buffalo would be gone and white settlers would cover the plains. He died in 1916 at age 89. He is buried in a crypt on Mission Hill in St. Albert.

From Lacombe we head for Ponoka, a community that started as Fort Ostell, one of the posts that the Alberta Field Forces built during the Riel Rebellion of 1885. Even before the fort was erected, the surrounding land along the Battle River had been an area of dispute between the Blackfoot and Cree that lasted over a century. The upper Red Deer River and Battle River valleys were traditional wintering grounds for the Blackfoot. In 1865, Father Lacombe was camped in the area with a small band of Blackfoot when a party of Cree and Assiniboine attacked during the night. In his attempt to quell the violence, Father Lacombe was wounded in the shoulder from a ricocheting bullet. The tribes stopped fighting when they feared they had killed their friend.

After the arrival of the CPR in 1891, Siding 14 was changed to Ponoka, a name Father Lacombe had suggested. The name comes from a Blackfoot term meaning "elk." In 1904 Ponoka incorporated as a town. In 1907, following the passing of the "Insanity Act" by the Alberta Legislature, Ponoka became the site for the Provincial Hospital for the Insane. It opened in 1911. The **Fort Ostell Museum** in Ponoka features exhibits on the local history, featuring artifacts in small, well-crafted contextual displays.

Continuing north of Ponoka along Highway 2A, we follow the Battle River valley through the Samson (Cree) reserve and Hobbema to the town of Wetaskiwin. A cairn two miles west of Wetaskiwin commemorates an event that brought peace between the Blackfoot and Cree tribes.

Flat Iron Building at Lacombe (R.L. Hursey)

The Legend of Wetaskiwin

In 1867, Blackfoot chief Buffalo Child and Cree chief Little Bear were both on reconnaissance and inadvertently chose the same hill that overlooked an area of dispute. When they discovered one another on the same hill, they fought a battle with no other weapons but hands and feet. When they had fought for almost an hour with neither having gained the upper hand, they agreed to rest awhile before resuming their fight. Buffalo Child pulled out his pipe and tobacco and began to smoke. Little Bear did the same, but when he discovered his pipe was broken, he threw it away in disgust. Buffalo Child took a puff on his pipe and held it out close to Little Bear to taunt him. Little Bear seized the pipe out of Buffalo Child's hand and smoked it. With horror, both realized the implications of the action—they had smoked a common pipe, a sacred pledge of peace. That day they agreed it had been a sign that they must remain friends and persuade their tribes to make peace. Each returned to their tribes to tell their story to the older chiefs. On the spot where they had battled, four Blackfoot chiefs and six chiefs of the Cree met together and passed the peace pipe.

During the Riel Rebellion in 1885, the Alberta Field Forces built a fort about five miles north of present-day Wetaskiwin on Big Stone Creek. Fort Ethier was named after Captain Ethier, commander of the fort.

In 1891 the CPR built Siding 16 and called it Wetaskiwin, an adaptation of the Cree word for "peace hills." Father Lacombe suggested the name to the CPR. In 1892 the townsite was surveyed and subdivided, and J.Z.C Miquelow opened a general store, Wetaskiwin's first business. He also became its first postmaster. In 1900, Wetaskiwin incorporated as a village; the following year, a town. Until local post offices were established in settlement districts, settlers went to Wetaskiwin for mail and supplies.

Wetaskiwin became an important detraining point for newly arrived immigrants who acquired homesteads east and northeast of the town. Immigration Hall provided living quarters and services for these newly arrived immigrants. Some of the more well-to-do settlers rented houses in Wetaskiwin for their families to live in while the men went off to build homes on their homesteads. The Native and pioneer history of the local area is portrayed at the **Wetaskiwin & District Museum** in the heart of the historic downtown area.

Immigrants arriving at Wetaskiwin. c1920 (Provincial Archives of
Alberta A5253)

Today Wetaskiwin is a major distribution and agricultural centre
as well as a centre for several automobile and farm equipment deal-
erships. One of the dealers, Stan Reynolds, began many years ago
amassing a large collection of early farm machinery, carriages, automobiles, trucks, and aircraft. He collected these monuments to
changing technology from all over western Canada. Many of these
deteriorate in the fields behind the dealership. My walk through this
strange crop of rusting skeletons gave me a vivid history lesson
about the transition on the prairies, from horse-powered vehicles
and equipment to steam and gas-powered machinery. Reynolds
himself restored many of these artifacts now on display at the
Reynolds Museum.

Just west of Reynolds Museum is the larger, provincially owned
**Reynolds-Alberta Museum and Canadian Aviation Hall
of Fame,** with collections based upon many acquired from Stan
Reynolds. This destination museum features authentically restored
artifacts in exhibits that tell the history of transportation and mecha-
nization in western Canada. Interpretive programs and multimedia
productions bring to life development of machines and the romance
of the automobile.

North of Wetaskiwin, the highway veers northwest through
lovely small farms, rolling wheat fields, and groves of aspen. The
village of Millet at Pipestone Creek comes into view. William C.
Van Horne, CPR manager, supposedly named Millet after the
French painter he admired—Jean François Millet. Some believe the
village was named after August Millet, a fur trader, who sometimes
travelled with Father Lacombe. It is well worth spending some time
in this community. The **Millet Museum & Exhibition Room**

contains an indoor "village" showing the story of Millet in period rooms, using artifacts related directly to the history of the area.

From Millet, 2A runs into Leduc, where the course of Alberta's history changed when Leduc #1 sparked the 1950's oil boom. In 1889, Robert Taylor Telford opened a stopping house along the C&E Trail. When the CPR reached there July 1891, the siding was named after the pioneer missionary priest, Father Hippolyte Leduc. Telford, born in Quebec in 1860, continued to run his store and started a hotel. In 1895, he became the community's first postmaster. He served as mayor of Telford during the World War I.

Leduc #1

On February 13, 1947, the Imperial Oil Company struck it big when an oil well on Mike Turta's farm brought in a gusher. The company had drilled over 130 dry wells before it finally made a major discovery. About 500 people witnessed the event. They first heard a rumble from deep in the bowels of the earth and then a roar as the huge geyser of oil, drilling mud, and water spewed out of the ground and blackened the sky when the oil was diverted and flared. Soon many other wells were drilled in the Leduc oil field, which eventually produced over 200 million barrels, ten times more than the Turner Valley oil field. Leduc #1 alone gushed in a record 72,000,000 barrels before it went dry. Although there were to be bigger discoveries of oil in future years, Leduc #1 changed Alberta from primarily an agricultural to an oil-based economy and shifted the province from a rural to urban population.

Leduc #1 (Glenbow Archives, Calgary, Alberta NA-555-5)

Leduc restored a home from the 1920s once owned by a local physician who practiced in the community in the 1920s and 1930s.

Dr. Woods House Museum provides a realistic look at the lifestyle of an urban, upper middle class family in the 1920s.

MUSEUMS ALONG the C & E TRAIL

☞ **Ellis Bird Farm** at Lacombe
Box 2980, Lacombe, AB T0C 1S0 * 8 km east and 8 km south of Lacombe
Governing body: Ellis Bird Farms Ltd.
Open June 15 to August 15, Tuesday to Sunday afternoons.
☎ (403) 346-2211 * Admission by donation * *Visiting time:* one hour

This bird farm has a collection of over 400 nesting boxes and a model wildlife garden. Indoor exhibits include the history of Ellis Bird Farm, wildlife gardening and cavity-nesting birds. This non-profit company carries on the work of pioneer conservationists Charles and Winnifred Ellis by maintaining a winter bird feeding program, bird banding, monitoring the nesting boxes, and producing publications and educational programs.

☞ **Lacombe Blacksmith Shop Museum**
Box 2179, Lacombe, AB T0C 1S0 * 5020 - 49th Street
Governing body: Maskipitoon Historical Society
Open May long weekend to September long weekend
☎ (403) 782-7333 * *Admission by donation* * *Visiting time:* one-half hour

The Lacombe Blacksmith Shop Museum is located in the former blacksmith shop that operated from 1902 to 1987. Until the shop closed, Jules Selvais and his son Roger owned and operated it. This living history museum interprets blacksmithing as a creative art form as well as utilitarian craft. Because the shop has been in continuous use for over eighty years, the machinery and equipment represent no one particular period, but show the transition of blacksmithing from wheelwright and plowshare work to modern welding, sheet metal and automotive work. The museum presents demonstrations by local and visiting blacksmiths and offers short courses in the winter in cooperation with Red Deer College.

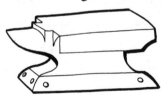

☞ **Michener House Museum**
Box 2179, Lacombe, AB T0C 1S0 * 5036 - 51st Street
Governing body: Maskipitoon Historical Society
Open September to May, weekdays; May to August, Wednesday to Sunday
☎ (403) 782-3933 * Admission by donation * *Visiting time:* one-half hour

This historic two-story house is the birthplace of Right Honourable Roland Michener, Governor-General of Canada from 1967 to 1974. It was built as a Methodist church manse in 1894 and declared a provincial historic resource in 1977. It has since been restored with period rooms with Mission furniture and other household artifacts that reflect the era of the 1910s and 1920s. On the second floor an exhibit of historic photographs tell the story of Roland Michener and his family. The museum also houses the archival collections of Lacombe.

☞ **Dr. Woods House Museum at Leduc**
Box 5201, Leduc, AB T9E 6L6 * 4801 - 49th Avenue
Governing body: Leduc and District Historical Society
Open summer: Tuesday through Sunday; Winter: Tuesday, Thursday, Sunday
☎ (403) 986 - 1517 * Admission by donation * *Visiting time:* 45 minutes

The museum is a historic house built in the 1920s by Dr. Woods, a prominent local physician. Part of his frame bungalow was used as a living quarters for him and his family. He used another part to practice medicine and perform surgery. The museum interprets the personal life and general practice of Dr. Woods and the town of Leduc of the 1920s and 1930s. The house reveals the level of comfort the urban professional enjoyed in the 1920s. A self-guided audio tour brings to life this family and puts a particular face on this historic moment. The restoration is well done, and even the plants in the garden are reminiscent of the period.

☞ **Millet and District Museum and Exhibit Room**
Box 178, Millet, AB T0C 1Z0 * 5120 - 50th Street
Governing body: Millet & District Historical Society
Open September to May: Tuesday, Thursday and Saturday afternoons; June to August: Monday to Saturday.
☎ (403) 387-5558 * Admission by donation * *Visiting time:* one-half hour

The museum is located in the town hall. The exhibit room on the main floor showcases six changing exhibits on a variety of subjects. During my visit, the museum had mounted an interesting display on Millet's local rodeo heroes. Downstairs is a replica village showing a one-room school house, a 1900s four-room home, an office and barbershop as well as a tool shed. You really get a sense of the history of this village, and the museum shows a high level of professionalism in the quality of the displays and care of artifacts. I found the summer staff well-trained and very friendly.

☞ **Fort Ostell Museum** at Ponoka
5320 - 54th Street, Ponoka, AB   T4J 1L8 * Centennial Park
Governing body: Fort Ostell Museum Society
Open May 1 to August 31, daily; September 1 to April 30,
Monday, Tuesday and Wednesday.
☎ (403) 783-5224/783-5968
Admission by donation * *Visiting time:* one half hour

Fort Ostell Museum features attractive thematic exhibits that tell the story of Ponoka and area. Collections include historical artifacts that depict the establishment of Fort Ostell and the pioneer era. An exhibition room shows travelling and temporary exhibits.

☞ **Alberta Central Railway Museum** at Wetaskiwin
RR #2, Wetaskiwin, AB   T9A 1W9
Governing body: Alberta Central Live Steamers Society
Open Victory Day weekend to first weekend in October, Wednesday thru Sunday
☎ (403) 352-2257/352-3202 * Admission fee charged
Visiting time: one hour

The Alberta Central Railway Museum, located in a replica of the Wetaskiwin CPR station, contains archives that depict CPR railway history in western Canada. Several examples of rolling stock are on display, as well as a 1948 mail-express car that houses a large collection of railway artifacts, a 1923 mail-express car, a 1949 caboose, and a 1923 former sleeper, now used as a cafe. Ride a Speeder, see how the semaphore works and take a self-guided tour of the grounds. Each month during the summer, the museum features a famous railway dinner in the cafe car.

☞ **Canada's Aviation Hall of Fame**
c/o Reynolds-Alberta Museum, Box 6360, Wetaskiwin, AB T9A 2G1
Reynolds-Alberta Museum Aviation Exhibit,
1 km west of Wetaskiwin on Highway 13
Governing body: Canada's Aviation Hall of Fame
Open year round, daily * ☎ (403) 361-1239
Admission fee charged * *Visiting time:* one half hour
🏆🏆🚗 ♿ 👫

This museum dedicates itself to recognizing individuals who have made a significant contribution to Canadian aviation. Displays feature the lives and accomplishments of the 144 members that have been inducted into the Canada Aviation Hall of Fame. Artifacts include a DC-6 flight simulator, uniforms, personal objects of the members, and restored aircraft on loan from the Reynolds family.

☞ **Reynolds-Alberta Museum**
Box 6360, Wetaskiwin, AB T9A 2G1
One kilometer west of Wetaskiwin on Highway 13
Governing body: Alberta Community Development,
Historic Sites and Archives Services
Open year-round, daily. * ☎ (403) 361-1351/ 352-5855
Admission fee charged * *Visiting time:* Two hours
🏆🏆🏆🏆🚗 ♿ 👫 ⛺ 🌲 ♿ 🍴 ━

Reynolds-Alberta Museum is a destination museum for anyone interested in the history of mechanized transportation in Alberta from the 1890s to the 1960s. The museum has a lot more going on than simply static displays of restored vehicles, aircraft and machinery. It is especially fun for children because of the numerous interactive activities and hands-on artifacts. Multimedia shows bring alive Alberta's transportation, agricultural, and industrial heritage. It also houses the Canadian Aviation Hall of Fame in the Display Hangar that shows vintage aircraft. Of special interest to antique car enthusiasts is the recent acquisition of a 1929 Duesenberg Phaeton Royale.

☞ **Reynolds Museum and Reynolds Aviation Museum**
4110 - 57 Street, Wetaskiwin, AB T9A 2B6
Governing body: privately owned and operated by the Reynolds family
Open May 15 to Labour Day, daily * ☎ (403) 352-5201/352-6201
Admission fee charged * *Visiting time:* one hour
🏆🏆🚗 ♿🍴 ━

This private museum features a large collection of antique tractors, steam engines, cars, trucks, airplanes, fire engines, war relics, and a variety of musical instruments and household items. The Reynolds Aviation Museum displays over 65 military and commercial aircraft and approximately 50 military vehicles. The museum actively collects and restores aircraft. Take the time to see the acres of rusted machinery. There are some real treasures awaiting restoration.

☞ **Wetaskiwin and District Museum**
5010 - 53rd Avenue, Wetaskiwin, AB T9A 0Y7
Governing body: Wetaskiwin & District Historical Society
Open September to May, Tuesday to Friday; June to August, daily.
☎ (403) 352-0227 * Admission by donation * *Visiting time:* one-half hour

---

The museum is located in the heart of downtown Wetaskiwin. Its artifact collections and displays feature Native and settlement history of Wetaskiwin and area. A series of travelling and changing feature exhibits are shown quarterly. The museum offers guided tours and walking tours of historic Main Street.

16

THE DAVID THOMPSON TRAIL
HIGHWAYS 11 AND 20

One of the most beautiful drives in the province is west from Red Deer to Rocky Mountain House. One leaves the relatively flat fertile parkland and enters the Boreal-Cordillerian forest. Lodgepole pine, white spruce, larch (tamarack), and aspen provide a rich habitat for large mammals like mule deer, white-tailed deer, moose and elk. The creeks and rivers, which flow in a southeasterly direction, offer the dry fly enthusiast with some of the best trout fishing streams in the province. Rocky Mountain House is located on the upper reaches of the North Saskatchewan River.

The area around Rocky Mountain House was traditionally Blackfoot country. During the 1790s the North West Company expanded into new areas of the Canadian West as regions further east became trapped out. In 1799, the NWC built a trading post at Rocky Mountain House; the Hudson's Bay Company followed closely on its trail and built Acton House the same year. Rocky Mountain House, the most westerly and southerly fur trading fort east of the mountains, was built at a time of fierce competition between NWC, HBC, and the XY companies. Liquor oiled negotiations with the Indians, who traded with whatever company gave them the best deal. Violence between the three companies was not uncommon. The fur traders stole each other's goods, damaged canoes, tore down each other's tents and fired shots at one another. Ruthless competition diminished somewhat after the NWC and XY Company merged in 1804, leaving the NWC and HBC to battle it out for supremacy until they also merged in 1821.

Chimneys of old Fort Rocky Mountain House 1913, (John Koch)

David Thompson (1770 - 1857)

David Thompson, western Canada's most famous surveyor-explorer, made the earliest, most detailed map of what is today's Alberta. Born in London in 1770 to a poor family, Thompson at an early age showed an aptitude for mathematics. At about 16 years of age, he arrived on the prairies and began to work for the HBC as a fur trader and surveyor, under the tutelage of James Gaddy. In 1785, he joined a group of Peigan Indians and wintered with them in the southwestern corner of Alberta. He left the HBC in 1797 because of its lack of interest in his surveys and joined the NWC. Two years later, at age 29, he married a Métis woman, Charlotte Small, daughter of a native woman and partner in the NWC. Charlotte and the growing family travelled with Thompson throughout many of his explorations. They eventually had 13 children.

Rocky Mountain House became Thompson's base for his explorations to find a navigable route to the Pacific. In 1807, he headed the NWC party that eventually crossed the mountains. Between 1807 and 1812 he surveyed the Kootenay and Columbia rivers and established posts south of today's 49th Parallel. His detailed notes on the geography and the people he met on his explorations appeared in his *Narrative of Explorations in Western America, 1784 - 1812*, published in the 1840s.

Rocky Mountain House continued operations throughout most of the 19th century. The importance of the fort declined by 1821, when the HBC and NWC merged. Between 1828 to 1861, Rocky Mountain House was open only in the winter for trade with the Blackfoot. The post was finally abandoned in 1875.

Rocky Mountain House remained deserted for many years before the first settlers began to homestead in the area. In 1904, George and Fred Fletcher decided to settle near the ruins, where a fire had destroyed the buildings a few years before, leaving only the stone chimneys. At first the Fletchers were squatters, but in 1906, after the land had been surveyed into townships and sections, they filed for homesteads. Another early settler was John Bertrand, considered the founder of the town of Rocky Mountain House.

These early settlers did not have an easy time preparing this forested land for crops. The Palliser Expedition of the 1850s had described the area around Rocky Mountain House as the western edge of the fertile crescent. The forest soils and the early frosts made the area unattractive to homesteaders until after the turn of the century when the better lands were already taken. The Rocky Mountain House area was suitable primarily for dairying and mixed farming. Homesteaders were required to live on their quarter section for at least six months of the year, and to gain full title to their land, they had to clear 30 acres. Settlers were able to clear only a few acres a year. Machine farming was impossible until large roots and stumps were removed.

Hauling logs for the Walker homestead. c1909. (Provincial Archives of Alberta A3476)

Coal brought the promise of prosperity and growth to Rocky Mountain House in 1911, when the Brazeau Collieries began operations at Nordegg, 96 kilometres west of Rocky Mountain House. Martin Nordegg, the mine's first president, named the town after himself. The following year, the Alberta Central Railway (ACR) and the Canadian Northern Railway (CNoR) started to build parallel lines west from Red Deer toward Nordegg. During this period, competition in railway building was keen, and companies often sabotaged each other's efforts. When ACR erected barriers to halt the progress of the CNoR line, the CNoR workers simply removed them in the middle of the night. In retaliation they sabotaged ACR's progress by dumping dirt and gravel on ACR's roadway below. The ACR filed an injunction against the CNoR and the railway commission had to settle the dispute. The CNoR was given permission to continue on to Nordegg, and the ACR got the green light to continue construction of its bridge across the North Saskatchewan River. By June 1912, track had reached Rocky Mountain House and John Bertrand, its founder, drove in the last stake.

You can travel in the footsteps of David Thompson and the early pioneers on the David Thompson Highway (Highway 11). **Rocky Mountain House National Historic Park** brings to life the fur trade period with interpretive displays and programs about the Native history and Thompson's explorations. Walking trails take the visitor to the sites where the original buildings were excavated. **Rocky Mountain House Museum,** located in a 1927 school building, offers many opportunities to learn about the settlement period of Rocky Mountain House, through hands-on exhibits and programs for all ages.

In Nordegg, the **Nordegg Heritage Centre** has begun restoration on several abandoned buildings of the former Brazeau Collieries. During the summer months, the Nordegg Historic Heritage Interest Group interprets the coal mining history of the area by providing tours of Nordegg's mine site and townsite.

Nordegg mine site in the 1920s. (Nordegg Historical Society)

For a scenic and historic side trip from Rocky Mountain House, go north from beautiful Sylvan Lake on Highway 20 to the town of Rimbey, which has two museums—**Pas-ka-Poo Museum and Park** and the **Smithson International Truck Museum.** Two provincial parks, one at Sylvan Lake and the other at Gull Lake, offer opportunities for watching wildlife.

Tracks and Traces: Pas-Ka-Poo means "blind man" in Cree. The Blindman River, a tributary of Red Deer River, got its name from the time that a party of Cree hunters, travelling through the area in winter, suffered severe snow blindness. They camped for several days beside the river until their sight improved.

MUSEUMS IN THE ROCKY MOUNTAIN HOUSE AREA

☞ **Breton & District Museum**
Box 696, Breton, AB T0C 0P0 * 4715 - 51st Street
Governing body: Breton & District Historical Museum Society
Open July and August, Tuesday to Saturday
☎ (403) 696-3862/696-3539 * *Admission fee charged*
Visiting time: one half hour

The Breton & District museum is housed in an old school annex building. The exhibits tell the story of the founding and development of Breton and area. Special focus is on the early Black settlers of the Keystone district and the importance of the lumber industry to the area.

☞ **Nordegg Heritage Centre**
Box 550, Rocky Mountain House, AB T0M 1T0
Office - 4340 - 47th Avenue, Rocky Mountain House;
Museum - Main Street, Nordegg
Governing body: Nordegg Historical Society
Open May to October, daily * ☎ (403) 845-7330
Admission fee charged * *Visiting time:* one hour

During the summer, the Nordegg Heritage Centre interprets the historic site of the Brazeau Collieries in a tour of the mine site, townsite and briquette plant. The restoration of approximately 20 structures is projected for completion by 1999. When completed, this historic industrial site will be the largest in western Canada.

☞ **Pas-Ka-Poo Museum and Park** at Rimbey
Box 466, Rimbey, AB T0C 2J0 * 51st Avenue and 56th Street, Rimbey
Governing body: Rimbey Historical Society
Open May 1 to October 31, daily *☎ (403) 843-2429
Admission fee charged * *Visiting time:* one hour

Pas-Ka-Poo Museum and Park has eleven historic buildings that have been restored. A large collection of farming and household artifacts, from old radios and cameras to a complete set of Model T Ford tools, can be seen in the main building. Better written labels and more historical photographs would be helpful. However, the resident interpreter and caretaker gives an excellent tour of the historic buildings, which include the Beatty House, a registered provincial historic resource; an Anglican church, barbershop, school, general store, and railway station. One of the best things about this museum is the park-like setting with its lovely flowers, trees, and foot bridge.

Barber Shop at Pas-Ka-Poo Museum, Rimby (R.A. Hursey)

☞ **Smithson International Truck Museum**
Town of Rimbey, Rimbey, AB T0C 2J0 * Next to Pas-Ka-Poo Park
Governing body: Town of Rimbey
Open May 1 to October 31, daily
Admission fee charged * *Visiting time:* one half hour

🏆 🚗 ♿ ⛩ ⛺ 🍴 ━

The museum houses a collection of pickups bought by the Town of Rimbey from a local collector. It features about twenty restored International Harvester half-ton trucks that show a transition of models that span a period of almost forty years. This collection, limited only to pickup trucks, would be of interest to those who owned International pickups or collect and restore vintage trucks and automobiles. The historical photographs on the surrounding walls, I think, are the most interesting part of the museum. These show a variety of local people engaged in various occupations and give a pictorial history of the area.

☞ **Rocky Mountain House Museum**
Box 1508, Rocky Mountain House, AB T0M 1T0 * 4604 - 49th Avenue
Governing body: Rocky Mountain House Reunion Historical Society
Open year-round; winter - Monday to Saturday; summer - daily
☎ (403) 845-2332 * Admission fee charged * *Visiting time:* one hour

---

Housed in the former Confluence School, this community museum has displays showing artifacts in their natural setting, including a pioneer kitchen, a Victorian parlour and a 1920s classroom. Several artifacts such as the rope-making machine and player piano are hands-on. On site is a forestry cabin. The museum offers programs that re-create many of the pioneer crafts and lifestyles. Tours are offered in French and English. Plans are to move the museum from its present location to the main highway next to the visitor information centre.

☞ **Rocky Mountain House National Historic Site**
Box 2130, Rocky Mountain House, AB T0M 1T0
7 kilometres west of the town, on Highway 11A.
Governing body: Parks Canada
Open mid-April to Thanksgiving weekend * ☎ (403) 845-5320
No admission fee *Visiting time:* one hour

This national historic site interprets the history of this important fur trading post built by the North West Company in 1799. The visitor centre's exhibits and artifacts explain the history and importance of this fort to the North West and Hudson's Bay Companies and portray the Native history of the period. Self-guided audio tours are available to use along the park trails, which lead to four archaeological excavation sites. As at most national historic sites, Parks Canada does an excellent job of bringing alive the people and their activities during the fur trade period. Group tours and summer programs are presented by friendly and helpful interpretive staff.

17

STETTLER & AREA—HIGHWAYS 12 AND 56

The Stettler area is appropriately called "the heartland of Alberta." It is in the heart of the parkland and Alberta's fertile crescent. Rich, alluvial soils and sufficient rainfall most years make this area an important centre for growing a variety of grain crops. Many lakes and marshes attract migratory waterfowl; and the "knob and kettle" terrain, dug by receding glaciers, provides ideal habitats for large game animals like white-tailed and mule deer.

Our heritage journey begins at Alix, west of Stettler, on Highway 12. The first settler to this area was Edward Parlby. In 1892, he and his brothers cut the first road from the Alix area to Lacombe, which became known as the Buffalo Lake Trail. Alix was founded by the Todd family, settlers who came from Michigan to homestead around the turn of the century. The community was then known as Toddsville until it was changed to Alix in honour of Mrs. Alice Westhead, the first white woman settler in the area. By 1906, Alix had become an important railway town. A 1910 advertisement in a Calgary newspaper listed Alix as "the railroad centre of Alberta" with its intersection of three lines—the CPR, the Grand Trunk Pacific, and the Canadian Northern Railway. Perhaps Alix's most famous early resident was Irene Parlby, a pioneer in achieving women's rights.

Irene (Marryat) Parlby (1868 - 1965)

Irene Marryat Parlby (Provincial Archives of Alberta A3353)

Born in England on January 9, 1868, to an upper middle class family, Irene Marryat lived a sheltered life until she came to the Alberta prairies, where she discovered that in Canada "women were useful." She spent part of her childhood in India where her father was in charge of building railways. She became an accomplished pianist, having studied in England and Germany. While living in London, she met Mrs. Alice Westhead, who invited her to come in 1896 to stay at the Westhead Ranch near Buffalo Lake. There Irene met Walter Parlby and married him the following year. Their first home was a sod hut. For the next 16 years she was a housewife, raising a son and gardening.

In 1913 she joined the Country Women's Club in Alix, which later became Local #1 of the United Farm Women of Alberta. She served as president of the UFWA until 1919 when she was appointed to the Board of Governors of the University of Alberta, a position she held until 1921. That year she was nominated to run as a candidate from the Lacombe Constituency in the next election. Winning a seat in the Alberta legislature, she became only the second woman in the history of the British Commonwealth to hold such a position. Furthermore, she became one of the "Famous Five," Alberta women who fought to have women declared as persons by the Supreme Court in 1929. This landmark decision made it possible for women to sit in the Senate. In 1930 she served on the Canadian delegation to the League of Nations before retiring from public life in 1935.

The settlement of the Stettler district preceded the arrival of the Canadian Pacific Railway by a couple of years. George Pattrick, one of the railway's surveyors, established a homestead about three kilometres north of the proposed townsite of Stettler in 1903. The same year a large group of Estonian immigrants settled about 16 kilometres south of Stettler, in what is known today as the Linda Hall district.

Stettler's founder was Carl Stettler, a German-speaking settler from Switzerland, who established a German Swiss colony in 1903 at Blumenau, where he was postmaster. The village consisted of two general stores, a blacksmith shop, and a few other businesses. When the CPR bypassed this hamlet to lay the line about 3 kilometres north, the businesses all moved to the new location in 1906. Carl Stettler became a CPR land agent, built a large hotel, became the first postmaster, and received the honour of having the community named after him.

The Métis Settlement at Buffalo Lake

About 20 kilometres northeast of Stettler lies Buffalo Lake, once the home of a large Métis settlement at Tail Creek. In 1875, when Company "A" of the NWMP arrived in the area, about 400 people lived there. Many of the Métis had moved from the Red River settlement in Manitoba following the Red River Rebellion of 1869-70. Métis from Lac Ste Anne and St. Albert would join them on annual hunts. It was an area where buffalo had winter feeding grounds, and the Tail Creek Métis used the area for drying meat, making pemmican, and processing hides. In 1875, four NWMP officers were stationed at Tail Creek to stop the whisky trade. By 1877, however, the Métis abandoned the site when the buffalo no longer appeared. Years later, a fire swept the community and destroyed most of the cabins. In the 1970s, archaeologists from the Provincial Museum of Alberta did a major excavation of the former Métis settlement.

One of the best ways to see the Stettler area is not by car, but by train. The **Alberta Prairie Railway**, operated by Alberta Railway Steam Tours Ltd., runs steam locomotive trips out of Stettler during the summer. The northern leg goes through Donalda, Meeting Creek, and Edberg; the southern leg through Big Valley, Rumsey, Rowley, and Morrin. The Alberta Prairie Railway also provides an eastern excursion, using an early diesel locomotive and passenger train. This run goes to Castor, Coronation, and Consort.

Alberta Prairie Railway steam locomotive. (R.A. Hursey)

The towns along today's Alberta Prairie Railway owe their existence to the railway building boom from the turn of the century to the First World War. So, all aboard for the southern excursion departing from Stettler! Our first stop is at Big Valley. It is worth spending some time walking around this community, once an important freight divisional point on CNoR's Vegreville line. You can see the remains of the old five-stall roundhouse, which could house up to 14 locomotives. The Roman Catholic Church overlooking Big Valley is well worth the walk to the top of the hill to see. The **Big Valley Station Museum,** located in the historic 1912 CNoR railway station, has railway artifacts and displays that interpret the history of the village. Back on board we roll on toward Rumsey, our next stop.

Big Valley Station Museum (R.L. Hursey)

Rumsey began as a cattle ranch. The Crooked Leg Ranching company, founded in 1900, ran 1000 head of cattle on open range. In 1904, the ranch lost its lease when the land was surveyed into sections and opened to homesteading. About this time a group of Russian Jews started a colony between Trochu and Rumsey. The Jewish Colonization Association, a resettlement agency, sponsored the colonists. After the First World War, several Polish Jews were absorbed into the colony, which struggled through droughts and financial problems in the 1920s. During the Great Depression, most of the colonists gave up the land and moved to Calgary. Only two families remained by the end of World War II.

South of Rumsey our train passes through a large marsh called the **Park and Moraine Ecological Reserve.** My scout and I experienced a lot of pleasure watching the hundreds of ducks, geese, and shorebirds that make this marsh their temporary home in the spring and summer.

Our final stop on the southern run is Rowley, a town that refused to die. Rowley was named after Lt. Colonel Charles Walsh Rowley of the NWMP. In 1911, when the CNoR put a line through from Stettler, George Swallow and his sons operated a store. The following year the community built its first school. In 1920, Sam Leung Ying built and opened a Chinese restaurant.

In the 1970s, when the village was about to disappear into prairie railway history, a group of enthusiastic farmers and ranchers formed a historical society and began restoring many of the buildings to their former glory. Ann Wheeler used it as a location for the film, *Bye, Bye Blues.* Rowley's **Yesteryear Artifact Museum,** located in a box car beside the track, is hardly worth the time to visit, but other artifacts are in buildings throughout the town. The town itself is really the museum. **Sam's Bar,** next to the Rowley Trading Post, is where one can go to talk with the locals about the work they are doing to make their hamlet an important Alberta tourist attraction.

Sam's Bar and the Rowley Trading Post. (R.A. Hursey)

The northern run includes stops at Donalda, Meeting Creek, and Edberg Creek. Donalda was first settled by Americans and Scandinavians in 1909 around the CNoR station. The name of the post office was Eidswold but was changed to Donalda in 1911, after Donalda Crossway. Donalda is home to a very unusual museum. The **Donalda & District Museum** calls itself "The Lamp Capital of Canada" and owns more than 800 household, industrial, and mining kerosene lamps. You can also take tours through the **Donalda Creamery**, a cooperative creamery that opened in 1924.

MUSEUMS IN STETTLER AND AREA

☞ **Alix Wagon Wheel Regional Museum**
Box 157, Alix, AB T0C 0B0 * Main Street
Governing body: Alix Wagon Wheel Museum Association
Open year-round; days vary * ☎ (403) 747-2462/747-2708
Admission by donation * *Visiting time:* one half hour

The museum features collections related to the history of Alix and region with local historical artifacts and photographs. It presents temporary exhibits on seasonal and topical themes.

☞ **Big Valley Museum**
Box 40, Big Valley, AB T0J 0G0 * Main Street
Governing body: Big Valley Historical Society
Open May 1 to August 31, daily *☎ (403) 876-2593
Admission by donation * *Visiting time:* one half hour

The museum is located in the original 1913 CNoR train station. Its collections include artifacts related to Big Valley's railroad, mining, farming, ranching, and petroleum history. A very good photographic display features the history of the community. Big Valley Museum is a stop along the Alberta Prairie Railway.

☞ **Castor and District Museum**
Box 864, Castor, AB T0C 0X0 * 5101 - 49 Avenue
Governing body: Castor & District Museum Society
Open year round: weekend afternoons *☎ (403) 882-3409
Admission fee charged

Castor & District Museum, housed in the former CPR station, features artifacts related to the local history to the town, railway, farming, ranching, and mining of the area. This museum appears to be mainly of local interest, as its hours are limited. When my scout and I were in Castor, we found the museum closed during the hours it was supposed to be open.

☞ **Donalda & District Museum**
Box 40, Donalda, AB T0H 1H0 * Railway Avenue and Main Street
Governing body: Village of Donalda
Open year round: Mid-May to Thanksgiving, daily;
rest of year, Tuesday to Friday * ☎ (403) 883-2345/883-2100
Admission fee charged * *Visiting time:* one hour

🏆🏆🚗 ♿ ⛽ ⛲ 🎪

Donalda & District Museum is located in the Donalda Village Office building overlooking the scenic Meeting Creek coulee. Known as "The Lamp Capital of Canada," this museum has a unique collection of kerosene lamps of every size and description, from parlour lamps to industrial and mining lamps. Of the 800-odd lamps in the museum's collection, the late Don and Beth Lawson donated 500. The oldest is a whale lamp dating back to the 1600s. Other artifact collections portray local history. The museum is a stop along the Alberta Prairie Railway.

☞ **Donalda Co-op Creamery**
Box 40, Donalda, AB T0H 1H0 * Railway Avenue and Main Street
Governing body: Village of Donalda
Open year round: Mid-May to Thanksgiving, daily; rest of year, Tuesday to
Friday * ☎ (403) 883-2345/883-2100 * *Visiting time:* one half hour

🚗 ⛽ 🎪 🍴

In 1990 the Donalda Co-op Creamery was designated a provincial historic resource. The creamery, home of award-winning "Donalda Maid Butter," operated from 1924 to 1987. The Donalda & District Museum conducts tours of this facility.

☞ **Meeting Creek Railway Station Museum** at Meeting Creek
Box 142, Big Valley, AB T0J 0G0 * End of Main Street
Governing body: Canadian Northern Society
Open July and August, daily * ☎ (403) 887-2189
Admission by donation * *Visiting time:* one half hour

🏆 🚗 ⛽ 🎪

The museum, housed in a third-class 1913 Canadian Northern railway station, has been refurbished to the 1940s era. The period rooms show a waiting room, operator's office, and living room. Collections pertain to CNoR and local history. In addition to its regular hours, the museum is open during arrivals of the Alberta Prairie Railway tours. Tours of the Meeting Creek grain elevator are also available.

☞ **Mirror & District Museum**
Box 246, Mirror, AB T0B 3C0 * 4910 - 53rd Street
Governing body: Mirror & District Museum Association
Open June through Labour Day * ☎ (403) 788-2166
Admission by donation * *Visiting time:* one half hour
🍷 🚗 🎪 ⚠

The Mirror & District Museum collections include local history and railway artifacts. An old wooden railway caboose is being restored. In the centre of town stands St. Monica's Anglican Church of the Mission of Lamerton, a registered provincial historic resource. It held services from 1895 to 1984.

☞ **Yesteryear Artifacts Museum** at Rowley
General Delivery, Rowley, AB T0J 2X0 * Main Street
Governing body: Rowley Yester-Year Artifacts Museum Society
Open July and August, daily; open weekends in spring and fall.
☎ (403) 368-3816 * Admission by donation
Visiting time: one quarter hour
🍷 🚗 🍴 🎪 ♿ 🍽

Artifacts pertaining to the local history of Rowley are housed mainly in a boxcar by the railroad tracks. Other artifacts appear in many of the original buildings that are being restored by the museum society. The hamlet of Rowley is a living history museum that is a stop on the Alberta Prairie Railway.

☞ **Alberta Prairie Railway Excursions** at Stettler
Postal Bag 800, Stettler, AB T0C 2L0 * 47 Street and 47 Avenue
Governing body: Alberta Prairie Railway Steam Tours Ltd.
Open weekends, June to October
☎ (403) 742-2811; toll free (April 1 to October 31) 1-800-282-3994
Admission fee charged * Excursions, four- to eight-hour round trips
🍷 🍷 🍷 🚗 🍴 ♿

This museum-on-wheels is one of the best tourist attractions in central Alberta. The Alberta Railway tours link several other museums along the former CNoR line, with terminals at Edberg, Morrin, and Coronation. Vintage steam locomotives and passenger cars provide a leisurely and nostalgic tour through railway history. Dinner excursions, live entertainment in the Lone Star Saloon, and murder mysteries are offered. Be prepared for occasional non-scheduled stops to cool an overheated bearing, and don't be surprised if you are held up by train robbers.

☞ **Stettler Town & Country Museum**
Box 2118, Stettler, AB T0C 2L0 * 6302 - 44th Avenue
Governing body: Stettler Town & Country Museum Society
Open May to September, daily
☎ (403) 742-4543 (summer); 742-4291 (winter)
Admission fee charged * *Visiting time:* Two hours

♥♥ 🚗 👫 ⊞ 🍴 —

This museum maintains a large collection of historic buildings arranged in a pioneer village, with a 1911 Class Two CNoR station at one end of the main street and on the other end, a courthouse with the original courtroom upstairs. Originally, a lot of work went into developing this museum, and some of the period displays are very well done. If one wants to see sheer volumes of artifacts from every possible source and topic, you'll enjoy this place. But seeing the poorly written labels, lack of adequate security, and deterioration of many fine artifacts saddened me. This museum obviously needs an infusion of money and tender loving care.

☞ **Veteran Museum**
Box 534, Veteran, AB T0C 2S0
Governing body: Veteran Museum Society * Open three afternoons a week
☎ (403) 575-2223 * Admission by donation
♥ 🚗 🎣

The museum's collection includes household items, school records, textiles, and other artifacts pertaining to the history of the Veteran community.

18

BATTLE RIVER COUNTRY
HIGHWAYS 21, 13, & 36

Battle River begins as an outlet of Pigeon Lake and meanders in a westerly direction through central and eastern Alberta until it joins the North Saskatchewan River at the Battlefords in Saskatchewan. The river wanders through fertile agricultural parkland and eventually carves a wide, deep valley into the prairie landscape of eastern Alberta. Poplars, white spruce, and willows line the river, providing ideal habitats for white-tailed deer, beaver, raptors (birds of prey), and small mammals.

In this chapter and the following, we will explore the fascinating history of the Battle River Country. First you will travel along Highways 21, 13 and 36, through communities that were settled mostly in the 1890s and early 1900s when the land was squared off into sections and the Canadian Pacific, Grand Trunk Pacific and the Canadian Northern railway companies began building branch lines from the centre of the province. You will want to make your first stop at Hay Lakes, which predates the coming of the railway but marks the beginning of telecommunications in western Canada.

In 1876, Hay Lakes became the western terminus of the first Dominion telegraph line across the vast stretches of western Canada, then known as the Northwest Territories. The Dominion Government started the line from Selkirk, Manitoba. It continued to Battleford, Saskatchewan, and on to Hay Lakes, where the Battleford Trail and the trail to Fort Edmonton joined. When James McKernon, the first telegraph operator, arrived at Hay Lakes, he discovered that no one lived there; but there were people living in Edmonton, 48 kilometres north. Why the government turned down Edmonton's petition to extend the line to the fort is as much a mystery to us as it was to the good people of Edmonton. They would have to wait three more years for a communication link with eastern Canada, and only after the Hudson's Bay Company provided the poles and labour to extend the telegraph line. Hay Lakes has commemorated the history of this most westerly telegraph station by establishing the **Hay Lakes Telegraph Park,** located next to where the Battleford Trail and the Hay Lakes trail to Fort Edmonton joined. You can still see remnants of these old wagon trails.

> **Tracks and Traces:** The first telegraph lines were strung from tree to tree in forested areas and on poplar poles in treeless areas. The lines were often down because of hail, wind, and ice storms, beavers and even buffalo herds, which liked to use the telegraph poles as rubbing posts.

South of Hay Lakes you leave Highway 21 and turn east on Highway 13 to Camrose, an important agricultural centre. This city of 13,000 is the home of the famous "Sunny Boy Cereal;" Camrose Lutheran College, and, in the last few years, the site of the Big Valley Jamboree, where over 100,000 enthusiasts come in July from all over western Canada to enjoy country and western music performers.

Camrose was settled largely by Norwegian immigrants. The first home in Camrose was a log shack built by Ole Bakken in 1893. Bakken came to Canada from Norway by way of Wisconsin. The same year, Peter B. Anderson, head of a group of Norwegian immigrants, detrained at Wetaskiwin and travelled by wagon to settle in the Bardo district. The year 1904 saw the beginnings of a hamlet on Stoney Creek when Duncan Sampson opened a small store with living quarters upstairs. On the west side of Stoney Creek, Charles Erickson had a stopping house at his farm, where settlers slept in the loft above his barn.

If you look at a railway map of circa 1915, you will get some idea of the importance of this community as a divisional point and railway centre. The CPR, GTP, and CNoR branch lines all converged at Camrose. In the summer of 1904, the CPR began to grade a roadbed east of Wetaskiwin to the Stoney Creek district. The community was first named Sparling, after Rev. Dr. Sparling, a physician from Winnipeg. By 1905 Sparling incorporated as a village. Because the name Sparling often got confused with other towns, like Sperling and Stirling, the village council changed the name to Camrose in 1906. Although the origin of the name is not clear, it may be derived from *cam rhos,* a Welsh term meaning "crooked moor."

Religion has always been an important part of life in Camrose. The Lutheran Church formed the centre of social and cultural life for the groups of Norwegian immigrants, who could hear sermons in their native language. In 1912, the Norwegian Lutheran community established the Camrose Lutheran College, with Rev. J. P. Tandberg serving as its first president. As there were no dormitories, the first students lived at a local hotel.

Camrose has two museums. The **Camrose & District Museum** tells the story of the history of agriculture and town life.

Its collection includes many beautifully crafted textiles and wooden objects, reflecting Norwegian heritage of the area. The **Camrose Railway Station Museum**, in the former CNoR station, shows an early waiting room and station office with telegraph equipment. This museum contains the archives and library of the Canadian Northern Society and is available to historians and researchers.

Camrose Railway Station Museum (R.L. Hursey)

Leaving Camrose, you continue east on Highway 13 where you pass through Daysland, a community originally settled by Edgerton W. Day, who bought 15 sections of CPR lands in 1904 and formed the Central Alberta Land Company. When early settlers asked the name of the area, the usual reply was "This is Day's land." So when the townsite was laid out, the name became official.

Your next stop is the village of Strome, named after an early Swedish family who settled in the region. Strome has one of my favorite community history museums, the **Sodbusters Archives & Museum.** Although the collections are not all that different from those of other museums in the area, the staff and volunteers have added a sense of fun to their displays by creatively using old store mannequins in humorous poses. On the grounds stands the original Strome jail house. The museum recently acquired a very large natural history collection of mounted specimens depicting birds and mammals of western Canada.

Sodbusters Archives & Museum- bathtub display (R.L. Hursey)

East of Strome you notice that the land becomes drier and flatter, and the aspen hummocks take on a stunted look. When my scout and I came through this area, we saw scores of red tailed hawks, Canada geese, and the occasional ferruginous hawk. Fourteen kilometres east of Sedgewick, you turn south at Killam on Highway 36 to Alliance, a town that owes its existence to the construction of a CNoR railway line that was supposed to go as far as Regina, but was never completed. The line terminated at Alliance in 1916.

Many communities along the Battle and Red Deer Rivers can claim, "Anthony Henday slept here." Henday, Alberta's earliest white man, camped on top of a hill in 1754, just west of present day Forestburg. His Cree companions sent smoke signals to the Blackfoot announcing their arrival—a wise thing to do as this was disputed territory between Blackfoot and Cree. Southwest of Forestburg is **Big Knife Provincial Park** on the Battle River. The park commemorates a time when a Cree warrior named Big Man and a Blackfoot named Knife battled and killed one another. Another important location in Native history is Iron Creek near the town of Lougheed.

The Manitou Stone

Reverend George McDougall, the Methodist missionary at Victoria Settlement, heard about a very powerful stone located on the banks of Iron Creek. Cree and Blackfoot regularly visited this stone and left offerings of beads and other objects because they believed the stone had great powers. In 1866, John McDougall moved the 386-pound rock by Red River cart to the Victoria Mission. The stone ended up at the mission's headquarters in Toronto and was later given to the Royal Ontario Museum. The stone turned out to be the largest meteorite in Canada and the third largest in the world. The removal of the stone caused great fear among the native people who believed a great disaster would happen. Within ten years of its removal, half the Native population of Alberta were decimated by small pox, the buffalo disappeared, and many died of starvation. The Manitou Stone now resides at the Provincial Museum of Alberta. In 1996, it will be on display in the new Indian Gallery. A cast of this magnificent stone can be seen in the museum's Earth Sciences gallery.

Near the junction of Big Knife Creek and the Battle River was the headquarters of one of the most notorious cattle rustlers in western Canadian history. The breakup of the gang's operations marked the end of an era, as the large ranches disappeared and were replaced by farms.

Jack Dubois, Cattle Rustler King

In 1902, Jack Dubois came from the United States and settled on Big Knife Creek, southwest of Galahad, where he organized a gang of cattle thieves that preyed upon the local ranchers for years, stealing cattle, altering brands and adding the stolen cattle to the gang's own herds.

In 1908, the Royal North West Mounted Police assigned Sergeant Robert W. Ensor to go undercover and gather evidence against the rustlers. Dressed as an ordinary cowboy, he rode from ranch to ranch gathering evidence against the gang. In 1909, Ensor and two other Mounties arrested Irven and Jim Holt, two members of Dubois' gang. Dubois, however escaped. He was finally arrested when he tried to board a train in Lacombe. He was arraigned and tried in the District Court at Red Deer. While the Holts received nine years in prison, Dubois, the brains behind the gang, received only nine months.

For the first time in Alberta, the Crown appealed the lower court ruling. The Supreme Court later overruled the decision and a new trial was set. Dubois received five years. He personally appealed the charges, which were thrown out of court on the basis that his 18-year-old son could have branded the cat-

tle. Dubois was ordered released. Soon after, he moved to

B.C., and the Holts were later
banished to the States.

In 1907, the area along the Battle River became an important coal mining centre when the Bish Brothers opened a coal mine near Forestburg. At the time, coal was needed to operate the great number of steam locomotives. In its heyday, the Castor coal field had 48 coal mines, mostly small claims that operated underground. In the 1940s strip mining became the standard mode of extraction. In 1949, Luscar Inc. took over mining interests in the area and started the Forestburg Collieries Ltd. The coal was hauled to the Alberta Power Plant on the Battle River. Today the Diplomat mine, 13 kilometres southwest of Forestburg, provides coal to generate electrical power. The **Diplomat Mine Interpretive Centre** portrays the history of surface coal mining on the prairies.

MUSEUMS ALONG HIGHWAYS 13 AND 36

☞ **Alliance & District Museum**
Box 101, Alliance, AB T0B 0A0 * On SR 602, west end of town.
Governing body: Alliance & District Museum Society
Open Summer, Tuesday and Wednesday afternoons
☎ (403) 879-3931 * Admission by donation
🍷 🚗 ⛱ 🍽

The museum is located in the old Roman Catholic church. Other buildings include a homesteader's log cabin furnished with period objects. This museum, with its limited hours, was not open during its scheduled time when my scout and I tried to visit it.

☞ **Camrose & District Museum**
Box 1622 * 46 Avenue & 53 Street
Governing body: Camrose & District Museum Society
May 15 to Labour Day, daily * ☎ (403) 672-3298
Admission by donation * *Visiting time:* one hour
🍷 🍷 🍷 🚗 🧍 🐎 🏛 ⛱ 🍽 ═

Located in a park setting, the main building has a large collection of household objects and farming equipment, a working scale model of a threshing outfit and two scale model steam locomotives. Some of the artifacts reflect the Norwegian heritage of the area, like the cutwork textiles and the *hardanger* wood furniture. Historic buildings include a log house and a log church, both with period furnishings, a 1907 country school, an old army hut, a fire hall with the first two fire trucks used in Camrose, and a machinery building with a working Case steam engine, early tractors and harvesting equipment. A replica of the 1908 Camrose Canadian Building, which published a local newspaper, has early printing machinery and equipment.

☞ **Camrose Railway Station Museum**
Box 142, Big Valley, AB T0J 0G0 * 4407 - 47th Avenue, Camrose
Governing body: Canadian Northern Society
Open July and August, daily
☎ (403)672-3099, Camrose; 876-2242, Big Valley
Admission by donation * *Visiting time:* one half hour
🏆 🏆 🚗 ♿ 🍴 ➖

The museum is housed in the restored 1911 Canadian Northern Class 3 station. It has a tea room, archives and library and period displays of a waiting room and station office, equipped with telegraph equipment. The Canadian Northern Society restored and refurbished railway stations at Rowley, Donalda, and Meeting Creek as well as Camrose. The archives and library are available for historians and researchers interested in railway history, particularly the CNoR and CN.

☞ **Diplomat Mine Interpretive Site** at Forestburg
Box 210, Forestburg, AB T0B 1N0
8 kilometres west of Forestburg on Highway 53,
and 8 kilometres south on SR 855
Governing body: Diplomat Mine Museum Society
Open May to September, daily * ☎ (403) 582-3668
Admission by donation * *Visiting time:* one half hour
🏆 🏆 🚗 👥

The Diplomat Mine Interpretive Site portrays the history of surface coal mining on the prairies. Forestburg Collieries Ltd., a division of Luscar Ltd., operated the Diplomat Mine from 1949 to 1986. The mine site displays various machines used for strip-mining coal. Its centrepiece is the mammoth Marion 360 strip-mining shovel—the world's largest mobile land machine when it was built in 1927. The 550-ton artifact is the first machine designated an Alberta Historic Resource. Other equipment like the Bucyrus-Erie 120-B coal loading shovel and the "Big Dipper" are also on display.

☞ **Iron Creek Museum** at Lougheed
Box 249, Lougheed, AB T0B 2V0 * 49th Street and 51st Avenue
Governing body: County of Flagstaff
Open summer, daily * ☎ (403) 386-3934
Admission fee charged * *Visiting time:* one half hour

The museum features local artifacts and archives with documents pertaining to the town, local curling clubs, and records of schools and principals dating back to the 1920s.

☞ **Sedgewick Historical Museum**
Box 450, Sedgewick, AB T0B 4C0
Governing body: Sedgewick Historical Society
Open year-round, Tuesday to Thursday afternoons
☎ (403) 384-3741/384-3070 * Admission by donation
Visiting time: one half hour

The museum's collections include small artifacts of local origin, photos, documents, maps, books and photo albums. Artifacts range from northern Native clothing to Depression glass, dolls, and antique jewelry.

☞ **Sodbusters Archives & Museum** at Strome
Box 151, Strome, AB T0B 4H0 * Main Street
Governing body: Strome & District Historical Society
Open May to September, daily; winter on Thursdays * ☎ (403) 376-3688
Admission by donation * *Visiting time:* one hour

Housed in the Memorial Hall, this dynamic small museum features a light-hearted look at its local history, with artifacts shown in the context of period rooms arranged in an open setting. The creative use of mannequins in humourous poses sets the displays apart from other museums of its size. The hall's stage serves as a work area for summer students who catalogue artifacts and are accessible to answer visitors' questions. In 1993, the museum acquired a new wing to house the large natural history collection the town purchased from the former Coutts Museum. The collection contains Native artifacts, fossils, and mounted specimens of birds and mammals.

19

BATTLE RIVER COUNTRY—HIGHWAY 14

As the Battle River approaches the Saskatchewan border, it begins to carve out deep canyons and badlands, much like one sees along the Red Deer River. This region is a transition zone between parkland and shortgrass prairie, with sandy soil and hummocks of stunted aspen and willows. This is mostly ranching and mixed farming country. Shorthorns, Simmental, and Charolais cattle cover the land where herds of buffalo once grazed. When my scout and I visited here in June of 1993, recent rains had turned the land a lush green, ending five years of drought. Geese and ducks peppered the sky as they commuted from one slough to another.

Highway 14, our main route, parallels parts of the old Battleford-Edmonton Trail used by freighters bringing supplies to Fort Edmonton. It also follows the railway line of the Grand Trunk Pacific (GTP). The end-of-steel reached Alberta by 1908, creating sidings that became hamlet stops and later towns. Steam trains were lifelines to these communities, bringing passengers and freight and hauling grain to eastern markets.

Your journey along Highway 14 will follow the path of the old GTP line from the Alberta-Saskatchewan border to the outskirts of Edmonton. About 30 kilometres west of the border, turn south on SR 894 to Edgerton, the first stop. The area was first settled around the turn of the century, and by 1907 the Ribstone post office was established. When the GTP line arrived the following year, the hamlet was named after H.H. Edgerton, a GTP engineer. By 1909 the community saw the erection of its first grain elevator. Edgerton incorporated as a village in 1917.

The **Edgerton & District Historical Museum** interprets the agricultural and railway history of the area. When we arrived here, the museum was closed; but within minutes "Scott," a volunteer, magically appeared to give us a tour of the museum and grounds. This fairly new museum appears to be doing some intelligent collecting and very good restoration of vintage farm machinery. Following Scott's suggestion, we drove SR 610, a scenic back road to Wainwright, which winds through rolling hills exposing prosperous farms and ranches to view.

Wainwright, the largest centre in this area of Alberta, experienced a fascinating history. Land speculation became a common practice for those who tried to anticipate where the railways would lay the track. J.H. Dawson from Winnipeg was one of these land gamblers who purchased land in 1906 on a high spot between Ribstone Creek and Battle River. There he built a stable and two-story rooming house, the beginnings of. Denwood. By 1907 Denwood had a post office, but in 1908 it was bypassed for a new townsite 4 kilometres farther east. On July 21, 1908, the GTP reached Wainwright, the new divisional point named after William Wainwright, the second vice-president of GTP. By the end of 1908 there were 450 inhabitants. In 1909, the Dominion government chose Wainwright as a National Buffalo Park.

Wainright National Buffalo Park, 1909 to 1940

In 1897, the Rocky Mountain Park at Banff maintained a small herd of buffalo, a popular attraction with tourists. When the herd developed an inbreeding problem, the federal government decided to buy bison from two Montana ranchers, Michael Pablo and C.A. Allard. These bison formed the nucleus of the Wainwright herd. In 1907, some 400 bison were rounded up from the Flathead Reservation in Montana, loaded into boxcars, and shipped to Elk Island Park, their temporary home until the nine-foot retaining fences at Wainwright were completed. When the herd was again rounded up and loaded into boxcars, a few bison eluded capture and eventually established the herd at Elk Island Park. On June 13, 1909, the bison arrived at Wainwright, with much fanfare and excitement.

Within a year the numbers totaled around 800, as other bison were brought in to add to the Montana herd. The park also supported small herds of elk and *yaks*! By 1921, more than 4,000 bison roamed the 620 kilometres^2 reserve and began to suffer from overcrowding and the destruction of their habitat. The park decided to hold its first roundup to thin out the herd. This launched a group called the Buffalo Park Riders, consisting of farmers and ranchers who took part in the first and subsequent annual roundups. Many bison were slaughtered or shipped to other parks in Canada, the U.S.A., and Europe. In 1925, a further 1625 bison were shipped by train and water transport to Wood Buffalo Park. In 1938, with the threat of war in Europe, Ottawa decided to turn Wainwright's Buffalo National Park into a National Defense area. The last roundup took place in 1940. Over 7000 buffalo were shipped to other national parks.

In the 1920s the wooden derrick became as common a landmark as the grain elevator, when British Petroleum and other oil companies began oil explorations in the Wainwright area. The first crude was shipped by rail in 1925.

Wainwright has few historical buildings. Fire swept through the original town in 1929, destroying most of the businesses, including the old Wainwright Hotel, a distinctive landmark. A replica of the hotel now stands on display at the Heritage Park Historical Village in Calgary.

During the Second World War, Camp Wainwright served as an artillery training ground. It tested tanks, rockets, grenades, and mortars. From 1944 to 1946, it became a German Prisoner of War camp, where 1066 German officers were interred. Today CFB Wainwright, with its 22 weapons ranges and two airfields, is the second largest training facility in Canada, covering 622 kilometres^2. In spite of its use as an artillery range, the area provides habitats for pronghorn, deer, coyotes, and other wildlife. On the base you can visit the POW tower and see some of the objects made by the POWs. Wainwright is the home of Canada's largest Peregrin falcon facility. It has also been a centre for heavy oil activity.

Wainwright & District Museum (R.A. Hursey)

To learn more about the heritage of the Wainwright area, you will want to visit the **Wainwright & District Museum**, located in a former CN railway station. The museum features displays that depict its multifaceted history: the coming of the railway, the history of Buffalo National Park, the oil industry, CFB Wainwright, and the agricultural settlement of the area. The **Peregrine Falcon Facility** raises and releases Peregrine falcons, an endangered species, and offers public tours of the facility.

Tracks and Traces: There is a saying that for every mile of railway construction, the life of a man is taken. During the building of the Fabyan Trestle Bridge, two men drowned after their suspension bucket hit the side of the bank, and they plunged to their deaths in the Battle River.

Leaving Wainwright and continuing west on Highway 14, you cross the beautiful Battle River valley at Fabyan. As you ascend the steep hill, you can get a glimpse of the famous Fabyan trestle bridge to the southeast (upstream). Construction on this trestle began in 1907 and was completed in 1909. It is the second largest trestle in Alberta (the largest is at Lethbridge). The Wainwright Museum can give you detailed instructions on how to get to the trestle. Continuing on Highway 14, we pass through several other communities that all owe their existence to the arrival of the Grand Trunk Pacific line in 1909, although settlement of the surrounding districts along the old Battleford Trail began as early as 1902.

The present town of Viking was originally two hamlets, Viking and Harland. When the GTP arrived, the two hamlets relocated at the new townsite. At first it was called "Meighen" but this proved unpopular with locals because it sounded too much like "mean." Although several names were put forward, the two most popular ones were the names of the original hamlets. On the day of voting, wily Ben Gray brought in the name "Viking" when he rounded up some Norwegian ladies to cast the winning votes. This strategy caught the opposition by surprise. Viking's local history is interpreted at the **Viking & District Museum.** Located in a former hospital, the museum contains everything from farm equipment to 800 sets of salt and pepper shakers.

Your next stop is Holden, a village that refused to die. In the 1970s and 1980s, many prairie towns began to lose their schools and service centres as improved highways siphoned transportation to larger centres. Jobs in cities attracted young people away from these communities where they were born and raised. When Holden faced losing its elementary school, residents of this picturesque village rolled up their sleeves, spruced up the main street, established a popular tea house, and began attracting new businesses to the community. They converted the former fire hall and Masonic Lodge into the **Holden Museum & Masonic Lodge Gallery.** The museum interprets the area's history and the building's former uses as a fire hall, a jail, and the Masonic Lodge. On the second floor you can visit the Masonic Hall.

Ryley, the next stop, was first settled in the 1880s by the Steele family and in the 1890s by settlers from eastern Canada and the midwest States. In 1911, the CNoR line joined the GTP just west of Ryley. This village of about 500 has **George's Shoe and Harness Shop**, a business that keeps alive the art of making objects from leather. The shop offers tours of the facility during its business hours. You can watch craftsmen making and repairing leather products, including harnesses and saddles.

West of Ryley, the town of Tofield is located on the shores of beautiful Beaverhill Lake, the largest lake in central Alberta. Tofield saw the arrival of the GTP in October 1909. Beaverhill Lake, surrounded by farms, has been a magnet for migratory birds and bird watchers since the early 1920s. The lake has never been developed for recreational uses until recently, when Tofield established the **Beaverhill Lake Natural Area and Nature Centre.** This centre provides birders with information about the local area as well as guided tours. The best time to enjoy the arrival of waterfowl and shore birds is during May. Huge flocks of Snow Geese and Canada Geese make their annual visit before flying south.

You may want to stop at Cooking Lake to enjoy a picnic or a boat ride. Cooking Lake is actually two lakes: North Cooking Lake and South Cooking Lake are separated by a narrow channel. This summer resort area has served the people of Edmonton since the 1910s, when vacationers rode the train to North Cooking Lake for weekend outings. In 1923, the Edmonton Yacht Club formed its headquarters at Cooking Lake. It remained there until 1940, when it moved to Seba Beach on Lake Wabamum. Cooking Lake held the first regatta in 1924. Wop May, the famous aviator, won second place in a dinghy race. The Cooking Lake airport was an adjunct of Edmonton's air harbor for seaplanes.

MUSEUMS ALONG HIGHWAY 14

☞ **Edgerton & District Museum**
Box 64, Edgerton, AB T0B 1K0
Old railway station on west side of village at junction of Highways 849 and 610.
Governing body: Edgerton & District Historical Society
Open summer months, daily * ☎ (403) 775-3963
Admission by donation * *Visiting time:* one half hour

The museum features artifacts representing the local agricultural and railway history. Historical buildings include a CN station and the Battle Valley School, both dating back to 1911, and Edgerton's first United Church. A large Quonset building displays restored farm machinery—part of an ongoing restoration project. A 1918 threshing machine is still operational. One of the best times to see the vintage farm machinery in operation is during the first week in July when the museum hosts a Tractor Show and Pull.

☞ **Holden Museum & Masonic Lodge Gallery**
Box 153, Holden, AB T0B 2C0 * 4928 - 50th Avenue
Governing body: Holden Historical Society
Open summer - Wednesday, Friday and Sunday afternoons
☎ (403) 688-3767 * Admission by donation * *Visiting time:* one half hour
🍷🍷🚗 &。↰ 🍴

The museum is located in the former fire hall. The first floor is the museum, with local historical artifacts arranged in period rooms such as an old time kitchen, living room, general store, one-room school house and a jail. The latter was the actual town jail. Upstairs, the Masonic Lodge Hall gallery is now open for public viewing.

☞ **Beaverhill Lake Natural Area and Nature Centre** at Tofield
On Highway 14, just outside of Tofield
Governing body: Public Lands Division, Sherwood Park
Open May to October * ☎ (403)662-3191; 464-7955
Admission by donation * *Visiting time:* one and a half hours
🍷🍷🚗 & 👥↰ ⛱

Beaverhill Lake Natural Area is an excellent location where birders can observe more than 253 species of birds. The lake has long been a stopover for migratory waterfowl like snow geese, Canada Geese, whistler swans, and many varieties of shorebirds. The Beaverhill Bird Observatory at the Natural Area offers instructional tours in the spring and summer. The Beaverhill Lake Nature Centre is the first stop for birders and visitors to get directions to viewing sites and other information about the area.

☞ **Viking & District Museum**
Box 270, Viking, AB T0B 4N0 * 5108 - 61 Avenue (north end of Main Street)
Governing body: Viking Historical Society
Open May 15th to Labour Day, daily * ☎ (403) 336-3066
Admission by donation * *Visiting time:* one half hour
🍷🍷🚗 & ⛱ 🍴 ⎯

The museum is located in Viking's first hospital built in 1922. Other historical buildings from the surrounding area form a small pioneer village.

Period rooms and displays appear in the hospital rooms. Some of these period rooms feature themes not usually exhibited in community history museums: early hospital equipment, a small natural gas display commemorating northern Alberta's first gas well in 1914, and a ham radio operator station. The museum also owns a very large teacup collection.

☞ **Wainwright & District Museum**
Box 2294, Wainwright, AB T0B 4P0
CN Railway Station at the end of Main Street
Governing body: Battle River Historical Society
Open year round, daily * ☎ (403) 842-3115
Admission by donation * *Visiting time:* one half hour

🍷🍷🚗 ♿ 👫 🎁 ⛩ ♿ 🍴 ⚊

Located in the 1929 CN Railway Station, the Wainwright Museum contains several galleries with artifacts and specimens featuring Native history, early pioneer life, the coming of the railway, Wainwright Buffalo Park, the oil industry, Camp Wainwright and the German POW camp. Find out what "cattalos" and "yakalos" are and see the hide of the world's largest cattalo. One exhibit features a large collection old radios and telephones. At one end of the railway station is the Galleria Restaurant, offering home-cooked breakfasts and lunches. In the restaurant model trains run up and down a model of the Fabyan Trestle.

20

YELLOWHEAD TRAIL WEST HIGHWAY 16

The Yellowhead Trail, or Yellowhead Interprovincial Highway, opened in 1970, providing an alternate Canadian transcontinental route from Portage La Prairie, Manitoba, to Prince Rupert, British Columbia. In Alberta the Yellowhead Highway (Highway 16) begins at Lloydminster and ends at the Alberta-British Columbia border at the western edge of Jasper National Park. The highway follows earlier trails first used by Natives, then fur traders, missionaries, gold miners, railroaders, and settlers.

The unusual name of this highway comes from an Iroquois Indian guide, Pierre Hatsinaton, nicknamed "the Yellowhead," (in French, "Tête Jaune"), who probably came with a group of eastern Indians around 1800. He worked for the Hudson's Bay Company off and on and had explored the mountain passes and Native trails all along the eastern flank of the Rockies between the Athabasca and Peace Rivers. The cache he built for his furs upstream of the present town of Tête Jaune Cache became a prominent landmark to the leather brigades that began to use the pass after the HBC and NWC amalgamated in 1821. His name has since become associated with a town, lake, river, mountain pass and a transcontinental highway.

If you want to follow in the footsteps of the fur traders, begin at the Alberta-B.C. border, where you cross over Yellowhead Pass (1131 m). Unlike other mountain passes in the Canadian Rockies, you will hardly be aware of having crossed the Continental Divide. From the west gate of Jasper National Park, you follow the heavily forested glacial valley of the Miette River until it joins the broad glacial valley of the Athabasca River. Your first stop is Jasper, a town of about 5000 and headquarters of Jasper National Park, the divisional point for the Canadian National Railway and the park's main tourist and service centre.

> *Tracks and Traces:* Ten thousand years ago, great glaciers carved out distinctive U-shaped valleys, like Athabasca Valley. Rivers carve V-shaped valleys.

In 1810, the famous surveyor David Thompson and his party ventured into the Athabasca Valley looking for a new route across the Canadian Rockies for the North West Company. The Peigan Indians stopped Thompson from using Howse Pass west of Rocky Mountain House, forcing him to find another route to New Caledonia (present-day B.C.). After leaving William Henry in the valley to care for the horses and build a cabin, Thompson and his party crossed Athabasca Pass in January 1811. This pass became the main crossing for the Columbia brigades, those hearty voyageurs who hauled provisions and furs to and from the NWC posts along the Columbia River. Jasper House, a small post built by Jasper Hawse and Françoise Decoigne in 1813, became a supply depot and a horse keep for the Columbia brigades.

Louis the Iroquois, "The Sun Traveller"

During the 19th century, Iroquois and Métis hunters lived a semi-nomadic lifestyle in the Athabasca valley. They worked part of the year as trappers, guides, packers, or horse keepers for the NWC and HBC. The best known was an Iroquois named Louis Kwarakwanté (also Karakonttie, Kalliou, Liroquoi, and Callihou), who left Caughnawaga with his brother Ignace Kwarakwanté and Ignace Wanyande. They arrived in the Grande Cache area about 1811. Louis had two wives and twelve children. In 1845, when Father De Smet sojourned in the Athabasca valley, he met Louis and his extended family at Jasper House and in his journals referred to him as "the Sun Traveller." Louis, who had not seen a priest for almost 40 years, had Father De Smet baptize his children and grandchildren, which numbered around 36. Many descendants of Ignace Wanyande presently live in the Grande Cache area, working as trappers, guides, and outfitters. Many Métis families living in communities along the Yellowhead Highway from Entrance to St. Albert can trace their ancestry to Louis Kwarakwanté.

Jasper House became an important stopping place for many 19th century travellers. Jesuit missionary Father de Smet, artist Paul Kane, botanist David Douglas, and Dr. W.B. Cheadle were guests of Colin Fraser, former piper for George Simpson and commander of the post. After 1870, Jasper House was rarely used, except once a year when an agent arrived to trade with the local Métis.

Before the 1850s, voyageurs canoed up the Athabasca River from Fort Assiniboine. André Cardinal, a Métis, was the first to pioneer a clearly defined trail overland from Lac Ste. Anne to Jasper House, linking up existing trails used by Natives. These "pitching trails" were hardly more than game trails. Father Lacombe used this overland route when he first visited Athabasca valley in 1852. The Overlanders also used Cardinal's overland route in 1862. This party of 175 men and one woman left Ontario in the spring to travel to the Cariboo gold fields of British Columbia. Few of this ill-fated group ever reached the Cariboo to mine for gold.

In 1872, Sandford Fleming was put in charge of a survey team to map the first transcontinental railway across Canada for the CPR. Fleming recommended a route through the Yellowhead Pass, which offered the gentlest grade of all the passes through the Canadian Rockies. In spite of his recommendation, Ottawa decided to abandon the route in favor of Kicking Horse Pass. Athabasca valley would have to wait another 30 years. Not one but two railways ran parallel lines through the valley: the Grand Trunk Pacific, in 1911, and the Canadian Northern Railway, in 1913.

Mary Schäffer, Woman Explorer (1861 - 1939)

Mary T.S. Shäffer was a frequent visitor to the Canadian Rockies and had a passion for unexplored valleys, lakes, and mountain passes. She called herself "a hunter of peace"; the Stoney Indians called her "Yahe-Weha," Mountain Woman. Born in West Chester, Pennsylvania, to a wealthy Quaker family, Mary T. Sharples first visited the Canadian Rockies in 1889. At Glacier, B.C., she met and married Dr. Charles Shäffer, a physician and botanist. Beginning in 1891, the couple made annual trips to Banff, where she assisted him in his research by painting and photographing wildflowers. After her husband's death, she returned to Banff in 1904 and sought solace in the craggy mountains by exploring many of the remote areas of the Rockies with Billy Warren, a trail guide and packer, whom she later married in 1915.

In 1907 she met Sampson Beaver, a Stoney Indian who had once visited Maligne Lake. Early fur trade journals had mentioned the lake, but its location was forgotton. Sampson drew from memory a map of the route he and his father took there when he was a child. The following season, Mary and her party set out on horseback and "discovered" the largest lake in the Canadian Rockies. In 1911 she returned with her sister and young nephew to survey Maligne Lake with equipment borrowed from D.B. Dowling of the Dominion Survey. She left an extraordinary written and photographic record of her trips to remote areas of the Canadian Rockies in her book *Old Indian Trails of the Canadian Rockies,* published in 1911. It was republished in 1980 in *A Hunter of Peace.*

Mary Shäffer in camp (Whyte Museum of the Canadian Rockies V439 PS2)

Although the Dominion government had established Jasper Forest Park in 1907, the park remained undeveloped until the Grand Trunk Pacific's end-of-steel arrived in September 1911. The previous year, the government had bought out the Métis residents. These settlers, who had occupied the Athabasca valley for almost a hundred years, were considered squatters. The families received a small payment for their buildings, but nothing for the land. Lewis Swift, the first white settler in Athabasca valley, refused to move, as he had already filed for a homestead. For many years he remained the only private landholder within the park.

In 1910, GTP engineers built a camp at Boss Hill, which overlooks today's townsite. By the end of the year, Mile 112 had the beginnings of a town, with three blacksmith shops, three stores and a veterinary shop. Mile 112 was named Fitzhugh after Earl Hopkins

Fitzhugh, vice president of the GTP. Two years later the name was changed to Jasper, after Jasper Hawse, who built the original Jasper House.

Each summer the GTP brought trainloads of wealthy tourists and mountain climbers from eastern Canada, the United States, and Europe. Outfitters like Curly Phillips, the Otto Brothers, and the Brewsters, who started as freighters for the GTP railway, made their living outfitting tourists and packing their supplies by horseback into the remote regions of the park. These businesses thrived until the 1920s, when roads brought in automobiles and a new type of tourist.

Curly Phillips, Outfitter (1884 - 1908)

Donald "Curly" Phillips, a woodsman from Ontario, came west in 1908 to work as a packer for the Grand Trunk Pacific. The following year Curly, who had never before climbed mountains, made a historic climb of Mt. Robson with Rev. George Kinney, a member of the Alpine Club of Canada (ACC). The climb was never officially recognized because they missed the summit by a few yards. Curly outfitted the ACC topographical survey expeditions and the ACC's successful climb of Mt. Robson in 1911. He became one of the most respected outfitters in the

area. He and his hired Métis guided tourists and hunters into remote areas of Jasper Park in the days when hunting was still permitted. He was also an excellent wood craftsman. In the 1930s, when roads and automobiles began to replace trails and horses, Curly built the boathouse at Maligne Lake and operated a boating concession until his untimely death in 1938. While on a skiing trip, he and another local resident, Reginald Pugh, died in an avalanche in Elysium Pass. Mt. Phillips (3231 m) was named to honor Curly Phillips.

During the hectic period of railway building (1909 to 1911), the GTP and CNoR surveyed lines west of Edmonton from Stony Plain and Lac Ste. Anne. Farther west, these lines often ran side by side, within a few yards of one another. The era of railway building often created wasted duplication of tracks. It became more lucrative to build a railway than to run one. Through the Athabasca valley, the GTP ran mostly along the east side of the river, whereas CNoR laid track on the west side; sometimes they would crisscross one another. During WWI, after the two railway companies merged, some of these tracks were removed and shipped to Europe, where steel rails were needed for the war effort. The Yellowhead Highway from the eastern entrance to Jasper National Park runs mostly along the old GTP roadbed.

Although most people come to Jasper National Park to enjoy the splendid scenery, wildlife, and year-round recreation, there is also much for the heritage hunter interested in the area's history. Unfortunately, few of the original fur trade sites remain. However, one site is within easy walking distance from town at the confluence of the Miette and Athabasca Rivers. A cairn at **Old Fort Point** marks the approximate location of Henry House built by William Henry, the first white person to winter over in the Athabasca valley in 1810-11.

To learn more about the fascinating human and natural history of the area, be sure to visit the **Jasper-Yellowhead Museum and Archives.** You will also want to stop at **Pochahontas,** at the eastern edge of the park, where you can take a self-guided tour of the area that once was a coal mining town, and **Miette Hot Springs**, which was first used by coal miners in the 1910s before it became a tourist destination. There are many historical buildings throughout Jasper. Inquire at the **Jasper National Park Interpretive Centre** in the old Parks Administration Building on Connaught Drive or at the Jasper-Yellowhead Museum and Archives on Pyramid Lake Road for information about these local historic sites.

Jasper National Park Administration Building, 1913 (R.A. Hursey)

With some reluctance, we leave the spectacular scenery and wildlife of Jasper National Park and venture eastward along the Yellowhead Highway, passing through many communities that originated as instant railway towns. These log-and-tent towns consisted of stopping houses, saloons, bordellos, and other businesses that encouraged the "navvies" to part with their hard-earned dollars. As the railways moved on, the instant towns pulled up stakes as well and relocated at the next end-of-steel. Places like Wolf Creek and Prairie Creek have disappeared into railway history, but some of these ends-of-steel, like Hinton, Edson, Entwistle, Evansburg, and Stony Plain, became permanent communities, as homesteaders, lumber men, coal miners, and businesses moved into the area.

Hinton, our first stop, was named after W.D. Hinton, a general manager of the GTP. Between 1911 and 1913, GTP ran a railway line south from Bickerdike (between Hinton and Edson) to connect several new collieries at Minehead (Robb) and Mountain Park. When the National Parks Policy of 1930 ended all mining within the national parks, these collieries in the Coal Branch area became the chief suppliers of coal to run the steam locomotives. In recent years the rich supply of timber around the Hinton area has made the community an important centre for forest products. Hinton is home of the Alberta Forest Technology School and the **Alberta Forest Service Museum**. This museum was established to depict the history of forestry and the work of the Forest Rangers in Alberta.

Edson, the next stop along the Yellowhead Highway, was another end-of-steel town that survived when it became an important link to the isolated Peace River country. Following the completion of the GTP line in 1911, the Alberta government opened the Edson-Grande Prairie Trail, where settlers could detrain at Edson and travel by wagon through 400 kilometres of "mud, muskeg, and mosquitoes" to the rich agricultural lands around Grande Prairie. The Edson Trail was used until 1915, when J.D. McArthur completed the Edmonton Dunvegan Pacific Railway line from Edmonton to the Peace River district. Edson has two museums. The **Edson School Museum** depicts the town's history, with artifacts from early Edson homes and businesses. The **Galloway Station Museum** in the old GTP railway station has railway and coal mining artifacts from 1910, as well as an operating telegraph station.

East of Edson we pass the town of Wildwood beside Chip Lake. On a 1915 railway map, the name of this community is marked Junkins. It became home to a large settlement of Black Americans who came to Alberta around 1908 to escape white racism in the South. The land was marginal for agriculture, and in the 1920s many younger blacks left the area to work in Edmonton and other towns. By the end of the Second World War, only a few black families remained in the area.

Continuing eastward, we pass the twin communities of Entwistle and Evansburg that straddle the deep, beautiful canyon of the Pembina River and on to Lake Wabamum, to the little summer community of Seba Beach on the lake's west shore. The settlement of Seba predated the arrival of the CNoR when two young men homesteaded the area and built the first cabin in 1906. Materials and supplies had to be hauled from the east end of the lake on a flatboat. After the railway pushed through the area, Seba Beach became a lake resort where families from Edmonton built cottages and spent the summers. In 1940, the Edmonton Yacht Club moved its operations from Cooking Lake to Seba Beach. Each August the community hosts a regatta. To learn more about the history of this small summer community, the small museum at **All Saints Heritage Place** has regatta trophies, photographs, and other artifacts related to the history of this resort village.

For a scenic side trip, take SR 765, east of Fallis, north to Darwell on the shores of Lac Ste. Anne and then turn east on SR 633 to Alberta Beach. This lake resort community has a much older history than the town. Natives have been coming to Lac Ste. Anne for hundreds of years. Some believe that its waters have curative powers. Father Thibault, the first Roman Catholic missionary in the province, established the **Lac Ste. Anne Mission** in 1842. It was to this mission that Father Lacombe first came in 1851 and where the first Grey Nuns in Alberta began their missionary work among the Natives. Each July thousands of pilgrims come from all over Alberta and the North West Territories to take part in the annual pilgrimage at Lac Ste. Anne. It is a religious and social gathering, where friends and families gather in peace and harmony. Even if one does not believe in the restorative powers of the waters, this is a mystical place to visit at this time.

Returning again to the Yellowhead Trail by continuing east on SR 633 and south on Highway 43, your final stop will be at the town of Stony Plain. The name comes from a former camp of the Stony Indians. The first settlers arrived in the area around 1881. In 1908 Stony Plain incorporated as a town. Now the town hangs its history on its buildings. The **Stony Plain Murals** (some 15 altogether) provide an exciting visual walking tour. The pioneer history of the community can be viewed throughout the town along Main Street and other locations. My favorite mural, at Shikaoi Park, depicts the multicultural heritage of the area. The **Multicultural Heritage Centre** is a distinctive multipurpose museum offering a host of interesting programs that portray the life, customs and traditions of pioneer and ethnic groups. The museum's "Homesteader's Kitchen" serves delicious traditional and ethnic meals.

Multicultural Centre, Stony Plain. (R.L. Hursey)

Tracks and traces: In 1907 Stony Plain's first sheriff, Israel Umbach, chained a railway locomotive to the tracks to persuade the GTP to pay its taxes. One of the Stony Plain murals depicts this man's temerity in taking on the railway giant.

MUSEUMS ALONG YELLOWHEAD TRAIL WEST

☞ **Alberta Beach & District Museum** at Alberta Beach (Lac Ste. Anne)
Box 68, Alberta Beach, AB T0E 0A0 * 4823 - 50th Avenue
Governing body: Alberta Beach & District Museum & Archives Society
Open July and August, daily; Winter, weekend afternoons
☎ (403) 924-3678/924-3489 *Admission by donation
Visiting time: one half hour
🍷 🚗 ⛩ ▲

The museum is located in a former Anglican church on Main Street. Its collections include artifacts and archival material pertaining to the history of Alberta Beach and district.

☞ **Devonian Botanic Garden**
University of Alberta, Edmonton, AB T6G 2E9
North of Devon on Highway 60 * *Governing body:* University of Alberta
Open May to September, daily * ☎ (403) 987-3054
Admission fee charged * *Visiting time:* two hours
🍷🍷🍷🚗 ♿ ⛲ ✝ 🎁 ⛲ ☕

The University of Alberta's botanic garden features hardy trees, shrubs, and flowering plants from all over the world that thrive in our northern climate. Natural areas as well as more formal gardens spread out over 190 acres of parkland forest. Special exhibits include the Kurimoto Japanese Garden, the Butterfly House, Alpine Garden, Alberta Plants, Native People's Garden, the Imrie Wetland Reserve, and many more. This is a place to return to each month over the season to observe the changes and catch the hundreds of species of flowers in bloom. University and high school classes as well as public education and nature interpretive programs are held here throughout the year.

☞ **Edson School Museum**
4818 - 7th Avenue, Edson, AB T7E 1K8 * In the Red Brick Arts Centre
Governing body: ECHO - Edson Cultural Heritage Organization
Open May to August, daily; Winter, Monday to Friday * ☎ (403) 723-3582
Admission by donation * *Visiting time:* one half hour
🍷🍷🚗 ♿ ⛲ ✝ 🎁 ☕ 🍴 ▬

The Red Brick Arts Centre is located in a 1914 brick school building, now designated a provincial historic resource. On the second floor is a school museum depicting a classroom of the 1910s and 1920s. The museum's collections include local domestic, school, and commercial artifacts, photographs, and other archival materials. Throughout the year, the centre hosts a variety of local and travelling art exhibits in its exhibition gallery. It also holds dramatic and musical performances in the new 141-seat theatre. A well-stocked gift shop features local artwork, crafts, and local history books. There is also a well-equipped studio for dance and aerobics classes. The Country Kitchen is a luncheon and tea shop.

☞ **Galloway Station Museum**
4818 - 7th Avenue, Edson, AB T7E 1K8 5425 - 3rd Avenue, Centennial Park
Governing body: Edson & District Historical Society
Open July and August, daily * ☎ (403) 723-5696
Admission fee charged * *Visiting time:* one half hour
🍷🚗 ⛲ 🍴 ▬

Located in a 1910 Grand Trunk Pacific Railway Station, the museum is next to the visitor centre. The museum's collections include railway artifacts, old railway maps, and an operating telegraph system. Other collections include artifacts from lumbering and coal industries.

☞ **Alberta Forest Service Museum** at Hinton
Forest Technology School, 1176 Switzer Drive, Hinton, AB T7V 1V3
East end of town on Highway 16. Park at pull-out for Forestry School Trail.
Governing body: Province of Alberta
Open Year round, Monday to Friday * ☎ (403) 865-8211
Admission by donation * *Visiting time:* one half hour

♥ ♥ ⚼ ⌗ ⑂ ▬

Although this is primarily a teaching museum for students at the Forest Technology School, the museum is open to the public in the summer months. The new Forestry School Trail is a 1.6 kilometer interpretive trail, with outdoor signage along the way. On the trail, an attractive two-story log building houses the Alberta Forest Service Museum. This is the only museum in Alberta with a large collection of artifacts related to the history of the Alberta Forest Service. Collections include fire-fighting equipment, saws, logging tools, forest service uniforms, saddles, and other forest service equipment. One of the displays features the interior of a forest service fire lookout tower. Adjacent to the site stands a log cabin that was once the Moberly Creek Ranger Station and temporary home to rangers during their patrols between Hinton and Grande Cache.

☞ **Jasper-Yellowhead Museum and Archives**
Box 42, Jasper, AB T0E 1E0 * 400 Pyramid Lake Road
Governing body: Jasper-Yellowhead Historical Society
Open Victoria Day to Labour Day, daily; Winter, Monday to Wednesday
☎ (403) 852-3013 * Admission by donation * *Visiting time:* one half hour

♥ ♥ ⛟ ♿ ⚼ ⊞ ⑂ ▲ ⑂ ▬

The museum interprets the history of Jasper, Jasper National Park, and the Yellowhead corridor from the fur trade period to the present. Collections include archaeology and ethnology material, early mountaineering and outfitter's gear, railway artifacts, Park Warden uniforms, mountain rescue equipment, and other objects depicting the town's history. The upstairs gallery features many interesting historical photographs showing the beginnings of Jasper National Park, the townsite, outfitters, railway people, and tourists. The archives contain documents, photographs, and history tapes of interest to researchers and historians. There is also an art gallery that features artwork by local and regional artists as well as travelling exhibits.

☞ **All Saints Heritage Place** at Seba Beach
Seba Beach, AB T0E 2B0 * 1st Avenue South
Governing body: Seba Beach Heritage Society
Open summer, daily except Sundays and holidays * ☎ (403) 420-6704
Admission by donation * *Visiting time:* one half hour

This small museum occupies the former All Saints Anglican Church built in 1946. It relates the story of the early homesteading, commercial fishing, and summer resort history. Seba Beach has been the home of the Edmonton Yacht Club from 1940 to the present. Artifacts include generic settlement period objects, regatta cups, religious objects, and a collection of interesting photographs that depict the history of the area.

☞ **Multicultural Heritage Centre** at Stony Plain
Box 908, Stony Plain, AB T0E 2G0 * 5411 - 51st Street
Governing body: Heritage Agricultural Society
Open year round, daily * ☎ (403) 963-2777

The Multicultural Heritage Centre is located in a 1925 brick school building and a provincial historic resource. This multi-purpose centre has a living museum furnished as a settler's cabin. Its interpretive collections are used for school and multicultural programming. The centre also contains local archives, a genealogy wall, a research library, and an art gallery showing monthly exhibitions. In the basement the "Homesteader's Kitchen" features ethnic meals. A large, well-stocked gift shop emphasizes local crafts and toys. Opperthauser House, a historic home of a unique construction, adjoins the centre. Inquire at the centre for a self-guided brochure of the Stony Plain historical murals.

21

YELLOWHEAD TRAIL EAST—HIGHWAY 16

If you are entering Alberta from Saskatchewan along the Yellowhead Trail, you will be following the route presented in this chapter. The eastern leg of the Yellowhead Trail in Alberta begins at Lloydminster and closely follows the original line constructed by the Canadian Northern Railway (CNoR) in 1905. Railway surveyors and building contractors seldom concern themselves with taking the scenic route. They are more interested in laying out gentle grades for roadbeds and bypassing sand hills, river valleys, and sloughs wherever possible. The region between Lloydminster to the Beaver Hills goes through dry, flat prairie interspersed with stunted looking aspen hummocks. What the area lacks in scenic wonders is more than made up for in its rich heritage.

The era of railway transportation changed the whole physical and cultural landscape of Alberta. Many of the towns and villages along the way owe their origins to the building of the railway. Although the area was settled prior to its arrival, the railway determined the location of the town sites. Business owners in existing hamlets had to move their buildings from the better, higher ground to less suitable areas. Villages and towns—such as Islay, Mannville, Innisfree and Ranfurly—began as stations, sidings, and divisional points along the CNoR. The more fortunate towns, like Lloydminster and Vermilion, became divisional points—places where railway crews lived and the steam locomotives were serviced.

Llyodminster, a city of 17,000, straddles the border of two provinces. About 10,000 live on the Alberta side and the other 7,000 live in Saskatchewan. The main street, Meridian Drive, runs right through the middle of Lloydminster. Its residents do not seem to have a problem sharing two time zones or living in one province and working in another. I have always wondered how they decide to set their watches. This prosperous small city began as the Barr Colony, the largest group of British settlers to come to the Canadian West as one group. About 2000 came together to start a farming colony. Very few had any experience in farming.

The Barr Colony

Two Anglican clergymen, Isaac Barr from Ontario, and George Exton Lloyd, a British veteran of the Riel Rebellion of 1885, conceived of the plan to start a colony of British immigrants to homestead the prairies. Their advertisements, placed in English newspapers, attracted thousands of land-hungry colonists—far more than they dreamed of. Most of the prospective colonists were from the urban lower middle classes, mostly with no farming experience. In 1903 over 1900 came in one group. Most were poorly equipped to face the rigors of pioneering. Problems began on the journey to Alberta; and Isaac Barr, a poor organizer and manager, was blamed. When Barr deserted the group, Lloyd succeeded him as leader. Many of the colonists gave up after the first year or two and moved to towns and cities to take up their former trades. Those who remained with Reverend Lloyd became competent farmers and ranchers. By unanimous acclamation, the colonists named their town after Reverend Lloyd. The name literally means "Lloyd's monastery," "minster" being the Old English name for monastery. Reverend Lloyd later became the Anglican Bishop of Saskatchewan.

Barr Colonists, (Provincial Archives of Alberta P444)

The Barr Colonists' choice of a townsite was right on top of the 4th Meridian. This would create a split personality for the town in later years when the meridian was chosen as the boundary dividing

Alberta and Saskatchewan. Finally an agreement worked out between the two provincial governments brought the community under Saskatchewan municipal legislation. The **Barr Colony Heritage Centre,** physically in Saskatchewan, portrays the fascinating history of the Barr Colony and the development of this border city. One of the highlights of this museum includes the extraordinary paintings of Berthold Von Imhoff, who immigrated to St. Walburg, Saskatchewan, in the 1920s. This farmer, professionally trained as an ecclesiastical and portrait painter in Europe, created religious frescos and murals in churches in the area. The Barr Colony Centre owns more than 250 of his works.

Back on the trail of the CNoR surveyors and "navvies," we leave Lloydminster and proceed along the old right-of-way to Islay, where it intersected with the old Battleford Trail. Islay, formerly the hamlet of Island Lake, incorporated under its new name in 1907. Farther down the track is Ranfurly, a small town named after the former governor of New Zealand, Lord Ranfurly. Both Islay and Ranfurly have small museums that depict the history of their communities.

Islay's Station Agent Too Busy for a Holdup

[From the *Vermilion Signal,* June 1907.]

Islay's station agent Waterfield looked up from his work to find himself staring along the barrel of a revolver pointed at him.

"What had you in mind?" asked Waterfield.

"This is a hold-up," said the holder of the revolver.

"I'm busy," said Waterfield. "Could you call around again when things aren't so rushed?"

"This is a hold-up," repeated the man with the revolver. "Hands up."

Waterfield took hold of the would-be hold-up artist, lugged him over to a box-car, and locked him up. Then he wired to the Mounted Police in Vermilion to come and get him. Somehow the man escaped from the box-car, but was later recaptured. This time he was taken to the best room in the hotel—the one with the best lock—and held there.

Presently Constable Short arrived from Vermilion and delivered the prisoner back there. From identifiable scars it was determined that the man was a much-wanted criminal who had been in and out of American jails since 1888. He was James P. McQuillan, who had just been released from jail after serving time for a robbery at Olds.

On the road again, we head toward Vermilion. This town incorporated in 1905 after the existing hamlet moved its post office, store, blacksmith shop, and a stopping place to the new townsite in the fall of 1905. In 1906 the Paradise Valley Land Company was formed and advertised, enthusiastically, that the area had "a splendid climate, the richest soil, pasturage, and wonderful rainfall that has never failed in thirty years." In 1912, Vermilion was chosen as the site for a government demonstration farm and school. Vermilion Agricultural College (the forerunner of today's Lakeland College) opened on October 28, 1913, and offered five-month courses. In 1918, a disastrous fire swept through town, destroying many of its frame and log buildings. Later brick structures replaced the ruined buildings. One such building is a 1928 brick school that now houses the **Vermilion Heritage Museum**, which effectively tells the story of the community. It also displays a remarkable collection of more than 20,000 buttons.

The largest centre along the old CNoR line between Lloydminster and Edmonton is Vegreville. On the eastern edge of town, the "world's largest pysanka" (Easter Egg), proclaims the Ukrainian heritage of the region and Vegreville's claim as the Ukrainian capital of Alberta. The history of Vegreville actually predates the arrival of Ukrainians to Canada. "Old Vegreville" began as a French community. Its first settlers were French Canadians from Kansas who arrived with Father Morin in 1894. In 1896, the hamlet was named after Father Valentin Vegreville, an Oblate missionary who had served in western Canada for over 50 years.

In 1905, "New Vegreville" was founded after the CNoR built the line 2.4 kilometres northeast of the hamlet. The low-lying site turned out to be an unsatisfactory location, as spring thaws and four sloughs nearby turned the town into a sea of gumbo. Although Vegreville retained its French Catholic character in the early years, several other ethnic groups began to move into the area in the 1920s, replacing the original settlers. In 1911, Jewish immigrants began to move into Vegreville. Most of them worked at trades or opened businesses. They interacted successfully with the growing Ukrainian community, as both groups shared a common eastern European background.

By the inter-war years, those of Ukrainian heritage surpassed other ethnic groups in numbers, when many Ukrainian-Canadian families moved from submarginal lands in Manitoba and drought areas in Saskatchewan to buy up land around Vegreville. Each year the community hosts an annual Ukrainian Festival in August, attracting visitors from all over western Canada to share in the cultural heritage of Alberta's third largest ethnic community.

World's largest pysanka, Vegreville (R.L. Hursey)

Vegreville has two museums open to the public. **Vegreville Museum** is the community's local history museum with artifacts depicting the settlement era and development of the community. The other museum, the **Vegreville International Police Museum,** displays a unique collection of police uniforms, weapons, badges, and paraphernalia representing police departments from all over the world.

Before the turn of the century, Scots from Scotland and Ontario originally settled Mundare, a town 15 kilometres west of Vegreville. The town was named after one of the earliest station agents, when the CNoR built a railway station in 1906. The first Ukrainian settlers in Alberta homesteaded in the Edna district (around today's Star) in the early 1890s. Aspen parkland and black soil, similar to that found on the Steppes of the Ukraine, attracted them.

In 1902, Father Filias of the Basilian Fathers, a Ukrainian Catholic religious order, took up a homestead east of Mundare and founded a religious community. The farming was done by volunteer labor. Accompanying the Basilian Fathers were four Sisters Servants of Mary Immaculate, who came to serve the Ukrainian people, sharing their poverty and hardships and providing nursing care, education, and care for orphans.

The Basilian Fathers' Monastery at Mundare established their first museum in 1953. In recent years they have built a larger museum to hold their extraordinary collection that claims national and international importance. These treasures include ancient illuminated manuscripts, icons, religious vestments, and folk art objects. The **Basilian Fathers' Museum** is definitely a destination museum for the heritage hunter interested in learning about the religious life of the Ukrainian-Canadian people. Another destination museum, located about 30 kilometres west of Mundare, is the **Ukrainian Cultural Heritage Village.** This heritage park and living history museum recreates the life of the Ukrainian people from 1892 to 1930. Many heritage buildings destined to destruction by time and human progress have been brought from surrounding farms and communities and restored. Of particular interest are the dwellings, which show the transition of architecture from the earliest sod dwellings to two-story frame houses. Interpreters dress in period costumes, perform domestic tasks, and tell stories about the early lifestyle and culture of the Ukrainian-Canadian people.

Basilian Fathers' Museum (R.L. Hhurey)

Elk Island National Park is our last stop on this stretch of the Yellowhead Trail. This national park may be small compared to others, but the high density of wildlife in this transitional parkland wilderness provides many opportunities for visitors to learn about the natural history of the parkland ecosystem. This was the temporary home to the Plains bison brought from Montana in 1907 until they were shipped to the final destination at Wainwright Park. A few of these bison eluded capture and formed the nucleus of the herd that roam the park today. A drive-through paddock allows the visitor to observe safely some of the hundreds of plains and wood bison living in the park. Other wildlife include about 400 moose, 1600 wapiti (elk), and 2000 beaver as well as over 200 species of birds. Over 100 kilometres of trails offer the hiker and cross-country skier a year round venue for enjoying nature.

MUSEUMS ALONG THE YELLOWHEAD TRAIL EAST

☞ **Ukrainian Cultural Heritage Village (Provincial Historic Site)** at Elk Island Park
c/o 8820 - 112th Street, Edmonton, AB   T6G 2P8
On the Yellowhead Trail just east of Elk Island Park.
Governing body: Historic Sites & Archives Service,
Alberta Community Development
☎ 403-427-2022 Open May 15 to Thanksgiving Weekend, daily
Admission fee charged * *Visiting time:* two hours

This living museum has over 30 historical buildings that depict the era of the largest Ukrainian settlement from 1892 to 1930. These buildings have been relocated from farms and towns in the east-central part of Alberta, where most Ukrainians first settled. These restored buildings include three onion-domed churches, thatched roof dwellings, barns, a grain elevator, and many other commercial structures. Together they form a model of a Ukrainian homestead and a rural town. The restoration of these buildings is of exceptional quality. Interpreters in period costumes role-play, encouraging visitors to interact with them as they go about their daily activities—baking bread, weaving, tending to the garden. Special events, including religious festivals, are held here throughout the year. In this beautiful setting there is always something new to see and do.

☞ **Morrison Museum of the Country School** at Isley
Box 4, Isley, AB   T0B 2J0 * Isley
Governing body: Morrison Museum Association
Open May to September, on request * ☎ (403) 744-2260/744-2271
Admission by donation * *Visiting time:* one half hour

This museum has artifacts and archival material used in country schools.

☞ **Barr Colony Heritage Cultural Centre** at Lloydminster
5011 - 49th Avenue, Lloydminster, AB S9V 0T8
Highway 16 East at 45th Avenue, *Governing body:* City of Lloydminster
Open year round; May to September, daily; September to April, closed Monday and Tuesday. * ☎ (306) 825-5655
Admission fee charged * *Visiting time:* one hour

🍷🍷🚗 ♿ 🛆 ⛴ ▲ ♨ 🍴 ━

This multipurpose centre houses a museum and an art gallery. The museum has an extensive collection of artifacts related to the Barr Colony, including farm machinery, horse-drawn carriages, heritage buildings, and domestic artifacts. The art gallery displays the permanent art collection of Berthold Imhoff, a European-trained painter who immigrated to St. Walburg, Saskatchewan.

☞ **Basilian Fathers' Museum** at Mundare
Box 379, Mundare, AB T0V 3H0
5419 Sawchuk Street, across from the monastery
Governing body: Order of St. Basil the Great in Canada
Open Year round, Monday to Friday; July and August daily
☎ (403) 764-3887 * Admission by donation * *Visiting time:* one hour

🍷🍷🍷🍷🚗 ♿ 🛆 ⛴ ▲ 🍴 ━

The Basilian Fathers' Museum is housed in an inspiring architectural structure. The museum contains collections of religious and folk life artifacts from Ukraine as well as farm and domestic objects used by early settlers. Rare religious objects include illuminated manuscripts as early as the 15th century, liturgical books, icons, relics, vestments, and sacramental objects. Exhibits portray artifacts depicting the everyday life of the Ukrainian people as well as their religious life. Of special interest are exhibits that portray festivals, "The Life of a Monk" and the Sisters Servants of Mary Immaculate. This is a destination museum with a unique collection. Some labels should perhaps be added to give the non-Ukrainian visitor a better idea of the symbolic meanings of the religious artifacts.

☞ **Ranfurly & District Museum**
Box 162, Ranfurly, AB T0B 3T0
School building west of the Ukrainian Catholic Church
Governing body: Ranfurly & District Recreational and Agricultural Society
Open May to September, daily * ☎ (403) 658-2208/658-2107
Admission by donation * *Visiting time:* one half hour

This museum displays artifacts reflecting the history of Ranfurly and area. Artifacts include farming tools and domestic objects.

☞ **Vegreville Museum**
Box 1283, Vegreville, AB T0B 4L0 * 5009-50th Avenue
Governing body: Vegreville Historical Society
Open year round, May through September daily; rest of year on Wednesdays
☎ (403) 632-2770 * Admission by donation * *Visiting time:* one half hour

---

The museum abounds with an amazing array of agricultural, ethnographic, and domestic objects from the local area. The museum has the town's first television. Because there are so few photographs, labels, and archival material displayed, it was difficult to get a real sense of the local history, especially the French- Canadian and Ukrainian heritage of the area.

☞ **Vegreville International Police Museum**
Box 1283, Vegreville, AB T0B 4L0 * 4843 - 49th Street
Governing body: Vegreville Historical Society
Open May through September, daily * ☎ (403) 632-2770
Admission by donation * *Visiting time:* one half hour

This museum features the private collection of Mike Mudryk, who spent years collecting uniforms, badges, weapons, and paraphernalia from police departments throughout the world. Anyone interested in history of police forces would find this museum a fascinating place to visit. Displayed are uniforms from all over North America as well as Tasmania, Germany, and other countries. These uniforms are attractively displayed with mirrors to reflect all sides of the uniforms. Some photographs, illustrations, and interpretive labels could be added to provide more information about the collector, the collection, and the police forces represented. See if you can find the "jaw cuff" used to restrain violent prisoners.

☞ **Vermilion Heritage Museum**
Box 1205, Vermilion, AB T0B 4M0 * 5310 - 50th Avenue
Governing body: Vermilion and District Historical & Multicultural Society
Open mid-May to Labour Day, afternoons daily * ☎ (403) 853-6211
Admission by donation * *Visiting time:* one half hour

For a museum that has only been in existence since 1991, Vermilion Heritage Museum possesses a large collection of local artifacts, which include agricultural and railway objects as well as some interesting surveying and woodworking tools. The society has done a good job of telling their story by showing artifacts in context, with clearly readable and relevant labels. The museum, located in a 1928 brick high school, was rescued from demolition by the historical society. The "button wall" has over 20,000 different buttons, sewn on a cloth by a local resident.

22

EDMONTON

E dmonton is Alberta's capital and has the largest metropolitan population in the province with about 840,000 people. It is located very close to the centre of the province in the fertile parkland valley of the North Saskatchewan River. The river carves a deep valley through eons of sediments, where dinosaurs roamed 60 million years ago, including the smaller carnivorous cousin of Tyrannosaurus Rex, named appropriately, Edmontosaurus. Edmonton sits on an ancient lake bed. "Lake Edmonton" was formed of melted ice from receding glaciers beginning 12,000 years ago. The **Provincial Museum of Alberta's** Quaternary Gallery features many of the extinct giants that lived in Alberta tens of thousands of years ago. Some resemble alien life forms, others seem vaguely familiar. One of the most complete and best-preserved mammoth tusks ever found was unearthed in the Clover Bar gravel pit east of Edmonton.

Edmonton's beautiful river valley has survived the impact of garbage heaps, coal shafts, miners' shacks and privies, gold-mining dredges, log booms, sawmills, and other destructive human developments for almost two centuries. Every 25 to 50 years the river reminds Edmontonians of their frailty with spectacular ice jambs and floods like the one in 1915 that almost washed away the Low Level Bridge. Beginning in the 1960s, the city began to buy river valley properties, install hiking and bicycle trails, and clean up old dump sites. Today Edmonton has a system of parks and wild areas that make it one of the most attractive urban park systems in North America. Wildlife abounds in the forested ravines and muddy banks. Beavers, deer, foxes, coyotes, migratory birds, and the occasional lynx and moose find the rich parkland vegetation a sanctuary, offering you many opportunities to observe nature.

To learn more about the variety of species that live along the river, the **John Janzen Nature Centre** in Fort Edmonton Park provides many programs, exhibits, and interpretive trails. The U of A's **Devonian Botanic Garden** and the **Muttart Conservatory** also feature plants that grow in a parkland environment. The Muttart Conservatory embodies four glass pyramid pavilions that feature tropical, desert, and temperate environments as well as an exhibition pavilion. The **Valley Zoo** is home to many species of mammals and birds that one finds in the river valley.

Edmonton has lived and prospered through two centuries of dramatic changes in human occupation, commerce, government, and transportation, owing to its strategic central location that serves as an axis for transportation routes. Much of its success had to do with the kind of self-reliant people who first settled here. A lot had to do with good fortune.

In the summer of 1795, the North West Company (NWC) built a fort on the North Saskatchewan River, thus getting the jump on their arch rival, the Hudson's Bay Company (HBC). They chose a location on the west bank near the mouth of the Sturgeon River, about two miles downstream of today's Fort Saskatchewan. In October, HBC's William Tomison and his party followed suit and built Edmonton House—the first Fort Edmonton—a short distance from Fort Augustus.

Both companies had been lured there by the promise of beaver and otter "...so numerous that women and children kill them with sticks and hatchets," and for acquiring provisions, such as pemmican from the Blackfoot and other northern Plains groups that came to the forts to trade. In 1802, both companies relocated to a site near Edmonton, east of today's Rossdale. The third site of the rival companies' forts was at the mouth of Whitearth River, east of Smoky Lake. It was built in 1812, but three years later those occupying the fort were back at Rossdale. By 1821 the two companies had amalgamated. In 1820-30, the HBC built the fifth post just below the present-day legislature building. For the next 50 years, Fort Edmonton was an important provisioning and distribution post for the northern posts in the Athabasca and Mackenzie districts and for posts further west in British Columbia. The fort was finally torn down in 1915.

John Rowand's Bones

John Rowand served as Chief Factor at Fort Edmonton, from 1826 until his death in 1854. Born in Montreal in 1789, he went to work in 1803 at the age of 14 as an apprentice with the North West Company. By 1821, when the two companies amalgamated, Rowand had advanced to Chief Trader at Rocky Mountain House. His pioneering of the Fort Assiniboine-Fort Edmonton Trail won him recognition, and Governor George Simpson appointed him Chief Factor of the Saskatchewan district in 1826.

During his long tenure at the fort, he built the biggest house west of York Factory. Nicknamed "Big House" and "Rowand's Folly," the three-story house offered hospitality to many sojourners, including missionaries and famous explorers. He dealt successfully with numerous frictions between Native groups that came to the fort to trade. In 1854, while on a trip with his son to Fort Pitt, Rowand died while trying to break up a fight between two of his boatmen. He was buried at Fort Pitt, but that was not his final resting place.

When his long-time friend, George Simpson, learned of Rowand's wish to be buried in Montreal, Simpson gave directions to have his remains exhumed. According to tradition, Rowand's bones were rendered of all flesh, packaged and taken to Norway House, where Simpson took personal charge of the package in his own canoe. At the Red River Settlement, Rowand's remains were repacked and transported to York Factory, then placed on a Hudson's Bay ship heading for England. Finally, four years after his death, Rowand's remains were shipped back to Canada and buried in Montreal's Mount Royal Cemetery on November 10, 1858.

John Rowand (Edmonton Archives EA-10-2773)

Be sure to visit **Fort Edmonton Park,** where you can learn more about the history of the fort and the people who lived and worked there. The fort is a full-sized replica of the one constructed in 1846.

In 1871, a hamlet began to grow above the fort. Reverend George McDougall erected a church and manse downstream of the fort. Several former HBC employees, like John Walter, Malcolm Groat, John Norris, and Richard Hardisty, began to take up river lots and establish homesteads and businesses. John Walter, an Orkadian, started a sawmill and coal mine across the river from the fort and operated Edmonton's first ferry in 1882. In 1876, Donald Ross, a gold miner who had prospected for gold in California, acquired River Lot 4, on the flats just below today's Hotel Macdonald. There he built Edmonton's first hotel.

In 1878, Frank Oliver bought the first town lot and built a log store, the first commercial enterprise outside the fort. John A. MacDougall, an independent fur trader, appeared in Edmonton in 1879 and opened a store near the Methodist mission. In 1880, Frank Oliver and Alex Taylor, a telegraph operator from Ontario, started the town's first newspaper, the Edmonton *Bulletin*. That year, Taylor was largely responsible for seeing that the telegraph line was extended from Hay Lakes to Edmonton. On January 1, 1880, he sent the first telegraph message from John Walter's offices to Inspector Jarvis at the NWMP station in Fort Saskatchewan. Five years later, Taylor started Edmonton's first telephone company. The Edmonton & District Telephone Corporation took over the operation in 1893.

By 1881, the growing hamlet started the first free public school in the North West Territories on land donated by the HBC. That year the HBC offered 100 lots for immediate sale. Flimsy frame buildings with false fronts began to pop up like rank weeds on both sides of Edmonton's muddy main street. By 1885, this isolated community, with roots in its fur trade heritage, boasted a population of about 200 people.

Showdown at the Land Titles Office

Within months of Edmonton's incorporation, Mayor Matt McCauley and the new town council faced its first crisis. In June of 1892, Ottawa ordered Dominion Land Agent "Timber Tom" Anderson to move the Land Titles Office across the river to South Edmonton, where the Canadian Pacific Railroad had its end-of-steel. Edmonton's merchants realized that such a move would be disastrous, as new settlers would bypass Edmonton altogether. Anderson soon attracted a crowd of angry citizens when he started to move books and records out of the building.

They surrounded his wagon, unhitched the horses, and removed the wagon wheels. Mayor McCauley fired off telegrams to Ottawa to try to rescind the order, but his request was refused.

Anderson sent for help from South Edmonton; but when the men crossed over on John Walter's ferry, they were met by a delegation and persuaded to return. McCauley issued an order for volunteers to bring arms and enlisted them to keep the peace (i.e., the Land Titles Office). When the situation threatened to get out of hand, Superintendent Griesbach of the

NWMP in Fort Saskatchewan sent 20 men, but he wisely stopped his troops at Rat Creek, just north of town and telegrammed Ottawa about the gravity of the situation. Ottawa finally reversed its order and set up a branch office in South Edmonton as a compromise.

The incident convinced Edmontonians that they needed their own local police to keep order. On June 20, 1892, Edmonton's first town council passed the bylaw to establish the first police constable position.

Since 1859, gold miners had tried their luck working the gravels of the North Saskatchewan River around Fort Edmonton. Tom Clover had panned for gold on a bar that bears his name. The Overlanders had come through in 1862 to reach the Cariboo. From time to time, parties of prospectors trickled through Edmonton on their way north to British Columbia and Yukon. But in the spring of 1897, Klondikers suddenly flooded Edmonton. They discovered that they could travel by rail as far as Edmonton and be considerably closer to the Yukon gold fields than by travelling up the Pacific coast by steamer to Skagway and trekking over the dreaded Chilkoot Pass.

When the first Klondikers arrived at Edmonton in April of 1897, the town was unprepared for the onslaught. But the Edmonton Board of Trade—always eager to promote the city and see new dollars flow into the hands of its businessmen—wasted no time in advertising their town as an all-Canadian route to the Klondike, the "Gateway to the North." There were basically two routes to the Klondike from Edmonton: the Athabasca-Mackenzie water route, via the Athabaska Landing Trail; and the Overland Route via the St. Albert Trail north to the Peace River country.

During the Klondike Rush of 1897-98, about 1500 men and women passed through Edmonton. Most were inexperienced and poorly prepared and never reached the Yukon gold fields. Nearly 900 discouraged Klondikers returned to Edmonton. Approximately 70 died of exposure, starvation, or scurvy on the trails. Diaries and letters found beside the bodies of these poor souls told the tales of their bitter end. The only ones who struck it rich during those two hectic years of the Klondike Rush through Edmonton were its merchants. The Klondike Rush may have put Edmonton on the world map, but historians would argue for years about whether Edmonton's boosters were indirectly responsible for the deaths of many of the gold seekers who, out of ignorance and inexperience, took the Edmonton route to the Klondike.

Mrs. Garner, first woman to pass through Edmonton enroute to the Klondike, 1897. (Provincial Archives of Alberta B5241)

Tracks and Traces: In 1900 Edmonton, a town of 4000, had one dog for every four humans. In the dog days of August, the newly appointed dog catcher rounded up a bunch of strays and locked them up. The night before the dogs were to be destroyed, someone broke in and set them all free.

After Alberta became a province in 1905, Edmonton became its capital, escalating the rivalry between Calgary and Edmonton, that probably began when the CPR went through Calgary instead of Edmonton. Calgary had the largest population and the transcontinental railroad. Edmonton was more centrally located and enjoyed the good fortune of having Frank Oliver, the fiery editor of the *Bulletin,* as the Liberal MP and Minister of the Interior at a time when Wilfred Laurier was Prime Minister of Canada. The first legislature had its temporary headquarters on the third floor of McKay Avenue School while construction began on the legislature building. A.C. Rutherford, a lawyer from Strathcona (formerly South Edmonton), was appointed Alberta's first premier, with George Bulyea its first Lieutenant Governor. Rutherford also became the first president of the University of Alberta.

If you are interested in learning more about Edmonton's roots as Alberta's provincial capital, visit the third floor of MacKay Avenue School, now the **Edmonton Public Schools Museum.** At the

Alberta Legislature Building, you can take a guided tour of the building and see the MLAs in action (or inaction) when the legislature is in session. **Government House,** the former Lieutenant Governor's mansion, also provides tours of the building. It is now used as a meeting place for the cabinet when the legislature is not in session.

Alberta Legislature Building (R.L. Hursey)

During the boom years between 1900 and the beginning of WWI, Edmonton and Strathcona began replacing their false-fronted wood structures with handsome, fire-resistant brick buildings. Strathcona and Edmonton amalgamated in 1911 at a time when thousands of immigrants from Great Britain, Europe, and the United States came by railway to Edmonton to buy cheap land for farms. Edmonton's economic prosperity in these years was largely due to its role as an agricultural service centre. Life had never been better for Edmonton, with two major railways, its own telephone and electric power companies, streetcars and motor cars, and new palatial houses like those of the McDougalls, Magraths, and Gariepys.

Beginning in 1914, Edmonton's river of prosperity slowed to a trickle. The First World War brought about social, political, and economic change. Edmonton's population dropped from 73,000 in 1914 to 54,000 in 1916. Between the two world wars, Edmonton's skyline changed very little. The city would have to wait until the oil boom of the 1950s to see a dramatic change in its skyline.

Edmonton's Incline Railway, 1909 (Edmonton Archives EA-10-1392)

The heritage hunter will find a number of museums in Edmonton that feature aspects of Edmonton's urban history. The largest is **Fort Edmonton Park,** where you can walk or ride along **1885 Street** and **1905 Street** to experience what life was like during Edmonton's expansion period after the turn of the century and before WWI.

In Old Strathcona, the **Telephone Historical Centre**, located in a 1913 AGT telephone exchange building, features Edmonton's telecommunications history. On the campus of the University of Alberta is **Rutherford House,** the elegant Edwardian home of A.C. Rutherford, Alberta's first premier and first president of the university. Furnishings of the period decorate the rooms. The **John Walter Museum** in Kinsman Park has three original homes that belonged to John Walter, one of Edmonton's most noted settlers. The **Old Strathcona Foundation** provides guided and self-guided walking tours of the area's historic buildings and sites.

Throughout the downtown area, a few buildings still exist that remind us of Edmonton's former glory. Most, however, were demolished during the building boom of the 1960s and 1970s when oil was king. Available at the visitor centre is the **Historical Walking and Driving Tours of Downtown Edmonton,** which feature four self-guided walking tours. There are also historical walking tours of the Highlands and the Oliver District. In the downtown area the **Edmonton Police Museum and Archives** offers you the opportunity to discover the history of the Edmonton's finest. Tour pamphlets can be acquired at the Edmonton Convention Centre and at many museums throughout Edmonton.

Gibson Block flat iron building (Courtesy of Alberta Historical Resources Foundation, Medicine Hat Museum and Art Gallery and James Marshall)

If there was little physical change to the city, there was certainly significant social changes, especially for women. In 1912, Edmonton women had begun to play a greater role in politics when Bessie Nichols became the first woman elected to public office as a

Public School Trustee. The same year, Annie Jackson became the first woman police constable in Canada, when she joined the Edmonton Police Department. In 1916, Edmonton's Emily Murphy was appointed police magistrate for the Province of Alberta, a position she held for 15 years. The Edmonton Commercial Grads, a woman's basketball team formed in 1914 and coached by Percy Page, began their incredible 25-year record of provincial championships. From 1922 to 1940, the "Grads" played a total of 375 games, winning 355. They attended the Olympic Games in 1924, 1928, 1932, and 1936.

The Edmonton "Grads" (Edmonton Archives, EA-10-2849)

Edmonton's identity as "Gateway to the North" took on new dimensions when, in 1909, Reginald Hunt built and flew Edmonton's first airplane. Flying aces like Wop May, Punch Dickens, Grant McConachie, and Matt Berry came back from the Great War to kindle the imaginations of Edmontonians with the possibilities of Edmonton as a centre for commercial aviation. Again its strategic location put Edmonton on the map as a departure point for bush flying in the north. Edmonton's Blatchford Field (now Edmonton Municipal Airport) became Canada's first designated air harbour in 1926. During the Second World War, Edmonton's airport played a key role in the British Commonwealth Air Training Programme, the Northwest Staging Route, and for the building of the Alaska Highway.

The **Alberta Aviation Museum**, located in the Edmonton Aviation Heritage Centre on Kingsway, brings to life Edmonton's exciting bush pilot era and the development of commercial and military aviation in Alberta.

Leduc #1 ushered in a new era of prosperity for Edmonton. Again Edmonton experienced a long-awaited boom. The heritage hunter in us regrets that most of the beautiful Edwardian buildings— the old post office, the CN railway station, and the McDougall mansion—were demolished to make way for the giant tombstones that now dominate Edmonton's skyline. But Edmontonians were tired of the old brick buildings that dominated the downtown area for 40 years and were ripe for change. In the last ten years Edmontonians have expressed interest in preserving some of the city's early 20th century architectural heritage. Efforts to restore structures like Jasper Avenue's Gibson Block (one of two flat iron buildings in Alberta), the warehouse district, and the Macdonald Hotel will ensure that future generations will have a link to their past.

MUSEUMS IN EDMONTON

☞ **Alberta Association of Registered Nurses Museum & Archives**
11620 - 168th Street, Edmonton, AB T5M 4A6
Governing body: Provincial Council of AARN
Open year round, daily * ☎ (403) 451-0043
Admission by donation * *Visiting time:* one half hour
🍷 🚗 ♿ 👫 🍴 ╼

The museum has objects related to the founding and development of the Alberta Association of Registered Nurses, including uniforms, caps, pins, military metals, yearbooks, photographs and other documents. Of special interest is the Florence Nightingale Lamp, one of only three lamps in the world of this design used by Crimean nursing staff.

☞ **Alberta Aviation Museum**
11410 Kingsway Avenue, Edmonton, AB T5G 0X4
Edmonton Aviation Heritage Centre, Municipal Airport
Governing body: Alberta Aviation Museum Association
Open year round: Monday through Saturday * ☎ (403) 453-1078
Admission fee charged * *Visiting time:* one hour
🍷 🍷 🍷 🚗 ♿ 👫 🎁 ♨ 🍴 ╼

The museum collects and restores vintage aircraft relevant to Alberta's aviation history. It is located in Hangar 14, which was the 418 (City of Edmonton) Squadron hangar after World War II. Exhibits focus on the bush pilots and pioneer aviation in the North and the importance of commercial and military aviation in Edmonton's history. Emphasizing restoration of aircraft rather than static display or flying conditions, the museum has several on-going restoration projects that the visitor can observe in progess: the Cranwell LA4, two Stinsons, a Beech 18, and the de Havilland Mosquito Mk. B35, to name a few. The museum also has a large archives and library for the researcher of aviation history.

☞ Alberta Railway Museum
Box 6102, Stn. C, Edmonton, AB T5V 4K5
24215 - 34th Street; from downtown Edmonton, go north on 97th Street (Highway 28) for 20 kilometres, turn right on Highway 37 for 8 kilometres; turn right at 34th Street for another 1.6 kilometres to museum entrance. Route is well marked * *Governing body:* Alberta Pioneer Railway Association
Open Victoria Day to Labour Day, Thursday to Monday
☎ (403) 472-6229 * Admission fee charged
Visiting time: one and one half hours
🍷🍷🍷🚗 👬 🎁 🎋

The Alberta Railway Museum has its main building in St. Albert's former railway station (1909). It possesses an impressive collection of rolling stock including steam and diesel locomotives, passenger and box cars, and a variety of railroad equipment once part of the Canadian National, Canadian Pacific and Northern Alberta Railway companies. Special emphasis is on the restoration and operation of vintage trains. During the long weekends in the summer, visitors can enjoy taking train rides. This is a destination museum for the railway enthusiast and lots of fun for everyone else.

☞ Calgary & Edmonton (C&E) Railway Museum
10447 - 86th Avenue, Edmonton, AB T6E 2M4
Governing body: Junior League of Edmonton
Open Victoria Day to Labour Day, Tuesday to Saturday
☎ (403) 433-9739 * Admission by donation * *Visiting time:* one half hour
🍷🚗 ♿ 👬 ⚲ 🎋 🍶 ━

The museum is housed in a replica of the original 1891 C&E station. Exhibits include a waiting room, ticket office, and a working telegraph office, with many interpretive photographs of early railway stations. The working telegraph is on line to the Telephone Historical Information Centre two blocks away.

☞ **City of Edmonton Archives**
10440 - 108th Avenue, Edmonton, AB T5H 3Z9
Governing body: Edmonton Parks and Recreation, City of Edmonton
Open year round, Monday through Friday; closed Statutory and Civic holidays
☎ (403) 496-8710 * Admission by donation

🍷 🍷 🚗 ♿🍽 ⎯

The City of Edmonton Archives (COEA) is located in the historic Prince of Wales Armouries. It contains documents and photographs related to Edmonton's history. Among the documents are city government and private records, still and moving images, newspapers, maps, architectural drawings, and oral histories. Photographs include many images besides ones of Edmonton. The city and the Northern Alberta Pioneers and Old Timers Association (NAPOTA) acquired and preserved many of these documents and photographs. The archives also has a non-circulating library of current and historical publications.

☞ **Devonian Botanic Garden**
University of Alberta, Edmonton, AB T6G 2E9 * North of Devon on Hwy 60
Governing body: University of Alberta * Open May to September, daily
☎ (403) 987-3054 * Admission fee charged * *Visiting time:* two hours

🍷 🍷 🍷 🚗 ♿ 👫 ⚲ 🎁 ⛩ ☕

The University of Alberta's botanic garden features hardy trees, shrubs, and flowering plants from all over the world that thrive in Alberta's climate. Natural areas as well as more formal gardens cover over 190 acres of parkland forest. Special exhibits include the Kurimoto Japanese Garden, the Butterfly House, Alpine Garden, Alberta Plants, Native People's Garden, the Imrie Wetland Reserve, and others. This is a place to return to each month over the season to observe changes and see hundreds of species of flowers in bloom. University and high school classes as well as public education and nature interpretive programs are held throughout the year.

☞ **Edmonton Art Gallery**
2 Sir Winston Churchill Square, Edmonton, AB T5J 2C1
Governing body: Edmonton Art Gallery *Open year round, daily
☎ (403) 422-6223 * Admission fee charged * *Visiting time:* one hour

🍷 🍷 🍷 🍷 ♿ 👫 ⚲ 🎁 🍽 ⎯

Since 1924, the Edmonton Art Gallery has collected and exhibited outstanding works of art for Edmontonians to enjoy. The collections contain more than 2500 works, including Canadian historical art, contemporary Canadian and international paintings, sculpture, photography, drawings and performance art from around the
world. These collections appear in feature exhibitions and travelling
exhibits. The exhibition *From Sea to Sea: the Development of
Canadian Art,* featuring some of the permanent collection, is an enjoyable way to learn about the history of Canadian art. Special programs include studio courses for children and adults, group shows,
lecture and film series, and guided tours. The gallery shop offers art
rentals.

☞ **Edmonton Police Museum and Archives**
9620 - 103A Avenue, Edmonton, AB T5H 0H7
Governing body: Edmonton Police Service and
Edmonton Police Museum Board of Advisors
Open year round: Tuesday to Saturday * ☎ (403) 421-2274
Admission by donation * *Visiting time:* one half hour

🏆🏆 ♿ 👫 🎁

The museum has artifact and archival collections related to the
history of law enforcement in Edmonton and Alberta. The artifacts
include uniforms, equipment, firearms, trophies, and awards. The
archives keep a large collection of photographs and case histories.
Exhibits feature the history of the Edmonton Police Service since its
establishment in 1892. Children's interpretive programs are a feature
of the museum.

☞ **Edmonton Public Schools Archives and Museum**
10425 - 99th Avenue, Edmonton, AB T5K 0E5
McKay Avenue School
Governing body: Edmonton Public School Board No. 7
☎ (403) 422-1970 * Admission by donation * *Visiting time:* one hour

🏆🏆🚗 ♿ 👫 ⤴ 🍴 —

The museum is located in the McKay Avenue School, the oldest
standing brick school in Edmonton. Public tours are available to see
classrooms of the 1912 and 1950 periods. In 1906, the first
Legislative Assembly met on the third floor, which has been restored to Premier Rutherford's administration. On the grounds is the
original 1881 frame school building, the first public school in the

North West Territories. School programs feature classroom instruction as it was in the 1880s.

☞ **Edmonton Space & Science Centre**
11211 - 142nd Street, Edmonton, AB T5M 4A1
Governing body: Edmonton Space & Science Foundation
Open year round; Tuesday to Sunday; closed Mondays
☎ (403) 452-9100 * Admission fee charged * *Visiting time:* two hours
♥♥♥♥ 🚗 ♿ 🎪 ☷ ♨ 🍴 ▬

This multipurpose museum is a planetarium, observatory, IMAX theatre, and interactive display gallery rolled into one building that looks like a giant UFO spacecraft. The world-renown architect Douglas Cardinal designed this extraordinary architectural showpiece. The Edmonton Space & Science Centre has the largest planetarium dome in Canada, with 200 computer-controlled projectors. The Challenger Learning Centre provides programs for school children and families to take part in a simulated mission aboard a space station and control centre. For younger children, the Discovery Room provides many activities where they can learn about the space sciences. The exhibit room provides hands-on displays where you can learn about our solar system and the physical principles of astronomy and space sciences.

☞ **Fort Edmonton Park**
Box 2359, Edmonton, AB T5J 2R7
Corner of Fox Drive and Whitemud Drive
Governing body: City of Edmonton * Open May to September
☎ (403) 428-2992 * Admission fee charged * *Visiting time:* three hours
♥♥♥♥♥ 🚗 ♿ ⚎ 🎪 ☷ ♨

Fort Edmonton (R.L. Hursey)

Fort Edmonton Park is the largest living history museum in Canada. It provides fun for all while learning about Edmonton's heritage. The park features four time periods represented by the Fort, 1885 Street, 1905 Street, and 1920 Street. The Fort is a reproduction of the Hudson Bay Company's Fort Edmonton of 1846. Interpreters reenact the fascinating life of a fur trade fort. You can watch bread being baked in an outdoor oven, see a York boat repaired, or watch a blacksmith hammering red-hot iron. Hop aboard the Edmonton Yukon Pacific Railway. Ride a stagecoach or a horse-drawn wagon or a streetcar and learn about early transportation first hand. Numerous heritage buildings line the streets, having been moved to the site, restored, and furnished with period artifacts. Two other museums are located at Fort Edmonton Park—the **Edmonton Radial Railway Society,** whose members have restored ten former Edmonton streetcars to operating condition and the **Fort Edmonton Masonic Museum,** where you can see Masonic regalia and artifacts displayed in an actual Masonic Lodge room.

☞ **Girl Guides of Canada Archives and Museum**
3rd floor, 11055 - 107th Street, Edmonton, AB T5H 2Z6
Governing body: Girl Guides of Canada, Alberta Council
Open September to June, Tuesdays and Thursdays
☎ (403) 424-5510 * Admission by donation
♥ ⛟ ⵊⵊⵝ ⌗ ⵏⵏ ⏗

The archives and museum has archival materials and artifacts relating to the history and activities of the Girl Guides. Artifacts include uniforms, insignia, badges, pins, crests and other commemorative objects.

☞ **John Janzen Nature Centre**
Edmonton Parks and Recreation, Box 2359, Edmonton,AB T5J 2R7
Fort Edmonton Park, corner of Fox Drive and Whitemud Drive
Governing body: City of Edmonton * Open year round, daily
☎ (403) 434-7446 * Admission by donation * *Visiting time:* one hour
♥♥ ⛟ ♿ ⵊⵊⵝ ⵏ ⌗ ⵟ

The John Janzen Nature Centre interprets the natural history of Edmonton. Special features include a large teaching collection of mounted and study specimens. The centre provides guided and self-guided tours along the nature trails that border the river and Fort Edmonton Park. The signage introducing "The Wood Family's Nature Diary" is a very effective way of introducing the natural area to other families. A variety of programs and classes are offered throughout the year for people of all ages. These programs cover every imaginable topic, from building bird feeders to exploring the aquatic life of a pond or going on ecology and winter camp-outs.

☞ John Walter Museum
10125 - 97th Avenue, Edmonton, AB T5K 0B3
Kinsmen Park, south of Walterdale Bridge * *Governing body:* City of Edmonton
Open year round, Sunday afternoons; pre-booked school programs on weekdays,
from September to June * ☎ (403) 428-3033
Admission fee charged for school programs * *Visiting time:* one half hour

---

The John Walter Museum is on the original site where John Walter established his various businesses. The site includes three original homes in which the Walter family lived during different periods, built respectively in 1875, 1884 and 1901. Two houses are furnished to period and the third presents a photographic history of John Walter, one of Edmonton's earliest settlers. School programs, pioneer workshops, and special events breathe life into Edmonton's early history.

☞ Muttart Conservatory
Box 2359, Edmonton, AB T5J 2R7 * 9626 - 96A Street
Governing body: City of Edmonton * Open year round, daily *
☎ (403) 496-6951 * Admission fee charged * *Visiting time:* one hour

---

The Muttart Conservatory offers one of Edmonton's highlights anytime of the year. The conservatory features collections of plants from all over the world in four pyramids. Three feature plants from tropical, arid, and temperate environments; the fourth is an exhibition pavilion with changing floral displays. The large collection of orchids in the temperate pyramid is a pleasure to see, as are the colourful finches and parrots that make their home in the tropical pyramid. There is a tea shop and a well-stocked gift shop on the premises as well.

☞ Old Strathcona Model & Toy Museum
8603 - 104th Street, Edmonton, AB T6E 4G6
Governing body: Old Strathcona Model & Toy Museum Directors
Open Year round: July and August, daily; September to June, Wed. to Fri.
☎ (403) 433-4512 * Admission by donation * *Visiting time:* one half hour

In the heart of Old Strathcona stands a very unusual family-owned museum unique in Canada. All of the artifacts and collections are made of paper or cardboard. Exhibits feature castles, cathedrals, ships, airplanes, dragons, dinosaurs, fish, birds, and other creatures. Famous edifices like the Eiffel Tower, the CN Tower, and a Japanese pagoda as well as busts of famous composers and prime ministers are but a few of many types of models crafted from paper. A special feature is a working paper model railroad that winds through a paper village. One of my favorites is the RCMP Musical Ride, with two dozen Mounties on horseback. This enchanting little museum provides fun for children of all ages. For the hobbyist interested in learning the ancient art of paper craft, there are classes and supplies available in the gift shop.

☞ **Provincial Archives of Alberta**
12845 - 102nd Avenue, Edmonton, AB T5N 0M6
Next to Government House in same building as Provincial Museum of Alberta
Governing body: Historic Sites & Archives Service, Alberta Community Development * Open year round: Tuesday to Saturday * ☎ (403) 427-1750

The Provincial Archives of Alberta is a storehouse of archival materials pertaining to just about every facet of Alberta's history. Archival materials include documents, maps, photographs, moving images, tapes, ledgers, registers, provincial government records, and private manuscripts. Its library has a complete selection of Alberta's local history series as well as other historical publications difficult to find elsewhere.

☞ **Provincial Museum of Alberta**
12845 - 102nd Avenue, Edmonton, AB T5N 0M6 * Next to Government House
Governing body: Alberta Community Development, Historical Resources Division * Open year round: summer, daily; winter, Tuesday to Sunday
☎ (403) 453-9100 * Admission fee charged * *Visiting time:* two hours

---

The Provincial Museum of Alberta (PMA) is a multidisciplinary museum, with extensive collections related to the natural and human history of Alberta. The museum occupies a large two-story building on spacious grounds overlooking the North Saskatchewan River. Its facade contains Tyndall stone, a beautiful sandstone rich with palaeozoic invertebrate fossils. The first floor Habitat Gallery features dioramas of wildlife and vegetation found throughout the five natural regions of Alberta. The painted backgrounds of these dioramas reveal some of the best you will find anywhere. On the second floor, "Treasures of the Earth" features nature's artistry with extraordinary mineral specimens from around the globe. The Quaternary Gallery features fossils of giant mammals that roamed western Canada during the ice age. Children will be delighted with the Discovery Room and the popular "Bug Room," which includes live insects and butterflies of every color. Expect to find examples of beautiful treasures, like those in the McDougall collection and the magnificent Blackfoot collection of beadwork. But don't expect to find much about the history of the province. In general, the museum's exhibits are long on magnificent collections but short on communication about what makes Alberta distinctive from other Canadian provinces.

☞ **Rutherford House Provincial Historic Site**
c/o Historic Sites & Archives Service, 8820 - 112th Street
Edmonton, AB T6G 2P8 * 11153 Saskatchewan Drive
Governing body: Alberta Community Development, Historic Sites & Archives
Service * Open year round, daily * ☎ (403) 427-3995
Admission by donation * *Visiting time:* one half hour

The stately residence of Alberta's first premier, Dr. A.G. Rutherford, is a three-story Edwardian home built in 1915. It reflects the understated elegance and taste of this period, in contrast to the extravagance and busyness of Victorian houses. Period furnishings and costumed interpreters give us a picture of the lifestyle of this distinguished Edmonton family. The Friends of Rutherford House operate a Tea Room and gift shop on the premises.

☞ **Telephone Historical Centre**
Box 4459, Edmonton, AB T6E 4T5
10437 - 83rd Avenue, in the heart of Old Strathcona
Governing body: The Edmonton Telephone Historical Information Centre
Foundation * Open Monday to Saturday
☎ (403) 441-2077 * Admission fee charged * *Visiting time:* one hour

---

Housed in the original 1913 brick telephone exchange building, the museum is the only accredited telephone museum in Canada. Antique telephone displays show a progression of styles and technologies, beginning with a model of Alexander Graham Bell's first telephone. This centre makes learning about telecommunications lots of fun. The visitor starts with an excellent multimedia slide show that tells the story of telecommunications in Edmonton and western Canada. Although it focuses mainly on telephone history, the slide show also presents the visitor with a delightful introduction to the history of Edmonton and its people. Most of the displays in the main exhibit gallery are interactive and show the progression of technology from a working telegraph station and step-by-step switching technology to the latest video telephones. A favorite with children is an old-fashioned telephone operator's station where they can take turns playing operator and connecting calls between their friends.

☞ **Ukrainian Canadian Archives & Museum of Alberta**
9543 - 110th Avenue, Edmonton, AB T5H 1H3
Governing body: Ukrainian Canadian Archives & Museum of Alberta
Open year round: Tuesday to Saturday; closed statutory holidays
☎ (403) 424-7580 * Admission by donation * *Visiting time:* one half hour

🍷🍷🚗 ♿ 🚻

This is the largest of the three Ukrainian Canadian museums in Edmonton. It portrays the rich cultural heritage of the Ukrainian people in Alberta through artifacts and photographs. Collections include traditional apparel from the western regions of Ukraine, musical instruments, folk art and traditional crafts including kylyms (woven rugs), pysanky (Easter eggs), embroidery, ceramics and wood carvings. Icons, banners, Slavonic bibles and liturgical objects reflect the importance of religion to the Ukrainian people. A special exhibit features costumes of renowned women from Ukrainian history. The UCAMA operates an extensive archives and library, with over 12,000 books in Ukrainian and English and an on-going program of collecting and preserving archival material for use by researchers.

☞ **Ukrainian Catholic Women's League of Canada Arts & Crafts Museum (UCWLC)**
10825 - 97th Street, Edmonton, AB T5H 2M4
Lower floor of St. Josaphat's Cathedral
Governing body: Ukrainian Catholic Women's League of Canada, Edmonton Eparchy * Open May to August, Tuesday to Saturday
☎ (403) 424-7505 * Admission by donation * *Visiting time:* one half hour

This small museum has been collecting, preserving and promoting Ukrainian culture for over 40 years. It functions primarily as a teaching museum to promote the learning of traditional crafts. Collections include historical costumes, hand woven textiles and kylyms, embroidery, ceramics, wood carvings and Easter eggs. The museum also owns a large collection of embroidery patterns and samplers and a series of dolls that show the variety of historical costumes from each province of Ukraine. Classes in traditional Ukrainian crafts, such as embroidery, weaving, Easter egg painting, and traditional baking are offered throughout the year.

☞ **Ukrainian Museum of Canada, Alberta Branch**
10611 - 110th Avenue, Edmonton, AB T5H 1H7
In back of St. John's Cathedral
Governing body: Ukrainian Women's Association of Canada
Open by appointment only * ☎ (403) 483-5932 * Admission by donation
♥ 🚗 ⅲ 🍴 ━

This museum celebrated its 50th anniversary in 1994. It is a branch of the Ukrainian Museum of Canada in Saskatoon. There is another branch in Calgary. This Alberta branch of the Ukrainian-Canadian museum has more than 50,000 artifacts on Ukrainian culture, many of which are over 100 years old. The collection includes some early paintings by internationally renowned Ukrainian-Canadian painter William Kurelek and over 200 pysanky (Easter eggs). Since the museum does not advertise and it is only available by appointment, the heritage hunter will need to make prior arrangements to see the collection.

☞ **University of Alberta Museums**
c/o Department of Museums & Collections Services, Ring House #1,
University of Alberta, Edmonton, AB T6G 2E1
Governing body: University of Alberta
Open year round, weekdays * ☎ (403) 492-5834 * Admission by donation

---

One of the University of Alberta's well-kept secrets is its numerous museums—about 30 in all—and other collections scattered throughout the campus in over 20 academic departments. The University of Alberta maintains one of the largest and oldest collections in Canada, with over 4 million specimens, artifacts, and works of art. These are primarily used as teaching and research collections for students, but there are several museums, collections, and exhibits that are readily accessible to the heritage hunter. A complete list of these museums can be acquired from the Department of Museums & Collections Services. Listed below are some of the museums, collections, and exhibits fairly accessible to the public:

• *Clothing and Textiles Collection*, Home Economics Building, B-6, ☎ 492-2528 for hours.

• *Origins of Dentistry exhibit,* Dentistry-Pharmacy Centre, fourth floor
• *Classics Museum,* Humanities Centre, 1-14, ☎ 492-2338 for hours.
• *Topics in Anthropology exhibit,* H M Tory Building, main floor
• *Window on the Collections exhibit,* Biological Sciences Building, main floor, centre wing
• *Museum of Zoology,* Biological Sciences Building, ☎ 492-4622 for appointment
• *Vascular Plant Herbarium,* Biological Sciences Building, ☎ 492-5523 for appointment
• *Soil Monoliths of Canada exhibit,* Earth Sciences Building, second floor, east hall
• *Mineralogy and Petrology Museum,* Earth Sciences Building, B-08.
• *Paleontology Museum,* Earth Sciences Building, B-01.
• *Historic Chemistry Equipment exhibit,* Chemistry Building galleria
• *Mechanical Engineering Collection,* Mechanical Engineering Building, first and second floors
• *Forest Science Collection,* Agriculture & Forestry Building, second floor foyer and hall
• *Sporting Heritage exhibit,* Van Vliet Centre, second floor, east entrance

---

☞ **Valley Zoo**
Box 2359, Edmonton, AB T5J 2R7 * 13315 Buena Vista Road
Governing body City of Edmonton, Parks and Recreation
Open May 1 to Labour Day, daily * ☎ (403) 483-5513
Admission fee charged * *Visiting time:* one and a half hours

---

The Valley Zoo, located in the river valley in a park setting, is primarily adapted to families with young children. The zoo keeps over 350 exotic and domestic mammals, birds, fish, and reptiles representing 115 species. Featured are Asian and African elephants, Siberian tigers, zebras, and many domestic animals like the wood bison, Canada lynx, and cougar. For children's enjoyment, the zoo features storybook characters throughout the park. A petting zoo, rides on camels, ponies, and a miniature train are all available to the delight of children. Interpretive programs, classes, and demonstrations are held throughout the summer.

☞ **Victoria Composite High School Museum and Archives**
10210 - 108th Avenue, Edmonton, AB T5H 1A8
Governing body: Edmonton Public School Board No. 7
Open summer, daily; winter, Monday to Friday * ☎ (403) 426-3010
Admission by donation * *Visiting time:* one half hour

The museum has collections related to the history of Victoria Composite High School from 1903 to the present. Artifacts and archival material include textbooks, photographs, uniforms, banners, flags, furniture, yearbooks, trophies, student records, and other memorabilia.

W.J. Magrath mansion, built in 1912 (Courtesy of Alberta Historical Resources Foundation, Medicine Hat Museum and Art Gallery and James Marshall)

23

STURGEON RIVER COUNTRY

The Sturgeon River, a tributary of the North Saskatchewan River, begins as a tiny stream in the hills southeast of Evansburg. Its waters flow into Lake Isle and Lac Ste. Anne and on to Big Lake. It wanders through the city of St. Albert, then begins to drop into a substantial valley until it joins the North Saskatchewan River a few miles downstream of the town of Fort Saskatchewan. You will find no sturgeon in the river today, but these fish were once caught near its mouth. Along its shores you will see an amazing variety of wildlife and parkland vegetation. Take a leisurely walk or bike ride along St. Albert's **Red Willow Park** trails to capture the essence of the riverine parkland or to observe the abundant variety of bird life, especially migratory waterfowl. You can acquire a pamphlet, the *Natural History Tour of St. Albert,* at the visitor centre or the Musée Héritage Museum at St. Albert Place.

The Sturgeon River Valley has been occupied by humans for at least 5000 years. Stone tools and points that date back at least 5000 years have been found along its banks. Permanent settlement of the Sturgeon Valley, in the area of today's St. Albert, began in 1861, when Father Albert Lacombe, the famous Roman Catholic priest of the Oblates of Mary Immaculate, established a mission for the Métis people.

St. Albert Mission is the oldest agricultural settlement in Alberta. Father Lacombe had foreseen a time when his beloved Métis would need to have a permanent home. He persuaded Bishop Alexander Taché to allow him to establish a mission for the devout Roman Catholic Métis. Although Lac Ste. Anne had been an excellent hunting and fishing area, its soil was unsuitable for agriculture. On January 14, 1861, Father Lacombe and Bishop Alexander Taché stopped at the hilltop overlooking the Sturgeon River; and the bishop chose the location for the first chapel, naming the mission after Father Lacombe's patron saint.

The first Métis to settle along the river were Michael Normand, his wife Rose Plante, and an orphan girl named Nancy. Twenty other Métis families from Lac Ste. Anne settled on river lots near the mission and formed the nucleus of the first agricultural settlement in Alberta. The first two years were busy ones: the priest had his followers clear the land, plant the first crops, construct the small chapel, and build a bridge across the Sturgeon. When the fledgling community was very short of supplies, the priest organized 30 Red

River carts to bring supplies from St. Boniface. This cart brigade brought back the first grinding stone.

In 1863, Grey Nuns Sisters Zoe Leblanc-Emery, Adele Lamy, and Marie-Jacques Alphonse left Lac Ste. Anne to join Father Lacombe at St. Albert. On the hill overlooking the Sturgeon River, they established the first hospital on the prairies west of the Red River settlement. By 1870, St. Albert had about 900 occupants, mostly Métis.

At first the Métis continued their semi-nomadic existence, going on their annual bison hunts in the summer, after planting their crops, and again in the fall after harvest. Then in the mid-1870s, the disappearance of the buffalo brought hardship to the community, for these were poor crop years as well. Today many residents of St. Albert are descendants of those early Métis families. The names Bellerose, Beaudry, Belcourt, Cunningham, L'Hirondelle, Normand, Plante and Callihoo are still familiar surnames in the St. Albert area.

Father Lacombe Chapel and Mission Hill today. (R.L. Hursey)

Bishop Vital-Justin Grandin (1829 - 1902)

Bishop Vital Grandin was born on February 8, 1929, at St. Pierre-sur-Orthe in France, the ninth of fourteen children. At a young age he joined the Brothers of the Holy Cross, but his frail health, which was to plague him most of his life, forced him to return home. In 1851 he began his novitiate with the Oblates of Mary Immaculate and was ordained in 1854.

Although his dream was to work in China, he was sent to western Canada and posted at Fort Chipewyan in 1855 with Fathers Faraud and Grollier and Brother Alexis Reynard. In 1857, Vital Grandin was put forward as Co-adjutor of the Saskatchewan diocese, despite his reluctance. He felt he was too young and inexperienced. Between 1861 and 1864, this modest, devout man, who continually suffered ill health, visited remote missions throughout his immense diocese. In 1868, the Saskatchewan diocese was subdivided and Grandin became the first bishop of the St. Albert diocese. In 1871, St. Albert became his administrative centre. In 1881, the Grey Nuns began to build a new hospital and convent, but at some point in its construction, they decided to turn the building over to Bishop Grandin. In 1887, he moved into his new residence.

The bishop's residence in St. Albert still stands today on Mission Hill and is now the Vital Grandin Centre. Bishop Vital Grandin's tenure bridged a period of immense social change in western Canada: the Dominion of Canada's purchase of Rupert's Land from the Hudson's Bay Company; the disappearance of the buffalo from the Great Plains; and the signing of Treaty 6 in 1876, which opened up the land to homesteading. Bishop Grandin's remains reside in a vault beneath the St. Albert cathedral, along with his devoted followers, Fathers Lacombe and Leduc.

Tracks and Traces: The system of parceling land into river lots was borrowed from Quebec. These long, narrow strips of land ensured that all settlers had access to river frontage. After western Canada adopted the system of dividing land into sections and townships, a few areas like St. Albert retained the River Lot System.

During the 1870s and 1880s, a thriving hamlet grew up around the mission. The Hudson's Bay Company opened the first store in 1868, and a flour mill and saw mill were installed by 1878. The first post office in Northern Alberta opened in 1880, and by 1883, a telegraph linked St. Albert and Edmonton. When the Riel Rebellion broke out in 1885, the Métis of St. Albert chose not to join the charismatic leader. After two priests were killed at Frog Lake, Bishop Grandin called for the formation of a militia. The St. Albert Mounted Rifles formed, and 39 of the 45 who enlisted were Métis. Although no action occurred, the militia was prepared to protect the community in case of attack.

Around this time, people from Quebec began to settle around St. Albert. In 1898, St. Albert, with a population of over 1000, incorporated as a village and in 1904, a town. In 1907, the Canadian Northern Railway reached St. Albert. It remained a predominantly French-Canadian community and experienced stable population growth and development of businesses, industry, and services. Then in the 1950s and 1960s, the oil boom brought profound changes for the town when it became Edmonton's bedroom community. By the '70s, St. Albert's population reached 30,000, and on January 1, 1977, it became the City of St. Albert.

In spite of its proximity to Edmonton, St. Albert retains its unique Métis and French Canadian character, proud of its heritage, with roots as a small Métis agricultural settlement and Roman Catholic mission. You can experience some of the richness of this heritage by visiting the **Vital Grandin Centre** and the **Father Lacombe Chapel,** two provincial historic sites on Mission Hill. To learn more about the natural and human history of the area, be sure to visit the **Musée Héritage Museum** at St. Albert Place on St. Anne Street. The museum also has charge of two historic sites, the **Little White School House** and **St. Albert Grain Elevator Park**, a provincial historic site.

Little White School House. (R.L. Hursey)

Continuing north from St. Albert on Highway 2, you follow the overland route that the Hudson's Bay Company used after 1825. The brigades destined for the posts along the Columbia River travelled overland by horseback or dog sled from Fort Edmonton to Fort

Assiniboine, ascended the Athabasca River by canoe to Jasper House, and crossed the mountains into New Caledonia (British Columbia). In 1890, Father Morin used this trail to bring French settlers from Quebec. In 1897 and 1898, it became known as the Klondike Trail, when many attempted to travel the all-terrain route to the Yukon gold fields. Very few made it.

Our next stop is Morinville, the centre of one of the more successful colonization ventures in Alberta. Bishop Grandin and Father Lacombe petitioned Father Jean-Baptiste Morin from the Joliette diocese to bring immigrants from Quebec. In 1890, Father Morin organized "The Catholic Colonization Society of Canada" and brought out the first group of settlers, about 25 families, to take up lands north of St. Albert. They named their community Morinville, after its founder. The same year, the parish built its first chapel, and Father Harnois became the first parish priest. During the next few years, other Roman Catholic immigrants joined the colony; French Canadians from the United States and others from Belgium, France, and Germany. Houle, Morin, Boissonnault, Kieser, and Lutz—surnames of some of the earliest settlers—are common names of descendants who live in the Morinville area today. Morinville and nearby communities of Riviére Qui Barre, Legal, and Villeneuve still retain their French culture.

Morinville, 1910 (Provincial Archives of Alberta B2636)

In 1904, four Sisters of the Filles de Jesus (Daughters of Jesus) from Brittany, France, came to teach in Morinville. By 1909 they had built the Notre Dame Convent and boarding school for 120 full-time boarders and 22 Sisters. You can visit the lovely **Notre Dame Convent**, a provincial historic site. It is now a cultural centre.

Leaving Morinville, go east on SR 642 to Highway 28 through Bon Accord and on to Gibbons, our next stop. Gibbons was named after William Reynolds Gibbons, who opened a stopping place where the old Athabasca Landing Trail crossed the Sturgeon River. This was the first stopping place on the trail north of Edmonton. At Gibbons, the **Sturgeon River Historical Museum** interprets the history of the area. Several historical buildings, like a turn-of-the-century general store, have been preserved.

The Athabasca Landing Trail

When the Hudson's Bay Company began to use steamboats on the North Saskatchewan and Athabasca Rivers, the company constructed a cart trail from Fort Edmonton to the Athabasca Landing. Freighters conveyed goods in carts and wagons drawn by oxen and horses along the narrow trail. In places, the trees were so tall that they formed a tunnel over the trail and little light reached the ground to dry out the deep mud. In other places the trail was reinforced with cut timber to make corduroy roads. Teams would frequently get bogged down in the muddy ruts and potholes. Mosquitoes and black flies made travel in the summer almost unbearable for beast and human alike. Stopping places were little more than log shacks and barns where travellers could get a basic meal and some hay for their animals. Most of the time they slept on the floor, and if they were lucky enough to get a bed, they ran the risk of being infested by fleas, lice or bedbugs.

After the railroad reached Edmonton in 1891, the Athabasca Trail was a conduit for settlers heading for the Peace River country. During the Klondike Rush of '97 and '98, the trail was the first leg of the water route to the Yukon. Bootleggers, mostly freighters, smuggled whisky in and under their wagons and played a game of cat and mouse with the NWMP who patrolled the trail and the Landing. The Athabasca Trail fell into disuse after the Alberta and Great Waterways Railway replaced river transportation to Fort McMurray.

From Gibbons, go east on SR 645 to SR 825 and turn south toward Fort Saskatchewan. Just before you get to the bridge that crosses the North Saskatchewan River, you will see a sign that directs you to Lamoureux, a small community that overlooks the river and the town of Fort Saskatchewan. The Lamoureux settlement was founded in 1872. Joseph Lamoureux operated a ferry that took people, goods, and animals back and forth across the North Saskatchewan. It is worth the time to drive along the main street (and only street) of Lamoureux to see its lovely Notre Dame de Lourdes Roman Catholic church. Lamoureux established the first Roman Catholic school district in Alberta.

If you continue east from Lamoureux along the gravel road for about 4 kilometres, you will come to a large rock cairn of the Fort Augustus-Edmonton House site. Below on the river flats was the approximate location of the first Fort Edmonton. In the spring of 1795, Angus Shaw of the North West Company built Fort Augustus. Not to be outdone, the Hudson's Bay Company sent William Tomison to establish a rival post the following fall "within a musket shot" of the Nor'westers. This post was named Edmonton House, after Edmonton, Middlesex, England. At the time, these two forts were the uppermost posts on the North Saskatchewan River. I can imagine what Angus Shaw and William Tomison would say if they could look across the river from the cairn and see the huge chemical plants that now line the south shore. No doubt they would say "Aye, lass, that be commerce for ye!"

About 3 kilometres farther down the gravel road you will come to where the Sturgeon and North Saskatchewan Rivers join. This was a favorite spot for Natives to gather birch bark for repairing their canoes. From here you can continue on this road to where it connects with SR 825, or go back to Lamoureux and turn south on Highway 28 to Fort Saskatchewan, our next stop.

Fort Saskatchewan was the first North West Mounted Police post north of Calgary. It was built in 1875 under the direction of Inspector W.D. Jarvis. Edmonton wanted the post located there, but Jarvis chose the site 20 miles downstream in anticipation of the transcontinental railway crossing the river at this location. The Canadian Pacific Railway, however, went to Calgary instead, and Fort Saskatchewan would have to wait many years for another transcontinental railway to arrive. In the meantime, settlers, arriving by steamboat, began to take up homesteads in the area. A large group of about 300 from Parry Sound, Ontario, settled east of Edmonton near Fort Saskatchewan in 1892. Ukrainians and Germans settled farther east of the fort. Soon businesses began to set up around the police post, providing goods and services for the new settlements.

The Fort Saskatchewan Museum, located in the old courthouse built in 1909, brings to life the history of the police fort and town. Upstairs the original courtroom has been preserved. On the grounds a cairn marks the location of the original police barracks. A path from the courthouse leads to the old prison, which now stands awaiting demolition. Next to the museum one can see the old trail leading down to the river where there used to be a ferry landing. It is now a bike trail and a lovely park and picnic area.

Tracks and Traces: The difference between a derelict building and a historical building depends on whether people want to tear it down or preserve it.

MUSEUMS IN THE STURGEON RIVER COUNTRY

☞ **Fort Saskatchewan Museum**
10104 - 101st Street, Fort Saskatchewan, AB T9L 1V9
Old brick courthouse overlooking the river.
Governing body: Fort Saskatchewan Historical Society
Open year-round, daily * ☎ (403) 998-1750
Admission fee charged * *Visiting time:* one hour

🏆🏆 🚗 👫 👶 🏛 🎪 ♿

The Fort Saskatchewan Museum is now a registered provincial historic resource. Although the exhibits and collections and historic buildings on the grounds reflect many themes, a special collection of RCMP uniforms, guns, carriole, and other equipment will be of interest to the historian of the history of the North West Mounted Police. Upstairs is the original courtroom, with a special stairs leading down behind the Judge's bench. On the grounds a cairn marks the original location of the police barracks and a path, lined with a tall hedge, along which prisoners from the nearby penitentiary were led to the courtroom for their trial. Adjacent to the museum is the original trail to the steamboat landing by the river.

☞ **Sturgeon River Historical Museum**
Box 645, Gibbons, AB T0A 1N0 * 4709 - 48th Avenue
Governing body: Sturgeon River Historical Society
Open June to September, daily * ☎ (403) 923-3726
Admission fee charged * *Visiting time: one half hour*

🏆🏆 🚗 👫🎪

This museum is a small historical village, with a variety of buildings from the area. The centre piece is the McLean Brothers General Store, where you will find typical merchandise one could buy in the Teens and Twenties. Next to the general store, a log building holds most of the museum's smaller artifacts collected from the area. A small home is decorated in period furnishings of the 1920s.

☞ **Morinville and District Museum**
10010 - 101st Street, Morinville, AB T0G 1P0
In the Historical & Cultural Centre, northwest of St. Jean Baptist Church
Governing body: Morinville Historical Society
Open July 1 to August 15, daily; rest of year by appointment
☎ (403) 939-2955 * Admission by donation * *Visiting time:* one half hour
🍷 🚗 ♿ ⚘ 🍴 ▭

The Morinville and District Museum is located in the Historical Centre, northwest of St. Jean Baptiste Church. The centre used to be the Provincial House of the Filles de Jesus women's religious order. This lovely old building now serves as a cultural, community, and educational centre. The museum features exhibits and artifacts depicting the history of the community and the Filles de Jesus. Hours are limited, so it is best to call before visiting.

☞ **Centre Vital Grandin Centre** at St. Albert
5th Avenue St. Vital, St. Albert, AB T8N 1K1 * Mission Hill
Governing body: Missionary Oblates Grandin Province
Open May 15 to Labour Day, daily * ☎ (403) 459-2116
Admission by donation * *Visiting time:* one half hour
🍷 🍷 🍷 🚗 👫 🍴 ▭

This prominent landmark was the former Bishop's Palace, built by the Grey Nuns in the 1880s. The Sisters turned the building over to Mons. Vital Grandin, the first bishop of the St. Albert diocese, for his headquarters. This three-story building, one of the finest examples of Quebec architecture, was fully restored in 1982, and is a provincial historic resource. The upper floors serve as a residence for retired Oblate priests. The main floor has exhibits that feature the history of the St. Albert Mission. Featured are Bishop Grandin's hand-carved desk, with some of his personal objects such as his bishop's hat. The Brothers Room features hand-made tools, an early printing press used in Lac La Biche and Brother Antony Kowalczyk's artificial arm. (He lost his arm in a sawmill accident.) Guided tours are available in French and English.

☞ **Father Lacombe Chapel Provincial Historic Site**
8820 - 112th Street, Edmonton, AB   T6G 2P8 * Mission Hill
Governing body: Alberta Community Development,
Historic Sites & Archives Service
Open May 15 to Labour Day, daily * ☎ (403) 427-2022
Admission by donation * *Visiting time:* one half hour
🏆🏆🏆🚗 ♿ 🚹 🍽 ➖

The Father Lacombe Chapel was the first building erected by Father Lacombe and the Métis at the St. Albert Roman Catholic Mission in 1861. It is one of the oldest existing buildings in the province. The building is not on its original site, as it was used throughout the years for a variety of purposes, including a chicken coop and a museum. This humble building was restored in 1984 and contains religious artifacts representative of the 19th century. Guided tours are available in French and English.

☞ **Musée Héritage Museum**
5 St. Anne Street, St. Albert, AB   T8N 3Z9
The north end of St. Albert Centre
Governing body: Museum and Historical Sites Board of Management, City of St. Albert * Open year round: Summer, daily; Winter, Tuesday to Sunday
☎ (403) 459-1528 * Admission by donation * *Visiting time:* one half hour
🏆🏆🏆🚗 ♿ 🏛 🎎 🍽 ➖

This municipal museum building, located at the northeast end of St. Albert Place, was designed by Douglas Cardinal, Canada's foremost contempory architect. The museum has well-constructed and informative displays that tell the story of St. Albert as a mission to the Métis and the history of the town of St. Albert. Collections include natural history specimens, native and Métis objects, and artifacts related to St. Albert's agricultural and religious past. The museum is in charge of two historic sites within easy walking distance of St Albert Centre: The Little White School House, the oldest school building in St. Albert, and the St. Albert Grain Elevators on Meadowview Drive.

24

UKRAINIAN SETTLEMENT BLOC

One of the unique features of east central Alberta is the onion-domed churches along Highways 45, 28 and 36. To come across these Ukrainian Orthodox, Russian Orthodox or Ukrainian Catholic churches standing in the middle of a wheat field is to be transported to some distant land and time. A narrow track leading to the church is overgrown with grass and weeds. The tin cupola reflects the pink rays of the late afternoon sun; a rusting bell, toppled from its tower, no longer calls the faithful. Many of these stucco monuments and the cemeteries nearby show signs of care.

Ukrainian Orthodox church near Redwater (R.L. Hursey)

What manner of people built these churches? Why are they no longer in use, but so obviously cared for? I asked myself these questions when I first moved to Alberta eighteen years ago. I found myself returning to this part of Alberta many times, absorbing the beauty of the rolling hills and farms and the tranquillity of the cattail sloughs filled with coots, pintails, and mallards. But most of all I went to photograph these churches. To me they symbolized the whole experience of immigration to a strange land, in which beliefs and traditions were transplanted intact from the old world to the new.

The first wave of Ukrainians, some 170,000, immigrated to Canada between 1891 and the First World War. Those who came to

Alberta settled in a large area 100 kilometres east of Edmonton, between the North Saskatchewan and Battle Rivers, as far east as Derwent and the Buffalo Trail. The second wave, about 68,000, came between the wars. The third came after the Second World War, during the relocation of displaced persons from Europe's concentration camps. These displaced persons, about 34,000, refused to return to the Ukrainian Soviet Socialist Republic. Today, Ukrainian-Canadians form the third largest ethnic group in Alberta, after those of British and American origins.

Before the arrival of the first wave of Ukrainians, east central Alberta had been occupied by many other groups—Native hunters, fur traders, missionaries, and ranchers. It was the Ukrainians, more than any other group, who transformed the landscape into prosperous farmland. But before we explore the Ukrainian heritage of the area, let us first go back to a time when the Woodland and Plains Cree still owned the region.

In 1862, Reverend George McDougall, a Methodist missionary, selected a site along the North Saskatchewan River, about 100 miles downstream of Fort Edmonton, to establish a mission to the Cree. He named it in honor of Queen Victoria. In 1863, Rev. McDougall returned to the site with his large family and began to develop the mission. The mission attracted Indians as well as about 25 families of mixed-blood who had migrated from the Red River settlement in Manitoba and had begun to farm on river lots nearby. Within a few years Victoria Settlement included livestock, gardens, a church and a hospital. In 1864, the Hudson's Bay Company built an outpost close to the mission to discourage free traders in the area. Fort Victoria, only modestly successful, was finally closed by the company in 1897.

The small pox epidemic of 1870 that devastated so many Natives also claimed the lives of three of the McDougall children. The following year, the McDougalls moved to Edmonton to start another mission. The Victoria Mission, however, continued to operate for many years, serving the community's religious, educational, and medical needs. When the Dominion government opened a post office in 1887 at the site, the name was changed to Pakan, in honor of the Cree Chief Pakan, who did not join the Riel Rebellion of 1885.

In 1901, Reverend Charles H. Lawford, a missionary doctor, assumed leadership of the mission at Pakan. The Cree had by this time signed Treaty No. 8 and had moved onto reserves. New settlers, mostly Ukrainians, had begun to settle in the district. When Pakan declined in importance by the 1920s, Rev. Lawford moved his home and the hospital to Smoky Lake in 1922.

Today you can visit **Victoria Settlement Provincial Historic Site**, located off SR 855 south of Smoky Lake. There you can explore the lovely parkland site of the original Victoria settlement; the McDougall grave site, where George McDougall and his three daughters are buried; the **HBC Clerk's Quarters** (the oldest building in Alberta on its original site); and the **Pakan Church**, built in 1906.

HBC storehouse and clerk's quarters, c1895 (Provincial Archives of Alberta B2406).

Most of the best land had already been settled when the Ukrainians arrived in Alberta during the 1890s. The heavily forested areas they chose were considered by other settlers to be unfit for farming, but to the Ukrainians from the Galicia and Bukovina provinces of the former Austro-Hungarian Empire, forest and brush were features that attracted them as well as the rich black soils. In Ukraine a person who owned 10 acres was considered well-to-do. Most peasants had to work for the *pan* (the landowner). Large landowners controlled most of the land including the forests. When peasants needed wood to heat their ovens, they had to ask permission of the *pan* for the dead limbs and twigs that had fallen from the trees. To be able to own 160 acres of free land that had trees as well? Unimaginable!

Vilni zemli (free lands) may have attracted Ukrainians to Canada, but their motivation for leaving Ukraine was more involved than simply owning land. As serfs and peasants they had been bound to the land for thousands of years. For many immigrants the free land provided a way to improve their lives—never to have to ask permission of a *pan*; to see their children get an education, learn a trade or profession and eventually to be free of the land.

Ivan Pylypiw, the Ukrainian who led the way.

Ivan Pylypiw was born in 1859 in the village of Nebiliw, Galicia. Although his family was poor and there was no school in the village, he was taught by the local priest to read. The priest also persuaded his family to send Ivan to school. Even though his father cut short his scholarly career, Ivan acquired a much better education than most Ukrainian boys his age. He also became a life-long friend of John Krebs, a son of a German colonist who eventually immigrated to western Canada.

Ivan met and married the daughter of a well-off farmer who left her a sizable estate when he passed on. She set Ivan up in a number of businesses, but Ivan, who was not a good businessman, managed to go through most of his wife's inheritance. By 1890, he began to think seriously about emigrating and he wrote to his school friend, Krebs, who had immigrated to a settlement east of Medicine Hat. Krebs' reply was filled with enthusiasm about the free land in Canada. Although Krebs felt he had picked a poor site, there was plenty of better land available along the North Saskatchewan River.

Despite his wife's protests, Ivan decided to go to Canada and see for himself. He tried to talk several other men in the village into going with him, but in the end only Vasyl Eleniak accompanied him. They arrived in Montreal on September 7, 1891, boarded a CPR train for the West and arrived in Winnipeg, where an immigration agent armed them with maps, information about homesteading, and free railway tickets. Ivan filed for a homestead around Langenburg. He continued exploring the prairies farther west until his money ran low, and he returned to Manitoba to spend the winter working at odd jobs. In the spring, Ivan raised enough money for his return passage to Galicia. Vasyl stayed on in Manitoba to work in order to pay passage for his family to come to Canada. Both men eventually moved to Alberta to take up homesteads in the Edna-Star area.

Ivan's return to Nebiliw caused a sensation, but his promotion of Canada soon got him into trouble with the authorities. Ironically, his arrest and brief imprisonment effectively advertised Canada to a far wider audience, and he became a martyr in the eyes of many who had decided to sell their lands and emigrate. Ivan Pylypiw confirmed that *vilni zemli*, free land, was a reality. He ignited the spark that fired a dream.

Between 1892 and 1895, the first group of Galician immigrants arrived in Alberta to homestead in the Edna-Star district. When Dr. Josef Oleskiw, an agriculturist, toured Canada in 1895 and talked with government officials, he returned to Ukraine to write booklets promoting immigration.

Most of the early Ukrainian immigrants were poorly educated, and almost none spoke English. They arrived with little more than the clothes on their backs and "ten fingers," the ten-dollar fee for filing a homestead. Their money had been spent on transportation and provisions to get them from their homeland to seaports, where they were further fleeced by unscrupulous steamship and customs agents. Some arrived too late in the year to plant a crop or even to go out to see their homesteads and had to live in Edmonton in hastily built sheds. Once they settled onto their homesteads, there was the arduous task of clearing the land before they could plant a crop. The men had to work in coal mines and lumber camps in order to buy the necessary seed and tools for planting in the spring, while their wives and children remained on the land to clear the brush and dig up stumps. Most could not afford horses or oxen to pull a breaking plow, so they pulled the plow themselves. They survived on a bit of flour and bacon, berries, and the few rabbits and partridge they managed to snare. Many died during the first few years of disease, malnutrition, starvation, and perhaps for some, discouragement.

Most Ukrainian-Canadians were ill prepared for the cruelty and ostracism of their Anglo-Saxon neighbours, who looked down upon "Ruthenians" because of their poverty, humility, language, and strange clothing. An attitude prevailed that these people "in sheep skin coats" somehow were indifferent to hardship and oppression. By World War I, prejudice came to a head. Ukrainian-Canadians who had been born in the part of Ukraine that was controlled by Austria were considered enemy aliens (along with Austrians and Germans). Hundreds lost their jobs. Men who refused to join the Canadian army or were unemployed were put into internment camps. By 1915, over 5,000 were interned and 48,500 paroled; about half were Ukrainian-Canadians. About 10,000 Ukrainian-Canadians fought in the Canadian forces and many Ukrainian-Canadian communities, like Two Hills, raised funds for the war.

Like other ethnic groups in Canada, in which language, culture, race or religion set them apart, it was the second generation that bore the brunt of the rejection and hostility when they tried to assimilate into Canadian society. They provided the bridge between old and new world values, and in the end they succeeded, but not without a bitter struggle. Mostly the third generation began to preserve their material heritage and collect oral histories from early pioneers.

You will want to begin your exploration of the Ukrainian Settlement Bloc at Redwater on Highway 38. The first Ukrainians arrived in 1896 to the Cookville area. Polish settlers began homesteading in the Opal district in 1908, as well as French settlers from New England, who took up homesteads along the Redwater River. In 1909, mail service came to the district, and the first post office opened at Cookville. In 1912, four Japanese families bought farms in the area. By 1918, the Canadian Northern Railway had extended its line as far as Redwater, which became a flagstop and village.

At Redwater you can learn more about the history of the area by visiting the **Redwater Museum**. This small community history museum effectively tells its history through well-chosen artifacts set in informative thematic displays.

John Gavinchuk reading a newspaper in front of his home. c1917. (Provincial Archives of Alberta UV4)

East of Redwater, along Highway 45, you pass several stately Ukrainian Catholic and Ukrainian Orthodox churches. This is the Edna-Star district where Ukrainians first homesteaded. At Skaro (formerly Edna) a religious grotto built in 1919 by the local Polish community, is the site of annual pilgrimages.

Farther east along Highway 45, you pass through Andrew, the home of the world's largest mallard duck. Continue east to Willingdon and turn north on SR 857 to Shandro, your next stop. The **Historical Village and Pioneer Museum at Shandro** has over 20 historical buildings—homes, businesses and structures that tell the story of Ukrainian settlement in Canada. The authenticity and variety of the collections, from beautifully embroidered textiles to hand-made tools, is a pleasure to see. The centre piece is a Russian Orthodox church, built in 1904. A reproduction of a sod shelter did more to convey the story of the hardships that many homesteaders faced their first year than at any other Ukrainian museum I have visited.

Continue north on SR 857 to your next stop at Smoky Lake. Take the time to drive around this village and visit the lovely old Ukrainian churches and the local museum. The written history of the area predates Ukrainian settlement by about 80 years. The Woodland and Plains Cree used "Smoking Lake" as a meeting place. The origin of the name has two versions: one is that the haze rising from the lake gave the appearance of rising smoke; another holds that the lake was a place where warriors smoked their peace pipes. Between 1812 and 1815, the North West Company and Hudson's Bay Company operated trading posts where the Whitearth River joined the North Saskatchewan, east of today's Smoky Lake. In 1860, Reverend Thomas Woolsey, a Methodist missionary, established a mission on the north end of Smoky Lake. Peter Erasmus, the famous guide and interpreter with the Palliser Expedition, joined Woolsey to assist in building the mission.

In 1915, Smoky Lake established the first businesses. Peter Dubitz opened a general store the following year, eliminating the need for settlers to go all the way to Lamont or Fort Saskatchewan for their supplies. In 1919, Smoky Lake became a hamlet, and by 1923, a village. One of its citizens, Nicholas Gavinchuk, an accomplished professional photographer, left a vivid record of the town, its people and the surrounding community from the early 1920s to the 1950s.

Tracks and Traces: In 1879, a famous battle between the Cree and Blackfoot took place at Hairy Hill, about 20 kilometers west of Two Hills. The Cree raided a Blackfoot camp that had been hit with small pox. It proved a costly victory for the Cree, who in turn fell victim to the dreaded disease.

Your last stop will be Two Hills, where Highways 45 and 36 intersect. The first settlers around Two Hills arrived in 1894. By 1910, Ukrainian, Polish, and Romanian settlers had claimed most of the land. Pozerville became the first post office in 1908. The name was changed to Two Hills in 1913. A townsite was surveyed in 1926 by the Canadian Pacific Railway. By 1927, the first business, a restaurant, opened. In the town, the **Two Hills & District**

Museum focuses on the early settlement of the area and has relocated some of the town's first buildings.

In 1994, the area discussed in this chapter became part of Alberta's second ecomuseum (the first was established at Crowsnest Pass). Known as Kalyna Country, it was named after the *kalyna*, the high bush cranberry, a symbol of independence to Ukraine in the 10th century. Kalyna Country encompasses some 15,000 square kilometres east of Edmonton, corresponding roughly with the Ukrainian settlement bloc. The ecomuseum will celebrate not only the history of the Ukrainian people, but other ethnic cultures. Still in its early stages of development, the **Kalyna Country Ecomuseum,** a joint project of Historic Sites & Archives Services and the Canadian Institute of Ukrainian Studies, will sponsor research and work with local communities in developing their regional tourism potential.

Mrs. P. Gregorovich, Smoky Lake, c1930s. (Provincial Archives of Alberta G228)

MUSEUMS IN THE UKRAINIAN SETTLEMENT BLOC

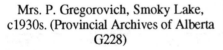

☞ **Redwater Museum**
Box 114, Redwater, AB T0A 2W0 * 4913 - 48th Street
Governing body: Redwater Museum Society
Open *year round: Friday, Saturday, and Sunday afternoons*
☎ (403) 942-3552 * Admission by donation * *Visiting time:* one half hour

The Redwater Museum is located in a small shopping centre next to the library. This museum achieved remarkable success in telling its community history through small thematic displays and well-chosen artifacts. In front of each thematic display is a scrapbook that contains photographs, quotes from oral histories, and stories about the local people. These stories do not dwell on sentimentalism or nostalgia, but tell the tragedies and hardships as well as the triumphs.

☞ **Smoky Lake Museum**
Box 302, Smoky Lake, AB T0A 3C0 * Town of Smoky Lake
Governing body: Smoky Lake Heritage Society
Open Victoria Day to Labour Day, weekends
Admission by donation * *Visiting time:* one half hour
♟ 🚗 🛖 ▲ 🍴 ⎯

Smoky Lake Museum features artifacts collected from the area.

☞ **Victoria Settlement Provincial Historic Site**
c/o Historic Sites & Archives Service, 8820 - 112th Street
Edmonton, AB T6G 2P8
10 kilometres south of Smoky Lake, off SR 855 and 6 kilometres east.
Governing body: Alberta Community Development, Historic Sites & Archives
Service * Open May 15 - Labour Day, daily
Admission by donation * *Visiting time:* one and a half hours
♟ ♟ ♟ 🚗 👥 👤 🏛 🛖 ♿

This provincial historic site is the location of the Victoria Methodist Mission to the Cree, founded by Rev. George McDougall in 1862. The site contains a number of restored historic buildings, including a Hudson's Bay Company clerk's quarters. Built in 1864, it is the oldest building in Alberta on its original site. A 1906 Methodist Church has also been restored and furnished to the period. You will also want to visit the grave site of Rev. George McDougall and his three daughters, who died in the 1870 small pox epidemic. This historic site rests on a beautiful parkland location overlooking the North Saskatchewan River, a great place to have a picnic. Interpreters in period costumes provide tours and programs. A good time to visit is during Fort Victoria Days in mid August for a weekend full of programs and demonstrations, bringing to life the history of this site.

☞ Two Hills & District Museum
Box 2, Two Hills, AB T0B 4K0 * 5910 - 51st Street
Governing body: Two Hills & District Historical Association
Open year round: April to August, daily; September to March, Tuesday and
Thursday afternoons
☎ (403) 657-2379 * Admission by donation * *Visiting time:* one half hour

🍷 🚗 👥

The museum displays turn-of-the-century artifacts, including tools, household articles, furniture and machinery. Some of the first buildings in the community have been relocated and restored.

☞ Historical Village and Pioneer Museum at Shandro at Willington
Box 102, Willingdon, AB T0B 4R0
9 kilometres north of Willingdon on SR 857
Governing body: Historical Village and Museum Society
Open July and August, daily * ☎ (403) 367-2133
Admission fee charged * *Visiting time:* Two hours

🍷🍷🍷 🚗 👥 ⚰ 🎁 🏕

This living history museum features over 20 buildings and structures that portray the Ukrainian pioneer heritage of east central Alberta. The museum, established in 1959, maintains outstanding collections of authentic historical buildings, embroidered clothing and textiles, hand-made tools, and domestic items that portray the early lifestyle of the Ukrainian-Canadians. A series of dwellings, starting with very basic, primitive sod dugouts, to more permanent homes constructed of white-washed, mud-plastered logs and thatched roofs, are furnished to the period. One of these houses exhibits festival breads and foods. Another displays tools used in yarn making and weaving. An early Russian Greek Orthodox Church, with its bell tower constructed entirely of timber, stands as the centre piece. It looks as if it were transported directly from the steppes of Ukraine. Built in 1902-3, this church has an exquisite interior, with illuminated icons, banners, and sacramental hardware. Another interesting building is a funeral home, with early caskets and mortician's equipment. An interpreter answers questions and provides the visitor with a map and audio tape and player, which give many details of the history of the buildings and background on the Ukrainian heritage.

25

THE KLONDIKE TRAIL

Heritage hunting is best when you can travel along historical routes and share vicariously some of the pioneers' insights and experiences. Modern highways do not always follow these earlier routes, but they often intersect or parallel them. You may want to trace the two main routes that the Klondikers took from Edmonton north: the overland route to Fort Assiniboine and the water route, or the Athabasca Landing Trail. Both are accessible by taking Highway 2 north of Edmonton.

School house, Fort Assiniboine Museum (R.L. Hursey)

Building overland trails good enough to accommodate horse-drawn wagons presented a monumental task in the parkland area north of Edmonton. Trees and brush had to be cut, stumps removed, and parts of the trail reinforced by corduroy roads. These trails had to be regularly maintained. It is little wonder that fur traders preferred to use water routes, in spite of the long and arduous portages between lakes and rivers. Overland trails generally followed the high ground on ridges above creeks and lakes and avoided boggy areas as much as possible. Trails also tended to follow established Native pitching trails—originally game trails. Throughout history, humans have tried to follow the paths of least resistance.

One of the earliest overland trails in northern Alberta was the Fort Assiniboine Trail. It was cut by the Hudson's Bay Company (HBC) in 1825 to convey supplies by pack train from Fort Edmonton to Fort Assiniboine on the Athabasca River. The Fort

Assiniboine Trail became a part of the new transportation system that George Simpson, Governor of the HBC, introduced to replace the older Beaver River-Lac La Biche Portage route. From Fort Assiniboine, the fur brigades ascended the Athabasca River by boat to Jasper House and crossed over the mountains through the Yellowhead Pass into New Caledonia (British Columbia).

The Snake Indian Woman

In 1830, a group of 37 Snake (Carrier) Indians were attacked by a party of Assiniboine (Stony) Indians, their traditional enemies. The Snake and Assiniboine Indians were camped on opposite sides of a stream near Jasper House which thereafter became known as Snake Indian River. The Assiniboines invited some of the Snakes to their camp, pretending they wanted to make a permanent peace. The Assiniboine warriors massacred several of the Snake people and took others hostage. Ten Snake Indians escaped and took refuge at Jasper House. Three young Snake women hostages were transported by canoe down the Athabasca River to Fort Assiniboine.

A Métis man named Bellerose witnessed the arrival of a canoe party of Assiniboine warriors and the three young women. Bellerose took pity on the women, who had been tied up in one of the teepees. That night he cut them loose and supplied them with a knife and a fire-bag containing a flint and some punk. After their escape the women split up and travelled in different directions, two of them with the fire bag, the other armed with the knife. The one with the knife survived. The other two disappeared.

The survivor made her way west to the foothills where she lived alone for two winters, living on berries and small animals. An Iroquois hunter discovered her, dressed in rabbit furs, living in an abandoned bear's den in the side of a bank. She fought like a wild animal until he convinced her that he meant her no harm. She returned to Jasper House with him where trader Colin Fraser and his wife took her under their care. The Snake Indian woman remained at Jasper House for two years before going off with some of her own tribe who had come into Jasper House to trade.

Tracks and Traces: The name Athabasca derives from the Cree word *athepescow*, which means a place of reeds and grass.

The old Fort Assiniboine Trail came into heavy use again during the Klondike Gold Rush of 1897-98. In the spring of 1897, Edmonton became the departure point for thousands of gold seekers on their way to the Yukon. There were several routes north from Edmonton, but the two main ones were a water route through Athabasca Landing and down the Athabasca and Mackenzie Rivers by scow or steamboat, and the overland route via the old Fort Assiniboine Trail, through the Swan Hills and into the Peace Country.

After the initial rush of gold seekers through Edmonton, the Edmonton Board of Trade began to lobby the Northwest territorial government to build a wagon road from Edmonton to the Peace Country. In September 1897, the territorial government sent T. W. Chalmers, a road engineer, to lay out the wagon road. Chalmers set out with Dan Noyes and ten horses. They travelled along the old Fort Assiniboine Trail, which he found in rough shape. By July of 1898, the wagon road had been completed as far as Lesser Slave Lake. By then, the Klondike Gold Rush was coming to an end. The wagon trail that Chalmers built became known as the Chalmers, or Klondike, Trail. Years later, settlers would use it to enter the Peace Country.

The Chalmers Trail was not only tough on men and women but it was hell on horses. There were few places for horses to graze between Fort Assiniboine and Lesser Slave Lake. Few Klondikers carried enough feed; and as a result, hundreds of horses died from starvation and abuse along the trail.

Parties of gold seekers were advised to haul feed for their horses when taking the Klondike Trail. 1898. (Provincial Archives of Alberta B5228)

Casualty on the Chalmers Trail

The only human casualty known to have occurred on the Chalmers Trail was the death of a three-month-old girl, who was buried six miles out of Fort Assiniboine. On the picket fence surrounding the grave site was an inscription: "In memory of a little girl buried here by her father in the days of the Klondike Gold Rush of 1898." There was no name to identify the baby or her parents. After a bush fire burned away the fence and marker in 1930, the Ladies Club of Doris erected a cross and painted the original inscription.

The other Klondike Trail out of Edmonton was known as the Water Route. It followed the trail from Edmonton to Athabasca Landing. Natives and fur traders used the trail as early as 1799. In 1875-76, the HBC widened the trail to accommodate ox carts and horse-drawn wagons, which hauled supplies and furs to and from Fort Edmonton. At Athabasca Landing, these supplies were transferred to York boats or scows and transported down the Athabasca River to link up with other steamboats along the Slave/Mackenzie River systems. Furs being shipped from the north to the south were conveyed by river boatmen tracking boats and scows up the Athabasca. When the Klondikers arrived at Athabasca Landing, with their two years' supply of goods, they booked passage on one of the HBC steamboats or built their own scows to float down the river. Many hired experienced Métis and Indian river boatmen to guide them over the Grand Rapids to Fort McMurray.

Transportation by steamboats and freight wagons eventually gave way to more efficient railway transportation in northern Alberta, beginning in the 1910s. The Chalmers and the Athabasca Landing Trails fell into disuse after the Edmonton Dunvegan & British Columbia Railway (ED&BC) was completed from Edmonton to Peace River Crossing and the Alberta & Great Waterways Railway (A&GW) reached Fort McMurray. These two railways would later be amalgamated into the Northern Alberta Railway in 1929 and operated jointly by the Canadian National and Canadian Pacific Railway companies. Many communities, such as Westlock, Barrhead, Thorhild and Boyle, began as railway towns.

You may want to follow in the footsteps of the Klondikers. You won't be able to follow their trail exactly and will have to backtrack a bit. First, you'll want to take the overland to Fort Assiniboine. Drive north from Edmonton on Highway 2 through St. Albert,

Morinville, and north as far as Clyde Corners. Then turn west on Highway 18 to Westlock, your first stop.

Westlock became a railway siding in 1913, when the ED&BC railway reached Mile 52.5 out of Edmonton. The railway company bought 80 acres of land from squatter William Westgate and another 60 acres from William Lockhart. The first four letters of each surname became the name of the town. The **Westlock & District Historical Museum** displays artifacts featuring the pioneer history of the Westlock area.

From Westlock, continue west on Highway 18 to Barrhead, your next stop. Here you will be very near to the original trail to Fort Assiniboine. Barrhead began as the end-of-steel town for the Pembina Valley Railway in 1927, but the Native and white settlement in the surrounding area was established much earlier. South of Barrhead is Lac La Nonne. During the 19th century the Indians and Métis who lived on this lake provided fish for the Hudson's Bay Company (HBC) as well as furs and pasturage for the company's pack horses. In 1870, the HBC established Lac La Nonne House, a trading post for the local Natives.

In 1910, about ten black families from mid-west United States came to Alberta to settle in the Campsie district near Barrhead. There were already a large number of white settlers from Ontario, Great Britain, and the United States in the area. By 1921, about 50 blacks lived in the Campsie district. As in a number of pioneer settlement districts, many of the second and third generations left the farms for other jobs, and these communities eventually disappeared. By 1985, only one black family remained in the area of Campsie. You will want to visit the **Barrhead Centennial Museum** where you can learn more about the settlement and railway history of Barrhead and district.

From Barrhead on Highway 33 to Fort Assiniboine, you will be following very closely the original Fort Assiniboine Trail and the main overland trail of the Klondikers. Fort Assiniboine was founded in the early 1800s by the North West Company as a small outpost on the Athabasca River. Thus it predates the establishment of the overland trail that the Hudson's Bay Company had cut through from Fort Edmonton in 1825. Fort Assiniboine served as a distribution post until the HBC ceased using the Fort Assiniboine Trail in favour of the overland route west from Fort Edmonton, via Lac Ste. Anne to Jasper House. The HBC post at Fort Assiniboine was finally abandoned in 1842.

Some fur trade artifacts from this early post were excavated by archaeologists when the town began construction of the Royal Canadian Legion Hall at today's Fort Assiniboine. Apparently, the hall now occupies the site of the original post. Hand-forged nails, ax heads and a copper billy pot are on display at the **Fort Assiniboine Museum**, next to the Legion Hall. The museum is a replica of an early fur trade post, with pole walls and palisades. The museum's exhibits tell the story of the fur trade fort and the more recent history of settlement and lumbering in the area. You might want to check at the museum for directions where you can hike along part of the old Klondike Trail. Sections of the trail have been identified and restored.

Fort Assiniboine Museum (R.L. Hursey)

From Fort Assiniboine you will need to head east on Highway 33 back to Clyde Corners and then head north on Highway 2 to Athabasca. Highway 2 parallels, but runs several miles west of the original Athabasca Landing Trail, the first leg of the Klondike Water Route. Modern Athabasca, with its population of over 2000, looks very different from the rough little hamlet that grew up around the Athabasca Landing, where HBC's steamboats, the *Graham* and *Athabasca* transported traders, missionaries, gold seekers, and settlers up and down the mighty Athabasca River.

In 1848, the HBC established a distribution centre and trading post on the Athabasca River. Supplies were transported from Fort Edmonton to Athabasca Landing by pack train, then loaded onto scows and York boats. In 1879, Athabasca Landing became one of the most important distribution centres in northern Alberta after the trail was widened for larger freight wagons hauled by horse teams and oxen. By 1883, the HBC was operating steamboats on the Athabasca River, starting with the *Graham,* which plied the river from the Landing to Smith's Landing (Fort Fitzgerald). For over 30 years, Athabasca Landing continued in its important role as entrepôt to the North.

This all changed when the Alberta and Great Waterways railway (A&GW) began laying steel in 1913 towards Lac La Biche and Fort McMurray. This marked the beginning of the end for Athabasca Landing as a distribution centre. After the completion of track to Waterways in 1921, steamboats were no longer needed to ply the stretch of river from Athabasca Landing to Fort McMurray. The A&GW track bypassed Athabasca Landing, and the Canadian National Railway (CNR) line that was to run north from Morinville to Athabasca was never built.

Athabasca continued, however, to exist as a service centre for homesteaders. The "Landing" was dropped from the town's name by 1904. Athabasca has weathered many changes, including a major fire that swept through the town in 1913. A provincial cairn marks the original location of the **Athabasca Landing Trail** on Highway 2 in Athabasca. The **Athabasca Brick School**, built in 1913, houses the Town Archives and is open to the public for viewing and research. Today, the town of Athabasca is the home of Athabasca University, which offers degree programs through correspondence to students all over the province.

Amber Valley

In 1910 and 1911, a large group of American blacks from Oklahoma settled in the Pine Creek district, east of Athabasca. It would later become known as Amber Valley. Many of these settlers were attracted to this isolated area of Alberta to escape the growing racism and discrimination in the United States. The land in Amber Valley was marginal for farming, but it had plenty of water and timber. The land was mostly bush, and few settlers were able to clear more than 30 acres for crops. Although they were experienced farmers, the black settlers were used to growing corn and cotton.

Despite the difficulties of climate and terrain, 75 of the original 95 families cleared enough land to receive their homestead patents. They had a strong sense of community and got along well with their Indian and Métis neighbours. Natives taught the black settlers how to live off the land, and the blacks taught the Natives to play baseball. For many years, Amber Valley's baseball teams were famous throughout Alberta.

MUSEUMS IN THE AREA OF THE KLONDIKE TRAIL

☞ **Barrhead & District Centennial Museum**
Box 4122, Barrhead, AB T7N 1A1
5629 - 49th Street, on sports grounds facing Highway 33
Governing body: Barrhead & District Historical Society
Open Victoria Day to Labour Day weekend * ☎ (403) 674-5203
Admission by donation * *Visiting time:* one half hour

The museum has artifact and archival collections that depict the settlement history of the area. Among the farm machinery is a 1920s binder that is operational.

☞ **Fort Assiniboine Museum**
Box 28, Fort Assiniboine, AB T0G 1A0 * In the Fort next to the Legion Hall.
Governing body: Fort Assiniboine Friendship Club
Open June to mid-September, afternoons daily
☎ (403) 584-3825 * Admission by donation * *Visiting time:* one half hour

---

The museum, housed in a replica of an early fur trade fort, overlooks a magnificent view of the Athabasca River. Its collections include archaeological, fur trade, and settlement artifacts that tell a comprehensive and interesting story of this very old settlement. Metal objects excavated from the site of the original fort are displayed. Of interest is a gold washer used by a local resident in the 1930s and a brick making machine. A one-room log school, used until the 1960s, stands within the palisades. On the blackboard, names of students who attended the school over the years are listed. Ask about directions for hiking part of the old Klondike Trail.

☞ **Lac Ste. Anne Historical Society Pioneer Museum**
at Rochfort Bridge * Box 525, Sangudo, AB T0E 2A0
Rochfort Bridge Trading Post on Highway 43
Governing body: Lac Ste. Anne Historical Society
July and August, daily * ☎ (403) 785-2674/785-3467
Admission fee charged * *Visiting time:* one half hour

The main part of the museum consists of a log building built in 1959. The museum houses a variety of artifacts depicting Native and pioneer history of the area. Historical buildings include a 1911 school, a log cabin, and a blacksmith shop.

Westlock & District Museum
Box 2637, Westlock, AB T0G 2L0 * 10216 - 100th Street
Governing body: Westlock & District Historical Society
Open year round, Friday and Sunday afternoons * ☎ (403) 349-2887
Admission by donation * *Visiting time:* one half hour

The museum interprets the history of Westlock and the surrounding area. Collections include pioneer farming implements and machines, WWI and WWII objects, and domestic items such as the Silknetter Hat collection.

26

THE LAKE COUNTRY

Many years ago, my scout and I camped on the shores of Pinehurst Lake, about 45 kilometres east of Lac La Biche. It was my first experience canoeing on a boreal forest lake, and I will never forget the joy of watching loons and red-necked grebes diving, and an osprey hovering above the lake surface looking for fish. One morning I took a walk along the lake shore and came upon the ruins of an old trapper's cabin and the remains of a sleigh with wooden runners. I wondered what person had built the cabin, and if he, like his cabin, had returned to the earth to become part of the bush again.

This is an ancient land, where there has been human occupation for over 8000 years. The magic of the boreal forest lake country is that it is circumpolar. Many species existing here can also be found in Norway, Siberia, or Hokkaido, Japan. So far, human effort to exploit, control, and modify the boreal forest has not managed to destroy it. Large areas still belong to the trees, muskeg, animals, and a few Natives and Métis who make this area their home.

Our exploration of the Lake Country of Alberta begins at Lac La Biche, one of the earliest settlements in northern Alberta. The name that appears on early maps and fur trade journals is "Red Deers Lake." Scottish explorers had mistaken the wapiti, or North American elk, for the European red deer. French-Canadian voyageurs called the elk "biche" irrespective of its sex. Early fur trade journals also refer to Portage La Biche, one the three gateways for traders to enter the Athabasca country. The other two entry points were by way of Methy Portage and a more northerly height of land east of Lake Athabasca. Portage La Biche came nearest to providing an all-water route from the Atlantic to the Pacific—the elusive Northwest Passage that early explorers like Samuel Hearne, Alexander Mackenzie, and David Thompson sought.

Portage La Biche was primarily used by fur traders travelling to the Lesser Slave Lake district. Between 1810 and 1825, the Columbia brigades en route to posts on the west side of the Canadian Rockies passed through the area and ascended the Athabasca River, over Athabasca Pass into the Columbia river system. David Thompson pioneered this water transportation route in 1810-12. He also established the first trading post at Lac La Biche.

Thompson arrived at Portage La Biche on October 3, 1798, and immediately set his men to building Red Deers Lake House. He spent the winter of 1798-99 trading with the Indians, mostly Cree, Assiniboine, and the occasional Chipewyan. In March 1799, he left Lac La Biche to go to Fort Augustus, where he launched an expedition down the Pembina River to survey the Athabasca country.

Thompson's presence at Lac La Biche did not go unnoticed by HBC's Peter Fidler, who had assisted William Tomison in establishing Buckingham House on the North Saskatchewan near NWC's Fort George. Fidler and James Bird mounted an expedition to Lac La Biche, but they encountered problems in trying to enlist men willing to go on the expedition and in trying to find the elusive trail used by NWC men. Fidler finally arrived at Lac La Biche on September 26, 1799, and established Greenwich House. The establishment of this post marked the beginning of intense rivalry between the two fur trade companies in the Athabasca country, a rivalry that lasted for twenty years.

Fidler, like Thompson, was a trained surveyor, and his detailed survey of Portage La Biche was used by both NWC and HBC traders on their way to and from the west coast. For 25 years, this route provided a vital link in the main highway to the posts along the Columbia River. It was also a link on the north-south route from Fort Edmonton, which provided pemmican to the brigades.

Tracks and traces: Pemmican was a staple for the brigades, who did not have time to hunt during their rush to and from Hudson's Bay or Montreal. Pemmican is a concentrated food made from dried buffalo or moose meat pounded into a powder, mixed with fat and sewn into rawhide bags. Dried berries were sometimes added for flavour. One pound of pemmican equaled about five pounds of fresh meat. Native women, essential to the operation of the fur trade, usually made the pemmican.

Very little documentation about Red Deers Lake House or Greenwich between 1800 and 1812 exists. It appears that fire destroyed both posts. The fire swept through the area a few years before Thompson returned to Lac La Biche following his explorations in 1812 of the Columbia district. In his journal, he made no mention of either posts other than that Dejarlais was living in two tents north of the "old house."

Portage La Biche continued to provide a vital link in the transportation route to the Pacific. As the fight to control the Athabasca country escalated between the two companies, HBC sent John Lee Lewis in 1817 to establish another post, Red Deers House II. When the companies finally amalgamated in 1821, this post was abandoned. However, the brigades continued using the portage until

Governor George Simpson changed the transportation route in 1825, instituting the York boat in place of the north canoe and having a horse trail made from Fort Edmonton to Fort Assiniboine on the Athabasca River.

Many freemen, no longer under contract with the companies, chose to settle on the shores of Lac La Biche, which abounded in whitefish, pike, and pickerel. The earliest were the Cardinals and Dejarlais, two names still common today in the area. These freemen increasingly cut into HBC's yearly profits, and the company decided to establish another post in 1853. Lac La Biche Post was located where the marina now stands. Peter C. Pambrun was placed in charge from 1853 to 1855. By the time the post was established, there were already Methodist and Roman Catholic missionaries on the lake.

In 1852, Father Lacombe and Alexis Cardinal travelled on horseback to visit the 15 Métis families living in Lac La Biche. Father René Remas arrived in the fall of 1853 to serve the Métis colony, but he was not adequately prepared to face the harsh winter. When Father Lacombe visited him shortly after, he found Remas almost starving and took him back to Lac Ste. Anne for the winter. In 1855, when Father Remas left Lac La Biche to take over the mission at Lac Ste. Anne, Fathers. Tissot and Maisonneuve replaced him. Deciding the mission was too close to Rev. Henry Steinhaur's Methodist mission, the two priests relocated on the south shore at its present location. Called the Notre Dame des Victoires, the mission became an Episcopal residence and an entrepôt for missionaries and supplies to Roman Catholic missions further north.

Alexis Cardinal, Métis Missionary (c1827 - 82)

Alexis Cardinal was born in Lac La Biche to Rose Grise and Joseph Cardinal, both devout Catholics. In 1852, Father Bourassa put Father Lacombe in touch with Alexis, who agreed to guide Lacombe into various Indian camps. Alexis probably suggested that Lacombe go to Lac La Biche. It was the beginning of many trips that the two would make together. Alexis assisted Fathers Lacombe and Remas, an Oblate from France, in learning the Cree language.

Over the next twenty years, Alexis and Father Lacombe travelled throughout today's Alberta, visiting the camps of the Plains Cree and Blackfoot, travelling overland to Jasper House to visit the Iroquois. They headed into the Peace Country by way of Swan Hills trail from Fort Assiniboine to Lesser Slave Lake. Together they travelled in all seasons, facing frost bite, starvation, illness, and danger of attack, during the continual battles between the Cree and Blackfoot over disputed territory. On one trip in the winter of 1865, they came upon three Blackfoot Indians. They had been killed by the Cree, who had scalped them and hung their hands and feet on nearby trees. On another trip, Father Lacombe received word in St. Albert that the Blackfoot had been stricken by scarlet fever. Lacombe and Alexis travelled by dog team to the Blackfoot camp and witnessed the course of this terrible disease.

During his later years, Alexis began to think of himself as a missionary, and he wore a black cassock. Many times he pleaded with Father Lacombe to allow him to join the Oblates as a brother, but he was refused. Perhaps Father Lacombe worried that Alexis' growing eccentricities made him unsuitable.

When Father Lacombe began to be called away from the prairies to Winnipeg and Quebec, Alexis was left behind. In 1872, Alexis went alone to start a mission to the Blackfoot. He built a shack on the Elbow River, about 20 miles west of Calgary, calling the mission Our Lady of Peace, the first Roman Catholic mission in the Calgary area.

Father Lacombe's increasing absences began to affect Alexis' mental stability. After the priest had been in Winnipeg for almost five years, Alexis decided to seek his mentor and went wandering the prairies, stopping at Indian camps and preaching. Once the fathers at St. Albert brought him back, but he soon left again to seek his divine mission. On his final mission, Alexis left for Cold Lake to try to find his former master and companion, and somewhere along the cart trail he died alone.

Lac La Biche Mission today. (R.A. Hursey)

In 1862, a group of Grey Nuns arrived to establish a school at the Lac La Biche Mission. By 1871, the mission had established the first sawmill in Alberta; and in 1877, Father E. Grouard brought the first printing press in Alberta to the Mission, where he printed books in Dene, Cree, and French.

Lac La Biche Mission is located about 10 kilometres northwest of the town. It is now a national historic site. This lovely restored mission should not be missed. The view of the lake from the point is alone worth the trip.

Lac La Biche had declined in importance as steamships on the Athabasca River replaced the traditional trade routes, until the arrival of the Alberta and Great Waterways Railway in 1916 revitalized the town. J. D. McArthur, builder of the railway line, had plans for Lac La Biche to become a resort area. Lac La Biche Inn, constructed of frame and fieldstone, overlooked the lake. Tourists from Edmonton began to arrive by train in early summer of 1916. During its second week, a sudden storm capsized a boat and four visitors drowned. Because of the tragedy and preoccupation with the war, the Inn fell on hard times and closed in 1918.

The Fire of 1919

After the Lac La Biche Inn closed, McArthur installed the Watsons, the station agent's family, as caretakers. They lived in some of the rooms on the bottom floor. For years Mrs. Christina Watson took care of the Inn and played host to railroaders, who often stayed there. In 1919, a forest fire devastated much of the village, destroying homes and businesses as well as telegraph and phone lines. No lives were lost. Most of the residents waded into the lake to escape the flames. The Inn was spared. When the flames died down, some 300 people had no homes to return to. Mrs. Watson opened the Inn to the homeless and organized donations of food and clothing for them. Within a few days a special train brought in Red Cross supplies, but it was Christina people remembered with fondness for her rescue efforts.

The Les Filles de Jesus (Daughters of Jesus), who had replaced the Grey Nuns in 1905, purchased the Lac La Biche Inn in 1937 and converted it into a hospital. St. Catherine's Hospital served the town for many years until a new hospital was built in the 1960s. In 1988, just when the grand Lac La Biche Inn was to be declared a provincial historic site, it caught fire and burned to the ground.

Today Lac La Biche is home to many ethnic groups. One is the relatively large Lebanese community. In 1905, two Lebanese immigrants arrived as peddlers and fur traders. They formed the nucleus of a growing Lebanese business community. After World War II, many others came. By the 1960s, the Lebanese community made up ten percent of Lac La Biche population and had established its own mosque.

From Lac La Biche head southeast on Highway 55, which parallels the Beaver River, the old fur trade water route to Cold Lake. The area played an important role in the fur trade and now serves as an important tourist centre. During the Second World War, Cold Lake became one of the British Commonwealth Air Training Program bases. Today it remains an important Canadian Forces air base for training fighter pilots, who fly routinely over the Cold Lake Air Weapons Range, a huge area that spans north-eastern Alberta and Saskatchewan. At Cold Lake stands the restored Clark's General Store, built in 1930. It is now a restaurant overlooking the marina and this beautiful lake. The communities of Grande Centre, Cold Lake and Medley formed the **Tri-Town Museum** and located it at Grande Centre. Its exhibits feature the aboriginals, local settlement, aviation, and oil and gas history of the region.

From Cold Lake we will head south on Highway 55 to Beaver Crossing and west on Highway 28 to our next stop, Bonnyville.

In 1789, Angus Shaw, a fur trader with the North West Company, ascended the Beaver River from Lac Ile-a-Crosse to Moose Lake, where he built Shaw's House, or Fort Lac de L'Orignal. For three years Shaw trapped and traded with the Natives around Moose Lake before moving on to the North Saskatchewan River, where, in 1792, he established Fort George, near today's Elk Point. Fort Lac de L'Orignal remained a minor post where emergency supplies were kept for fur traders using the Beaver River route to the Athabasca country. Today you can see some of the old fort's remains on the northwest end of Moose Lake, west of Bonnyville on SR 660. In 1910, Father Bonny established the first Roman Catholic Church near Moose Lake. The community is named in his honor.

At Bonnyville be sure to visit the **Bonnyville Historical Museum**, located in a reproduction of a fur trade fort. The impressive seven-meter-high wood statue of Angus Shaw, carved by Herman Poulin of St. Paul, dominates the spacious grounds in front of the museum. Among the attractions featured at Bonnyville Museum are the large collection of restored farm machinery and a unique collection of miniature figures made of paper mache and leather by the late Clementine Poitras.

While in the area, enjoy the **Bonnyville Wetlands**, where walking trails and viewing stands around Jesse Lake provide many opportunities to observe and photograph waterfowl and other wildlife. Over 150 bird species have been observed and recorded here.

From Bonnyville travel south on Highway 41 to our next stop— Elk Point. Here you will see another large wooden statue erected in 1992 to commemorate the 200th anniversary of Peter Fidler, famous explorer-surveyor for the Hudson's Bay Company and co-founder of Buckingham House on the North Saskatchewan River. Sculptor Herman Poulin used the sketches of Billie Milholland to carve the nine-meter-high statue.

Peter Fidler—Hudson's Bay Company Surveyor (1769 - 1822)

In 1787, at 18 years of age, Peter Fidler came from England to join the Hudson's Bay Company. In 1792, he helped William Tomison establish Buckingham House after the NWC built nearby Fort George. The same year, Fidler set out in November with some Peigans to explore the unmapped prairies. Although he was not the first white person to see the Rocky Mountains, he was the first to take compass bearings on them. On his return trip to Buckingham House in 1793, he discovered coal along the banks of the Red Deer River, the first recorded sighting in the Canadian West. In 1802, the

HBC sent Peter Fidler to the Athabasca-Peace country, where he established Nottingham House on Lake Athabasca and Mansfield House on the Peace River.

Peter Fidler learned surveying from Philip Turnor, teacher of David Thompson, Fidler's rival. These two adventurers had Native wives and mixed blood families who undoubtedly helped them in their explorations, but they are seldom mentioned. Like Thompson, Fidler left a legacy of accurately drawn maps and many observations of the area we now know as Alberta.

Thirteen miles southeast of Elk Point on SR 646 lies the original site of the two rival posts, NWC's Fort George and HBC's Buckingham House. They were the first posts built overlooking the beautiful North Saskatchewan River. They operated from 1792 to 1800, traded in this fur-rich area, and supplied the voyageurs with pemmican for their return trips to Montreal and Hudson's Bay.

Nothing remains today of the forts except the outlines of their buildings. The Provincial Museum of Alberta excavated these sites in the 1960s. In 1976 the ground on which the fur trade posts stood was designated a Provincial Historic Site.

Photograph of Poulin's statue of Peter Fidler (R.A. Hursey)

Fort George-Buckingham House Provincial Historic Site provides an interpretive centre operated by Historic Sites & Archives Services. Staffed by local interpreters, the service provides programs and group tours of the site. From the interpretive centre, you can take a self-guided tour along the system of pathways marked with informative signage. The magnificent view of the river alone is worth the walk.

For a scenic and historic side trip, you may want to continue east on SR 646 and then turn north on SR 897 to a cairn marking the site of the April 2, 1885, Frog Lake massacre that occurred during the Riel Rebellion. Nine white men were killed and two women taken prisoner by Big Bear's band of Plains Cree.

Returning to Elk Point head north again on Highway 41 and west on Highway 28 to our next stop—the town of St. Paul. This prosperous town has its eyes on the future and is prepared for any event of cosmic proportions. For Alberta's 75th anniversary, St. Paul built a landing pad for UFO's. When the little green men from outer space decide to land on earth, they will find St. Paul prepared to give them a hearty welcome. The landing pad has been used to host many events, including Mother Teresa's visit in 1982.

St. Paul originated as a Roman Catholic mission to the Métis. Father Albert Lacombe had been deeply concerned about the Métis, following the Riel Rebellion. The Métis had played a vital role in the fur trade, when western Canada was Rupert's Land, but their lifestyle changed forever when hordes of settlers came in the wake of the construction of the Canadian Pacific Railway. They had lost the battle for their own government, first in the Red River resistance of 1869-70 and again in 1885. Unlike the Plains Indians, whose land claims were settled by treaties and assigned reserves, the Métis received scrip. Not fully understanding the significance of scrip, most sold their land for a fraction of its value to unscrupulous traders and land speculators.

Tracks and Traces: Scrip was a coupon printed and issued by the Dominion Department of the Interior. It entitled the bearer to a parcel of Dominion lands (usually 80, 160 or 240 acres) or money instead of land, based on a value of one dollar per acre.

Father Lacombe dreamed of establishing an agricultural colony, where Métis could farm on land that could not be sold. The land remained in control of the Church. In 1896, Father Therien was sent to establish the St. Paul des Métis on four townships near today's Saddle Lake Reserve. Funding to continue its operation was always a problem, and Father Lacombe frequently had to go on begging trips to Quebec and the eastern United States for the mission's support. St. Paul des Métis Mission got off to a bad start when it was too late to put in a crop the first year, and the Métis had to support themselves with fishing and hunting.

The mission stumbled along for years on the brink of financial ruin. Many Métis, who were inexperienced and therefore disillusioned with full-time farming, began to leave the colony and take up their old lifestyle of fishing, hunting, and trapping. Perhaps the final blow came in 1905, when the Assumption Sisters' newly constructed boarding school burnt to the ground, and one of the young boarders died in the fire. In 1909, the mission closed and its land was opened for homesteading. The Church encouraged French-Canadian settlers from Quebec and New England as well as immigrants from France to establish homesteads.

St.-Paul-des-Métis became the centre of a large French-speaking community that served the needs of the new settlers. Although the community became incorporated into a village in 1912, the name was not changed to St. Paul until December 15, 1936, when it became a town.

To learn more about the history of St. Paul des Métis and the town of St. Paul, you will want to visit the **Musée Historique de St. Paul Historical Museum** located in the cultural centre beside the church on main street. This small museum is completely bilingual.

From St. Paul we head west on Highway 28 to St. Brides and south on Highway 36 for a couple of kilometres, to the turnoff on SR 652 to Saddle Lake Indian Reserve, our next stop. The Cree name *unechekeskwapewin* means "dark objects sitting on the lake." A Cree legend tells about a time when they could find no buffalo and were forced to make holes in the ice to fish. The crouching figures of fishermen on the ice may have resembled saddles from a distance.

The **Saddle Lake Museum** has many mounted specimens that portray the natural history of the area. It is one of the oldest native history museums in Alberta. Years ago when I visited this museum, I was impressed with its role in the cultural renewal of the community. The Saddle Lake Museum opens on weekdays, but it is best to call ahead to arrange a tour.

If you are heading south from Saddle Lake on Highway 36, you will come to the North Saskatchewan River. On the north bank, just below today's Brosseau, is the historic site of **St. Paul des Cris**, founded in 1866. Father Lacombe could not have picked a more picturesque location to establish his mission to serve the Cree and teach them farming. Like St. Paul des Métis mission, this was not one of Father Lacombe's lasting successes. The competition from the Methodists at Victoria Settlement upstream and the smallpox epidemic of 1870 had much to do with the decision to close the mission in 1874.

MUSEUMS IN THE LAKE COUNTRY

☞ **Bonnyville Historical Museum**
Box 6995, Bonnyville, AB T9N 2H4 * 54th Avenue and Highway 28
Governing body: Bonnyville & District Historical Society
Open May 1 to Labour Day, daily * ☎ (403) 826-4925
Admission by donation * *Visiting time:* one half hour

This community history museum is located in a reproduction of a fur trade post on spacious grounds that include a growing historical village, mostly reproductions of earlier buildings. The seven-meter high statue of Angus Shaw is one of many interesting objects

the museum displays. It maintains a large private collection of restored farm machinery. There is also a unique folk art collection of
leather and paper mache miniatures by the late Clementine Poitras.
The artist created these unique tiny figurines, which reflect an enchanting and whimsical imagination, 50 to 100 years ago.

☞ **Fort George-Buckingham House Provincial Historic Site**
General Delivery, Elk Point, AB T0A 1A0
13 kilometers southeast of Elk Point off SR 645
Governing body: Alberta Community Development,
Historic Sites & Archives Service
Open May 15 to Labour Day, daily * ☎ (403) 724-2003
Admission fee charged * *Visiting time:* one hour

🏆🏆🏆 🚌 ♿ ⛺ ⚲ 🍴

This interpretive centre and archaeological site portrays the history of the NWC's Fort George and HBC's Buckingham House
from 1792 to 1800. The facility reminds one of a WWII concrete
bunker. An introductory video is very informative, as is the theme
of presenting the history of the two forts from the viewpoint of native women. The staff are friendly and knowledgeable. My scout
and I felt disappointed, however, with the design elements in the
exhibits, particularly the use of abstract figures where representative
figures or photo cutouts might have been more effective. Overall,
the centre is not up to the usual standards one expects to find at
provincial historic sites operated by the Alberta government. The
trails leading to the site have good signage, and the view overlooking the North Saskatchewan River is breathtaking. Although nothing
remains of the original buildings, the foundations of Fort George
have been defined. The site of Buckingham House site, unfortunately, has been destroyed by local farming activity.

☞ **Tri-Town Museum** at Grand Centre
Box 11, Grande Centre, AB T0A 1T0
Governing body: Tri-Town Museum Society
Open year round: Saturday and Sunday afternoons * ☎ (403) 594-3480
Admission by donation * *Visiting time:* one half hour

🏆 🚌 ⛺ 🍴 ⛺ 🍽 ━

The Tri-Town Museum, a fairly new facility, displays aboriginal
life, local settlement, aviation history and the development of the oil
and gas industry. As this museum is still in its developmental stage,
it is best to check locally for any changes in its hours of operation.

☞ **Lac La Biche Mission Historic Site**
Box 1622, Lac La Biche, AB T0A 2C0
11 kilometers northwest of Lac La Biche
Governing body: Lac La Biche Mission Historical Society
Open summer months, daily * ☎ (403) 623-3274
Admission by donation * *Visiting time:* one hour

Lac La Biche Mission is a national historic site. Many of the buildings have been restored, including the convent, the church, and rectory. The present church was built after a tornado destroyed a larger frame church in the 1920s. This fascinating mission is located on a beautiful site, on a point overlooking the clear blue waters of Lac La Biche. The view alone is worth the visit.

☞ **Saddle Lake Cultural Museum**
Box 102, Saddle Lake, AB T0A 3T0 * Tribal centre, Saddle Lake.
Governing body: Saddle Lake Band
Open year-round; weekdays * ☎ (403) 726-3829
Admission by donation * *Visiting time:* one half hour

This museum is part of the ongoing cultural education program. Exhibits include mounted specimens of birds and mammals and Cree artifacts including beadwork, feather headdresses, paintings and historical photographs. The museum offers workshops and seminars to the Cree people. It is best to call ahead of time to arrange a tour.

☞ **Musée Historique de St. Paul Historical Museum**
Box 1925, St. Paul, AB T0A 3A0 * 4537 - 50th Avenue
Governing body: ACFA regionale de St. Paul
Open May to August, weekdays * ☎ (403) 645-3275
Admission by donation * *Visiting time:* one half hour

This community history museum is located in the Centre cultural building, which is operated by the French Association of Alberta (ACFA). Collections include Métis, Cree, and pioneer artifacts of the French-speaking settlers who homesteaded around St. Paul and St. Vincent. The museum's exhibits portray the history of St. Paul des Métis and the opening of the land for settlement. Labels are in French and English.

27

FORT CHIPEWYAN—FORT MCMURRAY

It is ironic that what was the hub of the fur trade in western Canada during the late 18th and much of the 19th centuries is now one of the most isolated communities in the province. To get to "Fort Chip" by automobile, you have to wait until the winter road is in place from Ft. McMurray or Ft. Smith, and its access varies from year to year depending upon the weather. Usually the road is in from mid-December until seasonal closure. The rest of the year, you can travel by airplane or chartered boat.

Fort Chipewyan, 1901 (Provincial Archives of Alberta B 2967)

Fort Chipewyan, established on the south shore of Lake Athabasca, at Old Fort Point in 1788 by the North West Company (NWC), was the earliest European-Canadian settlement in today's Alberta. The post was later relocated on the north shore at its present location. Fort Chipewyan sits upon the westernmost tip of the Canadian Shield. It is bordered on the west by Wood Buffalo National Park, with its confusion of rivers and channels that enter the vast Peace-Athabasca delta, one of the largest freshwater deltas in the world. Wood Buffalo Park is a UNESCO World Heritage site and home of the largest free-roaming bison herd in the world. The delta, with its meandering rivers and marshes, is a vital habitat for migratory birds like the whooping crane, sandhill crane, tundra swan, and peregrine falcon. Wolves, wood bison, woodland caribou, moose, beaver, and other fur bearing mammals also make this area a prime wildlife viewing area.

Before the construction of the Bennett Dam on the Peace River, the rivers that drained the delta used to change directions. Most of the year the Peace and Athabasca Rivers would flow north, joining the waters of the Slave River and the Mackenzie River. In the spring, however, this direction was reversed when the Peace, swollen with melted snow from the Rocky Mountains, overflowed its banks, causing waters to flow south into the rivers and flow into the Delta. When spring floods subsided, the rivers that normally drained Lake Athabaska and the delta would resume their northerly flow. This yearly inundation enriched the delta with fresh silt to generate new plant growth and in turn provide a rich habitat for its wildlife that has attracted Natives for thousands of years.

Wood Buffalo National Park is a UNESCO World Heritage Site and the home of the largest free-roaming bison herd in the world. The park provides unique opportunities to explore the biologically rich heritage of the Peace-Athabasca Delta. Founded in 1922 to protect the last remaining herds of wood bison, the park provides two visitor centres, one at Fort Smith and the other at Fort Chipewyan— departure points for exploring the 116,541 kilometre^2 park, the largest in Canada.

Lake Athabasca and the Peace-Athabasca Delta region have been home to Native peoples long before the first white man, Peter Pond, arrived in 1778 to establish the first fur trade post in northern Alberta. Archaeological evidence shows that Natives have frequented this region for over 8000 years. In the early 1700s, the area was inhabited by Chipewyans, who had migrated from the north, and Woodland Cree, who came from the east. These tribes had driven out the original inhabitants, the Slavey and perhaps the Beaver. Chipewyan and Cree served as middlemen to the Hudson's Bay Company and traded with tribes along the Mackenzie River. Each summer these enterprising Natives would make the long, hazardous trip to Fort Churchill on the Hudson's Bay to trade their furs.

Because the Hudson's Bay Company (HBC) had this pipeline to the Athabasca region, it had not attempted to establish a post until a group of Montreal "pedlars" began intercepting trade along this route by building posts on the lower Saskatchewan and at Lake Isle-à-la-Crosse. The independent traders were competitors at first; they were a hardy breed of highland Scots and Canadian voyageurs who were used to the rigors of a northern climate. In 1788 they came together to form the North West Company (NWC). Fort Chipewyan became their most important outpost west of the Great Lakes.

Peter Pond (1740 - 1807)

Peter Pond was born at Milford, Connecticut, in 1740. He spent several years trading around Detroit before venturing into the Canadian frontier around 1775. In 1778, the Montreal pedlars had decided to extend their trading efforts into the heart of the Athabasca region. Pond was the first white man to cross the Methy Portage and descend the Clearwater and the Athabasca Rivers.

Pond established the first trading post in today's Alberta, about 40 miles below Lake Athabasca. The exact location is unknown. He was respected as a capable, intelligent and aggressive trader, but his irascible temper implicated him in the deaths of two of his competitors. He had a keen sense of geography and drew a creditable map of western Canada in 1785. In 1787, the NWC sent Alexander Mackenzie to supervise Pond. Pond's dream of finding a freshwater route between the Athabasca and the Pacific triggered the imagination of Mackenzie, who went on to be the first white person to cross the entire continent north of Mexico. In 1788, Pond left the Athabasca for good and returned to Montreal. He sold his interest in the NWC and settled down at the place of his birth in Milford, Connecticut, where he died in poverty in 1807.

Alexander Mackenzie, having replaced Pond in the Athabasca area, sent his cousin, Roderick Mackenzie, to establish a post in a more convenient location on the south shore of Lake Athabasca. Pond's post was subsequently abandoned. The first Fort Chipewyan, known today as Old Fort Point, was established in 1788. In 1803, the NWC relocated their post to the rocky, barren north shore to be in closer proximity to where the company could trade with the Chipewyans, who occupied the lands along the Slave River.

In 1789, Alexander Mackenzie used Fort Chipewyan to launch his historic trip to the Arctic Ocean by way of the river that bears his name. Three years later he and his party of voyageurs left Fort Chipewyan, travelling up the Peace River and across the Rocky Mountains to the Pacific Ocean. Mackenzie and his party were the first to cross the entire continent north of Mexico. Later explorers, like Sir John Franklin, George Back and John Richardson also used Fort Chipewyan as a jumping off point for Arctic exploration.

In 1802, Peter Fidler started Nottingham House for the HBC and located it on English Island, across the channel from Fort Chipewyan. He maintained the post until eventually the powerful NWC drove him out. Not until 1815 did the HBC try again to establish a post, this time under the leadership of John Clarke, who established Fort Wedderburn on Coal (Potato) Island. The competition between the NWC and HBC finally became too counterproductive and violent, and they amalgamated in 1821 under the Hudson's Bay Company name. George Simpson, in charge of Fort Wedderburn, proved himself so capable of managing this difficult post that the company promoted him to Governor-in-Chief of all the HBC operations in North America. He held the position for over 40 years.

Tracks and Traces: A "made beaver" was a dressed skin of an adult beaver. It was used by the fur trade as a medium of exchange. For example, in the late 1770s at Fort des Prairies, a gun was worth 20 made beaver; a twist of tobacco, one made beaver, etc.

Fort Chipewyan remained exclusively a fur trade fort until the arrival of Oblate priest, Father Alexander Taché, in 1847, to establish a mission to the Chipewyan and Cree Indians. In the 1860s the Sisters of Charity of Montreal (Grey Nuns) arrived to serve the community. When the Dominion Government purchased Rupert's Land from the HBC in 1870, Fort Chipewyan became a centre for many government officials who worked in the North. Colin Fraser Jr. (whose father was George Simpson's famous piper) and other independent traders were attracted to the fur-rich area. In 1897, the NWMP sent Inspector Jarvis there when Klondikers began to pass through Fort Chipewyan on their way to the gold fields.

In 1899, the Canadian government decided to settle land claims, and Chipewyans and Crees came to Fort Chipewyan to sign Treaty No. 8. The Métis received "scrip" entitling them to 160 acres of land or $160.

Today, Chipewyans, Crees and Métis continue to make their home in Fort Chipewyan. Métis are the descendants of the early Scots and French Canadian fur traders and Native women who were important to Fort Chipewyan's history. Many continue to carry on the hunting, trapping, fishing, and trading activities that brought their ancestors together over 200 years ago.

Colin Fraser, with a season of furs. c1900 (Provincial Archives of
Alberta B10,018)

The **Fort Chipewyan Bicentennial Museum** offers the
visitor opportunities to learn more about Fort Chipewyan, its history, and what the community is like today. It is a full-size reproduction of the Hudson's Bay Company "Stores" building, where
trading took place. It occupies the site of the original fort, now an
archaeological and National Historic Site. No original buildings remain of the former post. The museum has a model of the fort as it
stood in the late 1800s, as well as Native and historical displays that
feature early exploration and fur trade.

Fort McMurray lies about 225 air kilometres south of Fort
Chipewyan at the junction of the Athabasca and Clearwater rivers.
Although the fur brigades passed through this area from Methy
Portage on their way to Fort Chipewyan, no permanent post was
established there until 1870. In that year, the HBC sent Henry John
Moberly to establish a new post. He named it after the Chief Factor
of Fort Chipewyan, William McMurray. Fort McMurray started as a
few log buildings, and indeed it almost ceased to exist when the
company built Fort McKay about 80.5 kilometres downstream. Not
until the HBC launched its first sternwheeler, the *Graham,* in 1884,
did Fort McMurray begin to come into its own. The *Graham* plied
the waters between Fort McMurray and Fort Fitzgerald, where furs

and supplies were taken over the 26 kilometres portage to Fort Smith. At Fort Smith, the HBC built another steamboat, the *Wrigley,* in 1885 to take passengers to the mouth of the Mackenzie River.

Around 1900, the HBC transferred its trading operations to Fort McKay. Fort McMurray remained a transportation terminus. At this time, independent traders had begun to establish posts in the area. One of these traders, William Gordon, established his headquarters at Fort McMurray in 1905 and ran a stopping house. His sister, Christine, became Fort McMurray's first white woman resident. She was there when the first group of Klondikers came down the Athabasca on their way to the Yukon in 1897. She was still there to see the first Alberta & Great Waterways train reach the end of steel south of McMurray in March of 1921. Christina Gordon was still around when Wop May, Cy Becker, and Punch Dickins made McMurray their headquarters for bush flying in the north in 1929. She probably rode the NAR's "Muskeg Mixed," a combined passenger and freight train that plied its way from Edmonton to Fort McMurray once a week. This famous train never ran on schedule and travelled perhaps the worst track in the province, but it served as a life line for many years to Indians, trappers, and settlers along its route and to the residents of Fort McMurray.

The Railway That Felled a Government"

The railway line between Edmonton and Fort McMurray has always had its problems and controversies. Its strongest promoter was James Kennedy Cornwall, known as "Peace River Jim." Cornwall had been a trapper, mail carrier, fur trader, and riverman who wanted the railroad to link with his new steamboat line. He obtained a charter from the Dominion government but was unable to acquire financing for the project, and he sold his option. Eventually a U.S.-financed syndicate, the Athabasca Railway Company, entered into negotiations with the fledgling Alberta government, who pushed through the Railway Act on the last day of the legislative session. The Act guaranteed the railway's bonds to $20,000 per mile and transferred control of railways from the minister of public works to the premier.

On October 7, 1909, the Alberta & Great Waterways railway was formed; and William Clarke, an American from Kansas, took charge of the project. Mismanagement and some shady financing soon got the company off to a bad start. When the legislature met again in February 1910, there was a split in the Liberal party over the

A&GW and strong opposition from the Conservative party, led by R.B. Bennett. The debate lasted a whole week. Bennett hinted that Clarke was engaged in pocketing some missing funds. Premier Rutherford appointed a royal commission to investigate the A&GW transactions. When the legislature reconvened in May, Rutherford announced his resignation. The Hon. Arthur Lewis Sifton succeeded him and repealed the Railway Act.

In the fall of 1913, railway builder J.D. McArthur took over the A&GW. The line went through extremely difficult terrain—sand hills, muskeg, and heavy forest. In February 1915, the line was completed as far as Lac La Biche, and by the following year the end of steel was within 29 kilometres of Fort McMurray. It took seven more years to complete the line to Old Waterways.

Development of the Athabasca tar sands finally put Fort McMurray on the international map. The existence of the oil sands had been known since the early 1700s, when a Cree trader called Captain Swan or Waupisoo brought a sample to York Factory. Natives and early traders used the oil sands to waterproof their birch bark canoes. In 1911, "Peace River Jim" Cornwall sent a scow-load of oil sands up the river to Athabasca Landing and overland to Edmonton to pave part of a road in Jasper. But the mystery of unlocking the oil from the sands would have to wait for several years.

In the 1920s, Karl Clark and Sidney Blair of the Alberta Research Council began experiments to find a way of extracting the bitumen from the oil sands. They came up with an experimental hot water extraction process. This led to the first commercial attempts at development of the oil sands, beginning in the 1930s. Max Ball, an American engineer, formed Abasand Oils and was producing synthetic crude by the beginning of World War II. The federal government took over the operation of this plant in 1943, but the plant burned down a few years later. In 1946, the provincial government built another plant at Bitumount and carried on experiments until 1950. Then in 1967, Sun Oil Company built the Great Canadian Oil Sands (GCOS) plant and began the first large-scale development of the oil sands. In the 1970s, Syncrude Canada Ltd., a company formed by heavy government and oil company investments, began building a plant north of Fort McMurray. It opened in 1978. During these boom years, Fort McMurray grew from a sleepy town of about 900 people in 1951 to a city of 33,700 by 1989, the average age being around 25.

Fort McMurray has two excellent museums. **Fort McMurray Heritage Park** features not only historical buildings, like Wop and Violet May's former home on Franklin Avenue, but Northern Transportation Company's yarding boat, *Radium Scout,* and some NAR rolling stock. The **Fort McMurray Oil Sands Interpretive Centre** depicts the fascinating history of tar sands development through many interactive displays and interpretive programs. This centre has the largest land-based heritage artifact in Canada—a bucketwheel Excavator 1202, used by Suncor to mine the Athabasca oil sands. Weighing 850 tons, it stands six storeys high.

Radium Scout riverboat at Fort McMurray Heritage Park (R.L. Hursey)

Tracks and Traces: The first official air mail to the North occurred on December 10, 1929. Pilots Cy Becker, I. Glen-Roberts, and Wop May made this historic 1,676-mile route, flying five tons of mail in a Lockheed Vega and two Bellancas. Mail travelled by train from Edmonton to Waterways-Fort McMurray. From there it was airlifted to 13 communities in the North, including Fort Chipewyan, Fort Fitzgerald, Fort Smith, Fort Resolution, Hay River, Fort Providence, Fort Simpson, Wrigley, Fort Norman, Fort Good Hope, Arctic Red River, Fort McPherson, and Aklavik.

MUSEUMS IN THE FORT CHIPEWYAN AND FORT MCMURRAY AREA

☞ **Fort Chipewyan Bicentennial Museum**
Box 203, Fort Chipewyan, AB T0P 1B0
Governing body: Fort Chipewyan Historical Society
Open year round, Monday to Friday; weekends by appointment
☎ (403) 697-3844 * Admission by donation * *Visiting time:* one half hour
🍷🍷🚗 👫 🎁 🎋 ⛏

The Fort Chipewyan Bicentennial Museum is located in a full-sized reproduction of the Hudson's Bay Company "Stores" building. It features exhibits depicting Fort Chipewyan's key role as a fur trade post. Exhibits and programs also feature traditional and contemporary lifestyles of northern communities, blending hunting, trapping and fishing with other occupations. The museum serves as a local visitor centre and houses the community archives and a reference and research library, focusing on regional Native and fur trade history.

☞ **Wood Buffalo National Park Visitor Centre**
Box 38, Fort Chipewyan, AB T0P 1B0 * Mackenzie Avenue, Fort Chipewyan
Governing body: Parks Canada
Open year round, Monday to Friday * ☎ (403) 697-3662
🍷🍷🚗 ♿ 🎋 ⛏

This reception centre features an exhibit on the park south of the Peace River, videos and park information on recreation, visitor facilities and guided tours of the area.

☞ **Fort McMurray Oil Sands Interpretive Centre**
515 Mackenzie Boulevard, Fort McMurray, AB T9H 4X3
Governing body: Historic Sites and Archives Service, Alberta Community Development * Open year round, daily
☎ (403) 743-7167 * Admission fee charged * *Visiting time:* one hour
🍷🍷🍷🚗 ♿ 👫 🎁 👕 🍽 ⎯

The Oil Sands Interpretive has exhibits and programs that feature the history and technology of the Athabasca oil sands industry. The new film presentation provides a good introduction to the oil sands and is shown on high definition video production using laser disc technology. One of the highlights of the centre is the Industrial Equipment Garden, with large industrial equipment used in the mining and extraction processes. Featured is Canada's largest land-based artifact, a giant bucketwheel excavator. The centre provides information about local and provincial historic sites, tours and fact sheets on the oil sands.

☞ **Fort McMurray Heritage Park**
One Tolen Drive, Fort McMurray, AB T9H 1G7
Governing body: Fort McMurray Historical Society
Open mid-May to Labour Day, daily * ☎ (403) 791-7575
Admission by donation * *Visiting time:* one hour
♟♟🚗 ♿ ⛲ 🎁 ⛾ 🍴 ⎯

The Heritage Park is a living history museum and historical village with original buildings and artifacts that play an important part in Fort McMurray's fur trade, river, railway and air transportation, salt mining and oil sands history. Collections include the first Roman Catholic Church, a log Anglican Church, Wop May's former residence, the riverboat *Radium Scout,* and NAR train cars and caboose.

☞ **Northern Life Museum** at Fort Smith
Box 371, Fort Smith, NWT, X0E 0P0 * 110 King Street
Governing body: Northern Anthropological and Cultural Society
Open Winter, weekdays and Sundays; Summer, daily
☎ (403) 872-2859 * Admission by donation * *Visiting time:* one half hour
♟♟🚗 ⛲ 🎁 ⛾ 🍴 ⎯

This museum features collections of Inuit, Dene, and Métis artifacts as well as objects featuring the natural, ethnological, and geological heritage of the area. Among its many activities is hosting travelling exhibitions and arts and craft shows.

☞ **Wood Buffalo National Park Visitor Centre**
Box 750, Fort Smith, NWT X0E 0P0 * Federal Building, 126 McDougal Road
Governing body: Parks Canada
Open year round, Monday to Friday * ☎ (403) 872-2349
♟♟🚗 ♿ ⛾ ▲

This reception centre provides a good introduction to Wood Buffalo National Park, with a 20-minute multi-media slide show, films, interactive exhibits and park information on recreation, visitor facilities and guided tours.

28

SOUTH PEACE COUNTRY

E arly fur traders and missionaries called this area *la grande prairie,* but it is hardly like the treeless grasslands of southern Alberta. However, to the traveller who had just spent weeks traversing by wagon some 563 kilometres of thick forest between Edmonton and Peace River Crossing and trekking another 201 kilometres south from Dunvegan, this region must have looked very much like a big prairie. The South Peace Country is part of Alberta's aspen parkland, with upland prairies, rolling hills, rivers flowing north to the Peace, and lovely blue lakes.

To get a spectacular view of the South Peace terrain, you will want to visit Saskatoon Mountain, the highest point, rising to 213.4 metres. Kleskun Hills Park and Pipestone Creek Park are well worth visiting also to see a rich variety of flora and fauna. Kleskun Hills Park, east of Grande Prairie off Highway 34, is more like the badlands of southern Alberta. Pipestone Creek Park, south and west of Grande Prairie, offers an interpretive display telling the story of the paleontological and archaeological finds of the area.

The South Peace Country covers much of northwestern Alberta; its geographic area extends from Lesser Slave Lake west to the foothills in British Columbia as far as Hudson Hope. To the north is the Mighty Peace and to the south is Swan Hills, covered with dense forests of white and black spruce, lodgepole pine, larch and aspen poplar. This crown forest divides the Peace River Country from the rest of Alberta. Early settlers were virtually isolated by this great green wall until the arrival of the railway in the 1910s. Even today, with good paved highways, the forest of Swan Hills forms a physical and psychological barrier. People living in the Peace River Country still speak of "going out" to Edmonton.

About 70 million years ago this area was a vast river delta that emptied into an inland sea. Herds of horned dinosaurs lived on subtropical vegetation and were stalked by meat-eating dinosaurs. Occasionally one died by a river bank and was quickly covered up by mud or silt and its bony remains were replaced by minerals. Amateur and professional paleontologists eventually resurrected these fossils. The late Robert Cochrane and others amassed a large collection of dinosaur fossils, excavated under the direction of Grande Prairie Regional College. You can see some of this collection, which includes both vertebrate and invertebrate fossils, at the **Grande Prairie Museum.**

In more recent history, vast herds of buffalo and elk fed on the rich grasses and peavine that grew in *la grande prairie*. In the late 18th and 19th centuries, the Beaver and Cree Indians occupied the area and traded dried meat, pemmican and furs to the trading posts along the Peace River. Some Iroquois had migrated from eastern Canada into the area by the late 1790s and began occupying the foothills and forests further south.

Until the amalgamation of the North West Company (NWC) and Hudson's Bay Company (HBC) in 1821, the rival companies established posts next to each other along the Peace River, as far upstream as Fort St. John and Hudson Hope. Although traders and missionaries had visited the open country south of the Peace, the first white person to actually live in the area was Thomas Kerr, a Scotsman who was sent by the HBC in 1881 to establish a post northwest of today's Grande Prairie. By 1898, a Roman Catholic mission had been built on Lake Saskatoon, and James Cornwall ("Peace River Jim") and Fletcher Bredin, independent traders, had set up a post in competition with the HBC. One of the most interesting characters to settle in the area was Alex Monkman.

Alex Monkman's Pigs

Alex Monkman arrived in the area in 1898 as a Klondiker who set out to seek his fortune in gold but never made it to the Yukon. When he reached the Peace River Country, he went to work for Cornwall and Fletcher at their trading post at Lesser Slave Lake. The following year Monkman went to help establish a post at Saskatoon Lake. He and Cornwall cut the first trail from Spirit River to Saskatoon Lake. Monkman operated the post from 1898 to 1906, when it was sold to Revillon Freres.

In 1903, Monkman had put in a small crop, and thus he became the first farmer in the area. According to historian J.G. Macgregor, Monkman had acquired the area's first herd of swine, descendants of a herd that Cornwall had brought from Edmonton. Monkman placed his pigs on an island in the middle of Saskatoon Lake and left them there to fatten up. He had either forgotten or had not realized that this island was a haven for bears. When he returned later in the fall to round up his herd, he found some very fat bears but no pigs.

> ***Tracks and Traces:*** Saskatoon Lake is named after the tall
> saskatoon bushes that border the lake. Natives used its sweet purple
> berries for berry soup. Dried, the berries were pounded into pemmi-
> can for flavour. The straight stems were useful for making arrow
> shafts. Settlers made preserves and pies with this berry. Today
> saskatoon berries are made commercially into jams, wines and
> syrups.

Bill Grant was another early settler who came up from Pincher
Creek in 1905 to establish a ranch west of Saskatoon Lake. Bill
Smith established a farm northwest of the Catholic mission in 1906
or 1907. About this time George Breeden opened the first stopping
house and blacksmith shop in the area of modern downtown Grande
Prairie. "Hotel Breeden," a log structure with a sod roof, was hardly
the Ritz, but to travel-weary settlers who had come over the Long
Trail, it must have seemed an oasis of comfort. These early buildings formed the beginnings of the hamlet of Grande Prairie, in 1914
incorporated as a village.

Caboose hauled by horse team, a common type of conveyance used by settlers to
the Peace River Country. (Provincial Archives of Alberta A9204).

In 1916 the Edmonton, Dunvegan & British Columbia
(ED&BC) had completed the line from McLennon to Spirit River.
Despite the "Dunvegan" in its name, the railway never reached the
old fur trade fort and mission. Instead, the line was extended from

Rycroft south to Grande Prairie. J.D. McArthur, general manager of the ED&BC established a "model farm" at Spirit River to demonstrate to new settlers the agricultural potential of the area. The railway brought waves of immigrants to the South Peace Country to take up homesteads along the railway. These newcomers did not have the glamour of those earlier pioneers who had come in by the "Long Trail" or the "Edson Trail." Town sites like High Prairie, McLennan, Fahler, Girouxville, Wanham, Sexsmith, Watino, and Wembley sprouted up along the railway. The old fur trade villages—Grouard, Bezanson, Dunvegan, and Saskatoon Lake—that had been bypassed by the ED&BC railway went into decline.

Wheat brought prosperity to the Grande Prairie region, which had a longer growing season than the lands north of the Peace River and had more open country suitable for mechanized farming. In 1915, the first shipment of wheat left Reno (a town south of Peace River) by rail. Other crops included barley, oats, and flax. W.D. Albright, superintendent of the Agricultural Research Station at Beaverlodge, had experimented with various grains and vegetables beginning in 1913. He also harvested the first apples in the area.

Beginning in the 1920s, farmers around Wembley entered wheat and oats in international competitions and won 18 world grain championships.

During the late 1920s and "the Dirty Thirties," the Grande Prairie region did not suffer the droughts that had devastated many parts of Alberta. Farmers that had "dried out" in Saskatchewan and southern Alberta relocated in the Peace River Country.

Following the attack on Pearl Harbor on December 7, 1941, the Northwest Staging Route and the construction of the Alaska Highway brought an influx of American service personnel into the South Peace Country. During one day in

W.D. Albright, 1931. (Provincial Archives of Alberta A6988)

June of 1942, some 500 planes passed through Edmonton and Grande Prairie on their way to Alaska. Over 500 Canadian and American Air Force personnel were stationed at the Grande Prairie

Airport during the war, when some 1500 P-39 Bell Air Cobras were transported to Russia. The Northern Alberta Railway (which had taken over the failed ED&BC in 1930) became an important link in moving supplies and troops to build the all-weather highway from Dawson Creek, Mile Zero, to Alaska in 1942. Many American soldiers who had worked on the Alaska Highway moved to the South Peace Country after the war. American military presence remained until recent years, when the operations of the radar station on top of Saskatoon Mountain was turned over to Canada.

American convoy on way to Alaska. (Provincial Archives of Alberta Bl 484/3)

You may want to begin your two- or three-day exploration of the museums in the South Peace Country by following the "Long Trail" that Klondikers and settlers used to enter the Peace Country before the arrival of rail transportation. The Grizzly Trail (Highway 33) from Fort Assiniboine to Kinuso parallels the old Klondike (Chalmers) Trail. Highway 33 goes through one of Alberta's largest stands of trees. Beyond the village of Swan Hills, you will descend into the Swan River valley. This was one of the worst sections of the trail, where many Klondikers lost their horses, hopes, and dreams.

Today's Grizzly Trail comes out at Kinuso. This area was settled by some gold seekers who gave up going to the Yukon and took up homesteads instead. At Kinuso, you will want to visit the **Kinosayo Museum**, located in the Agriplex. The museum has a mounted specimen of a huge Plains grizzly shot by a local hunter in the Swan Hills area.

From Kinuso, you should continue west on Highway 2 to the turnoff of SR 750, about 18 kilometres west of Joussard. Then go north to Grouard, your next stop.

Grouard began as a fur trade post. In 1801, John McGillivray established a post at Lesser Slave Lake for the North West Company. In 1816, HBC fur trader Françoise Decoigne built Fort Waterloo on the west end of the lake, near today's Grouard. When the NWC and HBC amalgamated in 1821, the company used Lesser Slave Lake House and closed Fort Waterloo.

Missionaries began to visit Lesser Slave Lake in the 1840s: Methodist ministers Rev. James Evans in 1841 and Robert Rundle in 1842 made visits to the west end of the lake. In 1870, the Roman Catholic church established the Lesser Slave Lake Mission, with the help of the local Métis. In 1909, the mission was renamed Grouard, in honor of Bishop Emile Grouard OMI, perhaps the most famous of all the Oblate missionaries in the North. He began his mission at Fort Chipewyan in 1862. For seventy years he travelled extensively throughout the North, administering to Indians and Eskimos, learning their customs and printing books in

Bishop Emile Grouard (Provincial Archives of Alberta A2345)

their languages. In 1891 he became Bishop of the Athabasca-Mackenzie diocese. In 1920 he made the mission at Grouard his permanent headquarters and remained there until his death in 1931 at the age of 91.

At Grouard you will want to visit the **Native Cultural Arts Museum**, primarily a teaching museum where you can learn about the story of this early fur trade and mission town. The museum exhibits historical and contemporary Native art work and artifacts as well as contemporary crafts. Tours are available to see the historic **St. Bernard Church**, which at one time was the Bishop's cathedral for the Athabasca-Mackenzie diocese.

Continuing your journey of the South Peace Country, you may want to stop at High Prairie and McLennan, both of which have museums that depict their local history. **High Prairie Museum** features mostly pioneer artifacts of the local area. McLennan's **Historical & Railway Museum** has a retired NAR coach, a caboose and other railway related artifacts. Also at McLennan is the **Kimiwan Bird Walk & Interpretive Centre** next to the museum, where the bird enthusiast can observe over 200 species of birds.

McLennan, the Station That Shouldn't Be

In 1911, Grouard had a population of 447 people, by far the largest community in the Peace River country at the time. You might think that the ED&BC railway should have gone through Grouard. But Grouard was bypassed altogether, and McLennan became the divisional point instead. In *Ribbons of Steel*, author Ena Schneider relates an interesting story why this may have happened.

Hughie Hunter was an Irishman who had settled at Grouard in 1898. Before the construction of the railway, ED & BC officials asked Hunter to take a sample of the water from Round Lake (Kimiwin Lake), north of to-

day's McLennan. He obtained the sample, but when he boarded the steamboat at Grouard, he discovered the water container was empty. Being a quick thinker, he promptly filled the container with water from Lesser Slave Lake. The water was later tested and found excellent for drinking and for use in locomotives. Later it was discovered that Round Lake contained noxious chemical compounds that made the water unfit for humans and steam locomotives alike. Despite the inferior water supply, McLennan became the second most important divisional point on the line.

In the early 1900s, Rev. Father Giroux OMI, another famous Oblate missionary of the north, was influential in attracting French Canadians from Quebec and New England to colonize the areas west of McLennan. Towns like Donnelly, Falher, and Girouxville began as a French agricultural colony. At Donnelly, **La Société Historique et Généalogique de Smoky River** has a large archives and genealogical records that focus on the French families and communities of the Peace Country. At Girouxville, be sure to make a point of visiting **Musée Girouxville Museum**. This fascinating museum defies description, with its eclectic collections and some 4500 small dioramas and displays. Housed in a massive Quonset building, the museum and archives is a treasure house of objects collected from all over northern Alberta, the Arctic, and other world missions. Diverse artifacts like forerunners of the snowmobile, a horse-drawn caboose, and religious objects including chalices, incense burners, and priest's vestments are displayed.

From Girouxville, return to Donnelly, turn south on Highway 43 to Valleyview, and then turn west on Highway 34, on past Sturgeon Lake to the village of DeBolt. The **DeBolt and District Museum** restored a historic log barn for its facility. On the grounds are an early United Church manse and a teacherage. There is also a spacious playground for children and a picnic area. While you are in the area, you may want to visit the **Bezanson Old Town Site** on the Smoky River.

Continuing west on Highway 34, your next stop will be Grande Prairie, the largest city in the Peace River Country, with a population of 30,000. You may notice while driving through this prosperous city that there are several signs depicting the Trumpeter swan, the world's largest waterfowl. This bird has become Grande Prairie's mascot. The surrounding lakes are nesting grounds for the largest breeding flocks of Trumpeter swans in Canada and the second largest in the world after Alaska. The smaller Tundra (Whistler) swan breeds in the Arctic and sojourns in the Grande Prairie area during spring and fall migrations. Because of their relatively small numbers, swans have been protected in Canada since 1916.

The best place to observe Trumpeter and Tundra swans is at Saskatoon Lake in autumn when the swans gather for a few weeks before flying south. There are camping facilities at **Saskatoon Island Provincial Park**, west of Grande Prairie. To learn more about swans and other wildlife in the area, visit Grande Prairie's **Muskoseepi Park Interpretive Centre**. To learn about the history of the area, **Grande Prairie Museum** has one of the largest and finest collections of artifacts related to the northern Alberta settlement. Its pioneer village features a number of historical buildings, including McQueen Presbyterian Church and Pipestone Creek General Store. This museum also maintains an extensive collection of fossils and mounted specimens of wildlife, including a white moose.

While you are in Grande Prairie, be sure to visit the **Prairie Gallery.** This art museum has a significant collection of paintings by Alberta and Canadian artists, including works by Robert Guest, Euphemia McNaught and Illingworth Carr.

Leaving Grande Prairie, head west on Highway 34 to Beaverlodge. If you have a raging thirst, you may want to stop at the **Beaverlodge Museum Tavern.** This famous local watering hole is known far and wide for its hundreds of wildlife specimens, but beware of the coyotes. Back on the road, our next stop is the **South Peace Centennial Museum** between Beaverlodge and Hythe. This is the largest agricultural museum in the Peace River country, and it has a unique collection of fully operational steam tractors and other mechanized machinery used in farming and lumbering. These restored artifacts include stationary steam engines, steam and gas tractors, a sawmill, shingle mill, planer mill, and a grist mill. Each year on the third Sunday in July, the museum puts on a threshing bee and demonstrations.

White moose at Grande Prairie Pioneer Museum. (R.L. Hursey)

From Beaverlodge you can either go back to Grande Prairie, then turn north on Highway 2 to Sexsmith, or you can continue going northwest on Highway 2 through Hythe and then turn east on Highway 59 to Sexsmith.

Sexsmith started as a railroad town in 1916, when the ED&BC completed its line to the area. The village was named after David Sexsmith, a Klondiker who first visited the area in 1898 and returned in 1912 to farm nearby. The **Sexsmith Blacksmith Shop,** a provincial historic site, is well worth taking the time to visit. This museum brings to life an era when the local blacksmith was an essential person in rural communities. You will see a blacksmith in action and learn about this versatile craft. Find out where

Dave Bozarth and Nels Johnson hid the moonshine from the Mounties during prohibition. Afterwards, take a stroll down Sexsmith's attractive Main Street and visit the shops along the way.

Sexsmith Blacksmith Shop (R.L. Hursey)

From Sexsmith, continue north on Highway 2 and turn west on Highway 49 to the town of Spirit River, the next stop.

In 1888, the Hudson's Bay Company established a ranch in the area with plans to sell beef and dairy products to settlers and the North West Mounted Police detachments. A herd of 35 cattle, including registered Aberdeen Angus bulls, were moved to the site. The ranch was not a success. There were problems with the water supply and an outbreak of disease among the cattle plagued the ranch for years. Finally in 1896, the HBC sold the ranch to Charles Brenmar and Peter Gunn. A sizable community of Indians and Métis had grown up around the ranch and two trading posts run by the HBC and Revillion Freres. When the Oblates closed St. Charles mission at Dunvegan in 1903, they relocated at St. Joseph's Mission at Spirit River. After 1907, settlers began to homestead in the Spirit River district. By the time that the end-of-steel had reached Spirit River in 1917, the ED&BC was already in financial difficulties. The railway line that was supposed to continue from Spirit River to British Columbia was never completed.

The picturesque village of Spirit River is built on a hill overlooking a dry lake bed. My scout and I hunted for the **Spirit River and District Museum** but had some difficulty, as the signage is not very good. The museum is worth the hunt, however. It maintains a pioneer village that includes a flour mill, a Ukrainian Orthodox church, and several other historical buildings that were moved in from the surrounding area. Two log cabins are of particular interest with their whitewashed interiors. One of the friendly women volunteers told my scout and me one version of how Spirit River may have gotten its name.

Tracks and Traces: The Cree name for Spirit River was, *chepeseepe* meaning "ghost river." Apparently the marshes near the river seeped methane gas, which at night gave off an eerie phosphorescent glow creating strange shapes. Some local Natives claimed that these were the spirits of the dead.

From Spirit River, the last stop in the South Peace Country is Wanham, on Highway 49, where, at the **Grizzly Bear Museum**, you will find early 1900s farm machinery and restored buildings, such as a 1924 farmhouse and a restored First Presbyterian church.

MUSEUMS IN THE SOUTH PEACE COUNTRY

☞ **South Peace Centennial Museum** at Beaverlodge/Hythe
Box 493, Beaverlodge, AB T0H 0C0
3 kilometres northwest of Beaverlodge on Highway 2
Governing body: South Peace Centennial Museum Society
Open mid-May to October 1, daily * ☎ (403) 354-8869
Admission fee charged *Visiting time:* one and a half hours

This living history museum and pioneer village spreads out over 40 acres. The museum employs a large corps of volunteers that operate a restored sawmill, flour mill, shingle mill, stationary steam engines, steam tractors, and much more. Historic buildings and artifacts reflect every facet of the history of the Peace country's rural life including mechanized farming, sawmilling, transportation, town life, religion, education, and domestic life. For antique car enthusiasts, the museum has a large collection of vintage vehicles, including a beautifully restored Model T Ford truck, a Model A car, and a Shelby Mustang from the early '60s.

☞ **DeBolt & District Museum**
c/o Box 447, DeBolt, AB T0H 1B0
Hubert Memorial Park on Virginia Avenue
Governing body: DeBolt & District Pioneer Museum Society
Open May to September, Monday, Thursday and Saturday
☎ (403) 957-3957 * Admission by donation * *Visiting time:* one half hour

The main part of the museum is located in a large log barn. Two historical buildings, a United Church manse, and a teacherage are also on the grounds. Although the artifact collection is relatively small, one gets a real sense of the history of the area through interesting photographs and well-chosen stories. One unusual display portrays the evolution of flour sacks.

☞ **Société Historique et Généalogique de Smoky River** at Donnelly
Box 221, Donnelly, AB T0H 1G0 * Main Street, Donnelly
Governing body: Societe Historique et Genealogique
Open year round, Monday to Friday * ☎ (403) 925-3801
Admission by donation * *Visiting time:* one half hour

♥♥ 🚗 👫 🍴 ⎯

This museum has a large archives with French-Roman Catholic records of the Peace Country. The researcher will find the largest collection of marriage indexes in Alberta and an extensive historical library, with classical French books dating from the 19th century.

☞ **Musée Girouxville Museum**
Box 276, Girouxville, AB T0H 1S0 * On Main Street
Governing body: Village of Girouxville * ☎ (403) 323-4252/323-4270
Admission fee charged * *Visiting time:* one hour

♥♥♥ 🚗 👫 🎁

The museum has an extraordinarily large and eclectic collection of natural history specimens, artifacts and artwork pertaining to Native, missionary, and settlement history. Of note is the wide range of religious artifacts. Early forerunners of snowmobiles, a horse-drawn caboose, a reconstructed trapper's cabin, early farm machinery, and a mission chapel are some of the displays and artifacts. Labels are in French and English.

☞ **Muskoseepi Park Interpretive Centre** at Grande Prairie
Postal Bag 4000, Grande Prairie, AB T8V 6V3
102nd Street and 102nd Avenue
Governing body: City of Grande Prairie
Open year round, daily * ☎ (403) 538-0451
Admission by donation * *Visiting time:* one half hour

♥♥ 🚗 ♿ 🚹 ⛱ 🍴 ⎯

This nature centre interprets the natural history of Grande Prairie and region, presents outdoor education programs and information on local wildlife and plants as well as travelling exhibits. Interpretive collections include mounted and study specimens for programs.

☞ **Grande Prairie Museum**
Box 687, Grande Prairie, AB T8V 3A8
102nd Street and 102nd Avenue, Muskoseepi Park
Governing body: Pioneer Museum Society of Grande Prairie & District
Open year round, daily * ☎ (403) 532-5482
Admission fee charged * *Visiting time:* one and a half hours

---

This large museum and pioneer village features wildlife specimens, fossils, rocks and minerals, Native artifacts, and objects representing settlement history and a variety of occupations from medicine to forestry. The quality and quantity of the collections is most impressive. The adjacent pioneer village is one of the best you'll find in the Peace River Country. Of particular interest are the 1911 McQueen's Presbyterian Church, Pipestone Creek General Store of hewn log construction, and a replica fire hall.

☞ **Prairie Gallery**
10209 - 99th Street, Grande Prairie, AB T8V 2H3
Governing body: Prairie Gallery Board of Directors
Open year round, daily * ☎ (403) 532-8111
Admission by donation * *Visiting time:* one hour

This art museum is located in a 1929 brick school that is a provincial historic resource. The galleries feature contemporary exhibitions of Alberta and Canadian and international artists. Its own fine collection includes paintings, drawings and prints of Euphemia McNaught, John Snow, Robert Guest, W.J. Phillips, Illingworth Carr and many others. The museum has a rental program and provides art education classes and workshops.

☞ **Native Cultural Arts Museum** at Grouard
General Delivery, Grouard, AB T0G 1C0
Alberta Vocational College, Mission Street
Governing body: Council of Community Education Committees Society
Open September through July, weekdays * ☎ (403) 751-3915
Admission by donation * *Visiting time:* one hour

This museum is located on the AVC campus at Grouard. It features the creative works of Native people of Canada and North America. The museum interprets Native historical and contemporary culture as well as the history of Grouard as an important fur trading, religious and transportation centre. Group tours are available to see St. Bernard Church by prior arrangement. This beautiful church contains murals originally painted by Bishop Grouard, and vestments, chalices, and other ecclesiastical artifacts. This teaching museum is an important part of the Native arts and crafts program at the college. It is best to call to make arrangements.

☞ **High Prairie & District Museum**
Box 1442, High Prairie, AB T0G 1E0
5300 - 49th Street, in public library building
Governing body: High Prairie & District Historical Society
Open year round, Tuesday to Saturday * ☎ (403) 523-2601
Admission by donation * *Visiting time:* one half hour
♟ 🚗 ♿ ⚲ 🍴 ━

This museum has collections of artifacts and photographs pertaining to the archeological and settlement history of the area. It features a "Community Corner" where local people may exhibit some of their own collections.

☞ **Kinosayo Museum** at Kinuso
Box 267, Kinuso, AB T0G 1K0 * In Agricultural Complex
Governing body: Kinosayo Museum Society
Open May 1 to August 31, daily * ☎ (403) 775-3774
Admission by donation * *Visiting time:* one half hour
♟♟ 🚗 ⚲ ⊞ ⛩ ▲

This museum has artifacts and mounted specimens depicting the history of the area, with some simple but effective small dioramas that show imagination and care. There is a good collection of tools reflecting the historical importance of commercial fishing, mink ranching, agriculture, and the forest industries of the area. Of particular interest is the upright mounted specimen of a huge Plains Grizzly, the largest taken out of the Swan Hills area.

☞ **Kimiwan Bird Walk and Interpretive Centre** at McLennan
Box 356, McLennan, AB T0H 2L0
On south shore of Kimiwan Lake, adjacent to Highway 2.
Governing body: Town of McLennan
Open May 1 to October 15, daily * ☎ (403) 324-2004/324-3065
Admission by donation * *Visiting time:* One hour

This interpretive centre and bird walk offer the visitor an opportunity to observe over 205 species of shorebirds, waterfowl and other bird species. Lake Kimiwan is at the junction of three major flyways. The town of McLennan has built a network of boardwalks, blinds, two telescopes, and signage for the bird enthusiast. The Centre offers guided tours, maps, and other information for the birder.

☞ **Northern Alberta Historical and Railway Museum**
Town of McLennan office, McLennan, AB T0H 2L0
There are two locations: the Museum Room in the Town Centre and next to the Kimiwan Bird Walk and Interpretive Centre.
Governing body: Town of McLennan
Open June to August * ☎ (403) 324-3653/324-3065
Admission by donation * *Visiting time:* one half hour

The Museum Room at the Town Centre displays artifacts related to the history of McLennan and area. The NAR Coach 18001 has railway artifacts and photographs depicting the importance of the railway to the development of the town into a divisional point for the NAR.

☞ **Sexsmith Blacksmith Shop**
Box 252, Sexsmith, AB T0H 3C0 * 9924 - 99th Street
Governing body: Sexsmith and District Museum Society
Open May 15 to September 5, daily * ☎ (403) 568-3681
Admission fee charged * *Visiting time:* one half hour

The Sexsmith Blacksmith Shop, which operated from 1916 to 1974, is now a provincial historic site. This living museum portrays the importance of blacksmiths in rural communities and the specific history of this shop, owned successively by Dave Bozarth and Nels Johnson. The collection includes thousands of objects related to the blacksmith trade. You can watch blacksmithing in action and learn about the evolution of blacksmith work, from making horseshoes and plowshares to doing repairs on the trucks used in the building of the Alaska Highway. The personal history of Nels is fascinating: he is a bit of a folk hero who defied the RCMP during prohibition days by hiding illegal booze in various parts of his shop.

☞ **Spirit River & District Museum**
Box 221, Spirit River, AB T0H 3G0
Corner of 48th Street and 44th Avenue. A little hard to find because of the lack of street signs.
Governing body: Spirit River Settlement Historical Society
Open May long weekend to September long weekend
☎ (403) 864-2180 * Admission fee charged * *Visiting time:* one half hour

� �e 🚗 🎁 🏕 ▲

This museum has a large collection of settlement and railway artifacts as well as a pioneer village component. Historical buildings include a small flour mill, a school, a Ukrainian Orthodox church, and two log cabins. The smaller of these was owned by a local bachelor and is furnished with his personal objects.

☞ **Grizzly Bear Prairie Museum** at Wanham
Box 68, Wanham, AB T0H 3P0
Governing body: Various organizations in the community
OpenJune to August, daily * ☎ (403) 694-3933
Admission by donation * *Visiting time:* one half hour

♟ 🚗 iⁱⁱ 🏕 ▲

The museum's collection includes artifacts from the area. They include farm machinery and tractors from the early 1900s, a restored farm house built in 1924, and a restored First Presbyterian church.

29

NORTH PEACE COUNTRY

I will never forget my first view of Peace River years ago, coming down the steep hill that overlooks the town. It was early autumn. The setting sun turned the river into a shimmering silver snake and painted the sky and cliffs in every shade of gold, russet and brown. Each time I return to the Peace River, its majestic beauty never fails to excite me.

Of the five major rivers in Alberta—the Milk River, the North and South Saskatchewan Rivers, the Athabasca River and the Peace River—only the Peace River begins its journey west of the Canadian Rockies, in British Columbia. All the others originate on the east slopes of the Rockies. The Peace River cuts a deep furrow through the mountains and out across the rolling plains. At Fort Dunvegan, the banks of the river rise to a height of about 800 feet. By the time the Peace arrives at Fort Vermilion, its banks are less than 100 feet high.

Tracks and Traces: The name Peace River is derived from an event that took place around 1784, some years before Alexander Mackenzie's sojourn at Fort Fork. At Peace Point near Lake Athabasca, the Cree and Beaver Indians settled their long dispute. The Beaver called the river "Unchaga," meaning peace.

In October 1792, Alexander Mackenzie, one of the wintering partners of the North West Company, travelled by canoe from Fort Chipewyan up the Peace River and arrived on November 1 at Fort Fork, near the junction of the Smoky and Peace Rivers. By the time he arrived at Fort Fork, the men he previously sent upriver had built the palisades and were preparing timber for the erection of his house. He moved into the house by Christmas and spent the winter trading and administering medical care to the local Beaver Indians. On May 9, 1793, Mackenzie, nine voyageurs, and two Indian guides left Fort Fork to ascend the Peace River to continue his westward journey seeking a water route to the Pacific. Mackenzie and his men reached the Pacific Ocean, at today's Bella Coola, B.C. Mackenzie was the first European explorer to cross the North American continent north of Mexico.

For 13 years, Fort Fork was an important provisions post on the Peace until abandoned in 1806, after the establishment of Fort Dunvegan further upstream. For years the exact location of Fort Fork remained a mystery, until Dr. J. H. Johnston rediscovered it in

1927 on Section 25, Township 82, Range 23. In the thick brush along the bank of the Peace River, he found a distinctive pile of stones. He had two men clear about an acre of dense forest around the stones and drew a map of the area. He also found a 1790s brass lantern on the site. Perhaps Mackenzie himself had used the lamp to write entries in his journal during his stay. Some salvage archaeological excavation was done by the Provincial Museum of Alberta in 1970. Archaeologists uncovered several small artifacts dating back to the time the fort had been in operation.

Today, nothing remains of the original fort, which the river completely washed away. The fireplace stones, lamp, and small artifacts from Fort Fork are on display at the **Peace River Centennial Museum.**

In March 1804, David Thompson snowshoed upriver from Fort Fork and wrote in his journal about a large area of flats, that would make a good location for a camp. The following year, the NWC erected Fort Dunvegan at this spot; and A. R. Macleod, the clerk in charge, and about 45 men were employed at the post. Like its predecessor Fort Fork, Fort Dunvegan served mainly as a provisions post, where supplies of furs, pemmican, dried meat, and leather goods were transported downriver to Fort Chipewyan. In the summer of 1818, John Clarke, a clerk with the HBC, established St. Mary's House at the confluence of the Smoky and Peace Rivers. The HBC closed this fort after 1821, when the rival companies merged.

Although Fort Dunvegan was never a very large post, it was strategically located in one of the richest fur trade areas in the northwest; and for many years, it supplied beaver, marten, lynx, and muskrat furs for the HBC. In the 1840s, the value of beaver declined, but the value of other furs remained high. The area eventually became depleted of these valuable furbearing mammals, as did the large herds of buffalo and elk used to make pemmican. After 1860, the HBC post began to experience competition from independent fur traders. One of the most famous of these was Twelve Foot Davis, who established a trading post across the river from Fort Dunvegan.

Twelve Foot Davis

In the early 1860s, a new breed of men started to invade the Peace River country; gold miners who had worked the gold fields of California and the Caribou started to move east across Rocky Mountain portage to try their luck along the banks of the Peace River. One of these prospectors was an American named Henry Davis. He got the nickname of "Twelve Foot Davis" after he struck it rich in the gold fields of British Columbia, when he staked a 12-foot-wide claim between two larger claims. On his small claim, he managed to extract $15,000 worth of gold.

He arrived in the Peace River country about 1865 and set up a trading post opposite Fort Dunvegan. It became the first of many posts he estab- lished along the Peace River. In later years, after he was blind, deaf and partially para- lyzed, he had a manservant help him. In 1900, he died and was buried at Lesser Slave Lake. Later, his long time friend, "Peace River Jim" Cornwall, had his remains moved to the hill overlooking the town of Peace River. His grave on Grouard Hill com- mands a breathtaking view of the town and the confluence of the Peace and Smoky Rivers.

Fort Dunvegan Provincial Historic Site (R.L. Hursey)

Missionaries began to arrive to the Peace River Country in the 1840s. James Evans, a Methodist preacher, was the first to enter the country in 1841. Robert Rundle also made a trip to Peace River in 1842. Evans was the inventor of the Cree syllabic form of writing. Father Joseph Bourassa was the first Roman Catholic missionary to travel the area in 1845. The first missionary to locate at Dunvegan was Father Christophe Tissier, an Oblate who founded St. Charles Mission in 1867. He was not very successful, having never learned the language of the Beaver Indians. Father Emile Grouard replaced him in 1883 and began constructing a church. St. Charles Church was completed in 1887. This church and rectory were restored in the 1970s and are now part of **Historic Dunvegan Provincial Historic Site**, located on the north side of the Dunvegan Suspension Bridge that spans the Peace. There is also a Visitor Centre and a restored HBC Factor's House west of the bridge.

Another missionary that left permanent tracks along the banks of the Peace River was Reverend Alfred Garrioch, an Anglican missionary, who founded the first mission at Fort Vermilion in 1876. Three years later, Thomas Bunn, a lay teacher, established St. Saviour's Mission at Dunvegan in 1879. In 1882, Reverend John Gough Brick arrived and remained there until 1884, when he left the mission to start a farm on the wagon road between Dunvegan and Peace River Crossing. Reverend Garrioch replaced Brick and stayed at the mission until 1891. In 1895, the mission house was dismantled and moved down river to the Shaftesbury settlement.

The Peace River Country was one of several routes explored for the Canadian Pacific Railway in the early 1870s. Sandford Fleming, in charge of the Dominion Survey, sent Charles Horetzky, the official photographer, and John Macoun in 1872 to see if the Peace River would be a practical route. The Peace River route, of course, was turned down in favor of the more southerly route through Calgary. The Peace River country would have to wait many years before it got a railway. Other surveyors and explorers visited the area,

Rev. A.C. Garrioch and his wife, 1886
(Provincial Archives of Alberta A4264)

including Alfred Selwyn in 1875, and George Dawson in 1879, both geologists with the Geological Survey of Canada. These sojourners recognized the agricultural potential of the Peace River valley, where vegetables had been grown as early as the 1790s at Fort Fork. The missionaries at Fort Dunvegan and Fort Vermilion had experimented with a variety of crops.

It was the rush to the Klondike in 1897-8 that opened up the Peace River country to large-scale agricultural settlement. In the spring of 1897, groups of men and women seeking fortune and adventure began to arrive by train in Edmonton to try their luck taking the "back door" to the Klondike. There were two main routes out of Edmonton. One was a water route that began on the trail to Athabasca Landing, then by steamboat or scow by way of the Athabasca and Mackenzie Rivers. The other route was the Swan River route along the old trail to Fort Assiniboine and overland through the vast green wall of dense forest and muskeg to Lesser Slave Lake at today's Kinuso and from there west to Grouard. From Grouard these parties broke up, following the old Cree War Trail to Peace River Crossing and to Grande Prairie along other trails leading west and north. This overland route was the shortest in mileage but by far the most difficult and hazardous. Most would-be-gold-seekers never made it to the Yukon, but turned back to Edmonton. Some died of starvation, overexposure, and scurvy. Some Klondikers who passed through the Peace River country and liked its looks returned later to take up homesteads and seek their fortunes in the rich soil.

Tracks and Traces: The Cree War Trail was an overland trail originating at the west end of Lesser Slave Lake and ending at the confluence of the Peace and Smoky Rivers. The Cree used this trail to make war on the Beaver. It later became the Grouard-Peace River wagon road, used by early settlers to reach the Peace River Country.

At the time of the Klondike Rush, the Athabasca-Peace region still belonged to the Beaver, Cree, Chipewyan and Dene. This sudden influx of inexperienced adventurers brought great hardship to the local Natives. Not only were areas depleted of game, but Klondikers brought in liquor and used poisoned bait, which killed many of the Indians' dogs. The Natives wanted the government to do something about these problems. The NWMP sent a number of Mounties to the area to assist the gold seekers, but mostly to assure the maintenance of law and order. In the wake of the Klondikers, the federal government sent a treaty party in 1899 and 1900 to negotiate Treaty No. 8. A few isolated groups, like the Lubicons, were overlooked. Today the Lubicons continue to agitate for settlement of land claims.

The Peace River country remained fairly isolated for many years. Before 1910, there were only about 5000 people, mostly Natives, living in the whole area. Then in 1911 the Grand Trunk Pacific had reached Edson. From 1911 to 1915, the Edson Trail provided the shortest distance to the Peace River country. Settlers then travelled to Edson, where they detrained and went overland by wagon on the Edson Trail. In 1915, J.D. McArthur completed the Edmonton Dunvegan and British Columbia (ED&BC) line to

McLennan by January. There the line split, one branch going to the village of Peace River, the other to Spirit River. McLennan became the divisional point.

Between 1915 and 1930, many farmers "dried out" in southern Alberta migrated to the Peace River country, along with settlers and immigrants from Ontario, Quebec, United States, Great Britain, and Europe. This was truly the "Last Best West," the most northerly agricultural area in Canada. In spite of improved transportation links to the North Peace Country, the area remained isolated regarding medical care and social services. The unusually high infant mortality rate gravely concerned the settlers. Beginning in the 1920s, a corps of pioneer women doctors—Drs. Emma Johnstone, Mary Percy Jackson and Margaret Strang Savage—brought desperately needed medical care to the area.

The Women Doctors of the Peace

Dr. Emma Johnstone was an English woman who had been born in India in 1879 and educated as a doctor in England. In the early 1920s, the Alberta government accepted her offer to practice in the North and sent her to Wanham. She lived in a tiny log cabin and travelled by foot and horseback, and hitched rides on passing wagons to get to her patients, scattered over hundreds of square miles. She returned to England to recruit other women doctors, one of whom was Mary Percy Jackson.

Dr. Mary Percy, a native of England, graduated from the University of Birmingham in medicine and surgery. She arrived in 1929 and became the Provincial District Doctor for the Manning area. She was the only doctor in a vast area that covered 906 kilometre^2. She also served as a dentist, nurse, druggist, and veterinarian. Her biggest battle was with tuberculosis, especially among the Native populations. In 1931, she married Frank Jackson and moved to Keg River, where she continued her practice until 1974, after 45 years in the North. At the time of writing this book, she is still living in Keg River.

Dr. Margaret Strang graduated from the University of Western Ontario in 1929, the only woman in a class of 25. The Presbyterian Church appointed her to serve as a medical missionary in the Dixonville area in 1931. While she was delivering babies and administering to the sick, she also served as the area's doctor and the first Presbyterian minister in the Dixonville district. When the community needed a cemetery, she wrote letters to the government, but her requests went unanswered. She arranged for the donation of land, which was fenced and divided into plots. Six people were buried there before a warning came from government officials that this was not a registered cemetery. Her reply to the bureaucrats was: "Come and establish a proper registered cemetery under fron-tier conditions and transfer the dead, if you wish." Obviously, the original cemetery remains. In 1934, she resigned as missionary when she married Douglas Savage, but she continued to serve as the community's doctor until 1943, when her family moved to Cold Lake.

For the heritage hunter, there is a variety of museums and historic sites that interpret the natural and human history of the North Peace Country. You many want to begin your explorations of this area at **Historic Dunvegan Provincial Historic Site** o n Highway 2, about 20 kilometres south of Fairview. This excellently restored site provides a beautiful view of the Peace River as well as the suspension bridge. The buildings have been furnished to the period of the 1880s. In St. Charles Church are altar murals that have been painstakingly repainted using black and white photographs and matching the colors from the side walls. The original paintings had been destroyed in a fire.

Travelling north on Highway 2, turn north on Highway 64 at Fairview and visit the **End of Steel Heritage Museum and Park** at Hines Creek, which commemorates the arrival of the railway in 1930. The historical village includes a trapper's cabin, a railway caboose, pioneer homes and church, and a nature trail.

Return to Fairview, where you can visit the **Fairview Agricultural Museum.** From Fairview to Peace River, you may want to take a side trip along the Shaftsbury Trail (SR 684), the original wagon road from Dunvegan to Peace River Crossing. A small park and picnic area commemorates the establishment of Fort Fork, which was actually located on the opposite side of the river. For an intimate view of the river, you may want to ride the Shaftsbury Ferry, one of two ferries that operate on the Peace River.

Peace River is a bustling town of about 6700 people. It used to be called Peace River Crossing in the 1880s and 1890s. It was an important stopping place for those travelling down river to Fort Vermilion. By the early 1900s, steamboats like the *Peace River* and *D.A. Thomas* carried passengers and freight from Hudson's Hope, B.C., to Fort Vermilion. At Peace River you will want to visit the **Peace River Centennial Museum and Archives**, where you can learn about the remarkable history of the area—the building of

Fort Fork, the town, and river and rail transportation. A large folk model of the *D.A. Thomas* steamboat is on display. The **NAR Railway Station**, built in 1916, and now a designated provincial site, has been recently restored and opened to the public. Be sure to drive up to the top of Grouard Hill to **Twelve Foot Davis Provincial Park** to see his grave site and a breathtaking view of the Peace River valley.

The D.A. Thomas steamboat (Provincial Archives of Alberta A2132)

Heading west on Highway 2 for about 20 kilometres, you will want to turn north on Highway 35 to High Level. The country along here becomes very flat and heavily forested. At Manning, the **Battle River Pioneer Museum** provides the opportunity to learn more about the North Peace country. Formerly called Aurora, the town's name was changed in 1947 to Manning, after Ernest Manning, premier of Alberta from 1943 to 1968.

Leaving Manning and continuing north on Highway 35 to High Level, you will be driving through the most northerly agricultural area in the province. High Level, a town of about 3000, has the spirit of a frontier town. The name may seem a bit of a misnomer, as it appears quite flat. However, in the early days, trappers used to meet at the height of land between the Hay River and the Peace River Valley. At High Level, be sure to visit the **Mackenzie Crossroads Museum and Visitors Centre,** located in a large log building reminiscent of a fur trade post. Here you will see a pristine collection of early containers and tins used for packaging food and dry goods. The museum also has a large collection of Medalta pottery.

From High Level, head east on Highway 58 to Fort Vermilion—the oldest European settlement in Alberta after Fort Chipewyan. Boyer's Post (Fort Vermilion) and the first Fort Chipewyan were founded in 1788 by the North West Company.

Fur Trade Wars 1815 - 1821.

The NWC had a virtual monopoly over the Peace River country until 1815, when the HBC sent John Clarke to establish Fort Wedderburn, across the channel from Fort Chipewyan. This was a troubled post from the very start. When the provisions became low towards winter, Clarke sent his men about the country to hunt their own meat. Clarke himself led a party of 50 men and 14 canoes up the Peace River. By the time they got to Fort Vermilion, they were reduced to eating squirrels, partridges and crows, as the Nor'westers had sent Indians ahead of them to scare away game. Clarke's men were forced to trade their goods for food from the NWC. Sixteen of Clarke's men starved during the winter. The following winter, A.N. Macleod of the NWC was armed with legal papers to put Clarke and his men under arrest.

In 1818, the HBC sent Colin Robertson, with Clarke second-in-command and more than a hundred men to establish a foothold in the Athabasca region. Robertson led his men up the Peace to establish two posts: St. Mary's, across from Fort Fork; and Colville House, a few kilometers downstream of Fort Vermilion. Back at Fort Wedderburn, Robertson was captured and held prisoner for most of the winter at Fort Chipewyan. He eventually escaped and found his way to Fort William. The bitter feud between the rival companies lasted until 1821, when they merged under the Hudson's Bay Company name. In 1830, the HBC established Fort Vermilion in its present location.

Fort Vermilion attracted many missionaries during the 19th century, beginning with Reverend James Evans, who visited here in 1842, and Father Bourassa in 1846. Rev. William C. Bompas, an Anglican priest, visited Fort Vermilion in 1868. He returned again in 1870, when he vaccinated 500 people against smallpox. Anglicans and Roman Catholics established the first permanent missions in 1876. E. J. Lawrence and his family came from Ontario in 1879 to set up a school and mission farm. In 1888, the Anglican Church held its first synod of the new Diocese of Athabasca at St. Luke's Church, and Reverend Richard Young became the first bishop.

The Fort Vermilion area probably has more historic sites per capita than just about any other community in Alberta. To walk around the hamlet is to step back in time. Along the river you may notice the layout of the town, which still retains evidence of the original river lot system. Most of the existing historical buildings date from the turn of the century to the 1930s and need attention if they are to be preserved. Perhaps the most impressive site is the **Old Bay House.** Downstream from Fort Vermilion is the site of NWC's **Boyer's Post,** which operated from 1788 to 1792. It is now a national historic site. To learn about the history of the local area, be sure to visit the **Fort Vermilion Heritage Museum.**

Be sure to pick up the *Fort Vermilion Heritage Guide* at the visitor centre to use on your driving or walking tour of the town. While you are in the Fort Vermilion area you may want to visit the **Fort Vermilion Experimental Farm**, founded in 1907. A few miles west of Fort Vermilion is **Rocky Lane School.** It contains a small museum curated by seventh grade students.

From Fort Vermilion pick up SR 697 west of town and head south to the hamlet of La Crete. The name comes from the French *crête* meaning crest of cock's comb. The Mennonites began to settle in the La Crete area about 1937. In 1992, the La Crete Mennonite Historical Society began building the **La Crete Mennonite Village** on a quarter section about 4 kilometres from the hamlet. This pioneer village shows the history and heritage of the Mennonite settlement. Several historical buildings, with construction unique to this area, have been moved on the property and are being restored. Among the buildings is a large 1950s farmhouse built by the Peter Wiebe family, a flour mill, and a Forest Service stopover cabin.

On your return to Peace River, you may want to continue south on SR 697 to cross the ferry at Tompkin's Landing. Be sure to check locally about road conditions, as it can be very slick during the rainy season.

MUSEUMS IN THE NORTH PEACE COUNTRY

☞ **Dixonville Trading Post Museum**
Box 154, Dixonville, AB T0H 1E0 * Main Street
Governing body: The Life Club
Open July and August * ☎ (403) 971-3750
Admission by donation * *Visiting time:* one half hour
♥ ᛁᛁᛏ

The Dixonville Trading Post Museum is known as "the smallest museum in the Peace River Country." This log museum was originally the first store in Dixonville, built in the early 1930s. The museum has artifacts and memorabilia related to the history of the town. If you are in the area, be sure to visit the historic Strang Presbyterian Church, a log church built in the 1930s by Dr. Margaret Strang, missionary doctor and minister.

☞ **Lac Cardinal Regional Pioneer Village Museum** at Grimshaw
Box 325, Grimshaw, AB T0H 1W0
West of Grimshaw at the Queen Elizabeth Provincial Park, Lac Cardinal Lake.
Governing body: Lac Cardinal Regional Pioneer Village Museum Society
Open May to September * ☎ (403) 332-4284
Admission by donation * *Visiting time:* one half hour

🍷🚗 іі† ⋗і ☷ ▲

This 20 acre museum opened in 1995. Historical buildings and early farm machinery are in various stages of restoration.

☞ **Historic Dunvegan Provincial Historic Site** at Fairview
c/o Historic Sites & Archives Service, Box 1334, Provincial Building, Fairview,
AB T0H 1L0, South of Fairview about 20 kilometres off Highway 2 at the
Dunvegan Suspension Bridge
Governing body: Alberta Community Development,
Historic Sites & Archives Service * Open May 15 to Labour Day, daily
☎ (403) 835-5244/835-4889 * Admission donation * *Visiting time:* one hour

🍷🍷🍷 🚗 іі† ⋗і ☷

This historic site was the location of the early NWC fur trade post, Fort Dunvegan, founded in 1805. It was also one of the earliest Roman Catholic missions in Alberta. St. Charles Church, rectory and the Factor's House have been restored to the 1880s period. The historic "Maples" park was the site of the Anglican church. Of particular interest is the beautifully restored altar murals in the church. Interpreters on the site give guided tours and present programs. Plans are to construct an interpretive centre and tea room.

☞ **Fairview Agricultural Society Museum**
Box 1994, Fairview, Alberta, T0H 1L0 * 10813 - 103rd Avenue
Governing body: Fairview Agricultural Society
Open May 15 to September 30, Tuesday to Saturday afternoons
☎ (403) 835-4044 * Admission by donation * *Visiting time:* one half hour

🍷🚗 ☷ ▲ 🍴 ━

The Fairview Agricultural Society Museum encompasses two sites. The *RCMP Celebrations Museum* demonstrates what a pioneer home was like and has exhibits of an early schoolroom, a general store, and the original home and jail of the RCMP, established in 1928. The *Fairview Pioneer Village* at Cummings Lake features historical buildings, including homes, schools, and stores reflecting the area's heritage. This is just a beginning of what the society plans to have on the site.

☞ **Fort Vermilion Heritage Museum and Archives**
Box 1, Fort Vermilion, AB T0H 1N0
Community and Cultural Complex, Tardiff Avenue
Governing body: Fort Vermilion Agricultural Society
Open May 15 to Labour Day * ☎ (403) 927-4603/927-3416 (visitor house)
Admission by donation * *Visiting time:* one half hour

🏆🏆 🚗 ⛺ ⤳ 🎪 ♿

The museum features Fort Vermilion and the fur trade. Collections include artifacts and memorabilia from the 1907 Fort Vermilion Experimental Farm, the 1988 Fort Vermilion and District Bicentennial, and the 1914 Fort Vermilion Board of Trade Collection. It also houses a large collection of family history photographs. While in the area, be sure to visit other sites around Fort Vermilion; i.e., the Old Bay House and the national historic site, Boyer's Post, which the NWC operated from 1788 to 1792.

☞ **Rocky Lane School Museum**
Rocky Lane School, Fort Vermilion, AB T0H 1N0
Governing body: Rocky Lane School
Open during the school year on weekdays
☎ (403) 927-3297 * Admission by donation * *Visiting time:* one half hour

🏆 🚗 ⛺

This museum is part of the school program. Each year, grade seven students become the curators of the collection and organize exhibits and programs. The grade eight students, who are experienced curators, become advisors to the new curators. The Rocky Lane School Museum provides a model for other school districts interested in having their students learn about their own family and community heritage by becoming actively involved in collecting, researching, preserving, and displaying artifacts. Be sure to call in advance for booking a tour.

☞ **Mackenzie Crossroads Museum and Visitors Centre**
at High Level
Box 485, High Level, AB T0H 1Z0
Large log building on Highway 35 at the east end of town
Governing body: Town of High Level
Open year round daily. Closed on Statutory Holidays.
☎ (403) 926-4811 * Admission by donation * *Visiting time:* one half hour

🍴🍷🚗 ♿ 👥 ⛲

The museum's primary exhibit is called "Northern Trading Post," which features a typical trading post and living quarters of the late 1800s. Artifacts include a very fine collection of packaged goods and tins reflecting what one would find at a general store from the 1920s to 1940s, as well as trading, trapping, farming, and natural history objects. This is an excellent place to come to find out about other museums, historic sites, and events happening in the area.

☞ **End of Steel Heritage Museum and Park** at Hines Creek
Box 686, Hines Creek, AB T0H 2A0
At the crossroads of Highway 64 and SR 685
Governing body: End of Steel Heritage Society
Open May to September, daily * ☎ (403) 494-3522
Admission by donation * *Visiting time:* one half hour

🍴🍷🚗 👥 📷 🏛 ⛲

This museum is a pioneer village that focuses on the homesteading period and the arrival of the NAR railway in 1930. Historical buildings include a railway caboose, pioneer homes, a general store, a log church and a trapper's cabin. Artifacts include agricultural machinery and a horse-drawn school bus.

☞ **La Crete Mennonite Village**
c/o Northern Lights Gas Co-op, La Crete, AB T0H 2H0
About 2 miles from town on West La Crete Road
Governing body: La Crete Agricultural Society
Open summer months, daily * ☎ (403) 928-3881/928-2442
Admission by donation * *Visiting time:* one hour

🍴🍷🚗 ⛲ 🍽 ▬

This pioneer village shows the history and heritage of La Crete's Mennonite settlement. Historical buildings include a large 1950s farmhouse with a barn attached, a flour mill, a blacksmith shop, and a Forest Service stopover cabin.

☞ **Battle River Pioneer Museum** at Manning
Box 574, Manning, AB T0H 2M0
1 kilometre off Highway 35 on SR 691, just south of Manning
Governing body: Battle River Pioneer Museum Association
Open May 15 to September 15, daily
☎ (403) 836-3114/836-2180/836-2281
Admission by donation * *Visiting time:* one hour

The Manning area is sometimes called "The Land of the Mighty Moose," and this museum has an albino moose as its mascot. The museum presents displays featuring wildlife, minerals, antique machinery, small tools, and domestic artifacts that portray the history of the area.

☞ **Peace River Centennial Museum**
10302 - 99 Street, Peace River, AB T8S 1K1
Follow the Museum logos through town to 10302-99th Street
Governing body: Town of Peace River
Open year round: Summer, daily; Winter, Tuesday to Sunday
☎ (403) 624-4261 * Admission fee charged * *Visiting time:* one half hour

This museum has a lovely park-like location at the junction of the Peace and Hart Rivers. It depicts the 200-year history of the area, beginning with Mackenzie's stay at Fort Fork and including the settlement and town history, river and rail transportation. There are some very interesting artifacts related to Fort Fork, including some of the fireplace stones, an 1800s brass lantern, a large fur press, and models of Fort Fork and the steamboat, the *D.A. Thomas*. In town also visit the 1916 NAR railway station, a designated provincial historic site, at 9309 - 100th Street.

☞ **Brownvale North Peace Agricultural Museum**
Box 3, Brownvale, AB T0H 0L0
Governing body: Brownvale Museum Society
Open July and August ☎ (403) 597-3950 * Admission by donation

The museum's collection depicts the history of agriculture in the Brownvale area. Plans are to restore several buildings in the hamlet in situ.

HERITAGE ORGANIZATIONS IN ALBERTA

The following are heritage organizations and associations that have a regional, provincial or national focus.

Alberta Archives Council
Contact: Elizabeth Denham, c/o City of Calgary Archives, Box 2100, Station M., Calgary, Alberta, T2P 2M5. Phone: (403) 268-8180; Fax: (403) 268-1585.

Alberta Community Development, Cultural Facilities & Historical Resources Division
Contact: Eric Waterton, 8820 - 112 Street, Edmonton, Alberta, T6G 2P8. Phone: (403) 431-2342; Fax: (403) 432-1376.

Alberta Family Histories Society
Contact: Lois Nicholson, Box 30270, Station B, Calgary, Alberta T2M 4P1 Phone: (403) 247-3455

Alberta Genealogical Society
Contact: Gordon Becker, 78 - Oberlin Avenue, Red Deer, Alberta, T4N 5A4. Phone: (403) 346-5160; Fax: (403) 342-6644.

Alberta Historical Preservation and Rebuilding Society
Contact: Roseleen Heddenger, President, c/o 4121 4 Street NW, Calgary, Alberta, T2K 1A3, Phone: (403) 277-6694/281-7526

Alberta Historical Resources Foundation
Contact: Mark Rasmussen, 8820 - 112 Street, Edmonton, Alberta, T6G 2P8. Phone: (403) 427-3184/431-2300; Fax: (403) 432-1376.

Alberta Main Street Programme
Contact: Merinda J. Conley, Suite 301, 525 - 11 Avenue SW, Calgary, Alberta, T2R 0C9. Phone: (403) 297-8940; Fax: (403) 297-2785.

Alberta Museums Association
Contact: Dr. Adriana Davies, Rossdale House, 9829 - 103 Street, Edmonton, Alberta, T5J 0X9. Phone: (403) 424-2626; Fax: (403) 425-1679.

Archives Society of Alberta
Contact: Margo Lainge, Administrative Coordinator P.O. Box 21080, Dominion Postal Outlet, Calgary, Alberta, T2P 4H5 Phone: (403) 246-2489; Fax: (403) 225-0889

Calgary Heritage Network
Contact: Harry Sanders, c/o 7123 - 7 Street SW, Calgary, Alberta T2V 1G1. Phone: (403) 259-8339; Fax: (403) 259-8339.

Canadian Rodeo Historical Association
Contact: Donna Wallace, Box 1268, 105 River Avenue, Cochrane, Alberta T0L 0W0
Phone: (403) 932-3911; Fax: (403) 932-3515

Central Alberta Heritage Network
Contact: Elizabeth Plumtree, Box 224, Red Deer, Alberta, T4N 5H2. Phone: (403) 346-0055.

Edmonton Heritage Network
Contact: Katherine Jaster, 11336 - 57 Avenue, Edmonton, Alberta, T6H 1B1. Phone: (403) 493-4798/438-3929.

Environment Canada: Parks Canada
Contact: Steve Whittingham, Chief/Heritage Communications, #520, 220 4 Avenue SE, Calgary, Alberta, T2P 3H8 Phone: (403) 292-6656; Fax: (403) 292-4242

Friends of Geographical Names of Alberta Society
Contact: Tracey Harrison, 8820 - 112 Street, Edmonton, Alberta, T2G 2P8.
Phone: (403) 431-2300; Fax: 432-1376.

Heritage Canada Foundation
Contact: Reg Crowshoe, Box 1857, Fort Macleod, Alberta, T0L 0Z0. Phone: (403) 965-3826.

Heritage Council of Alberta
Contact: Frances Blondheim, c/o Box 800, Red Deer, Alberta, T4N 5H2.
Phone: (403) 492-2642.

Historic Sites and Archives Service, Community Heritage Services Section, Alberta Community Development
Contact: Les Hurt, Deputy Director, Community Heritage Services, 8820 - 112 Street, Edmonton, Alberta, T6G 2P8, Phone: (403) 431-2342; Fax: (403) 433-3553

Historic Sites and Monuments Board of Canada
Contact: Trudy Cowen, 87 - Haysboro Crescent SW, Calgary, Alberta, T2P 1C2.
Phone: (403) 253-0250; Fax: (403) 253-4038.

Historical Society of Alberta
Contact: Katherine Ivany, President, Box 4035, Station "C", Calgary, Alberta, T2T 5M9
Phone: (403) 261-3662; Fax: (403) 269-6029.

Municipal Heritage Advisory Boards Network
Contact: Morris Flewwelling, Box 800, Red Deer, Alberta, T4N 5H2
Phone: (403) 343-6844; Fax: (403) 342-6644.

Petroleum History Society
3800 150 6 Avenue SW, Calgary, Alberta, T2P 3Y7
Phone: (403) 286-6721

Royal Canadian Mounted Police Veterans Association (Calgary Division)
Contact: Max Goulet, President, 75 Sunmount Crescent SE, Calgary, Alberta, T2X 2G3
Phone: (403) 256-1151/ 274-0040

Southeast Alberta Heritage Network
Contact: Jim Marshall, 97 First Street NE, Medicine Hat, Alberta, T1A 5J9.
Phone: (403) 527-2774; Fax: (403) 526-7680.

SPARE (Society of the Preservation of Architectural Resources of Edmonton)
Contact: Johanne Yakula, c/o Old Strathcona Foundation #4, 10324 - 82 Avenue, Edmonton, Alberta, T6E 1Z9.
Phone: (403) 439-2797 and (403) 433-5866

Spirit of the Peace Museums Association
Contact: Fran Moore, c/o Box 447, DeBolt, Alberta, T0H 1B0
Phone: (403) 957-3957

SELECTED BIBLIOGRAPHY

The following selection of sources will help you discover Alberta's fascinating heritage. Because most libraries and archives in Alberta have copies of local histories, they are included in this list.

Bolton, K., S.A. Fogarty, S. Saul and S. Ursan. *The Albertans.* Lone Pine Media Productions Ltd., Edmonton, Alta., 1981.

Brado, Edward. *Cattle Kingdom: Early Ranching in Alberta.* Douglas & McIntyre. Vancouver, B.C., 1984.

Cruise, David and Alison Griffiths. *Lords of the Line: the Men who Built the CPR.* Viking Penguin Inc., New York, 1988.

Ewing, Sherman. *The Range.* Mountain Press Publishing Co. Missoula, Mont., 1990.

Dempsey, Hugh A. *Indian Tribes of Alberta.* Revised edition. Glenbow Museum, Calgary, Alta., 1986.

Dickason, Olive P. *Canada's First Nations: A History of Founding Peoples from Earliest Times.* McClelland & Stewart Inc. Toronto, 1992.

Foran, Max. *Calgary: An Illustrated History.* John Lorimer & Co. & National Museum of Man, Toronto, 1978.

Francis, Daniel and Michael Payne. *A Narrative History of Fort Dunvegan.* Watson and Dwyer Publishing Ltd., 1993.

Fryer, Harold. *Ghost Towns of Alberta* Stagecoach Publishing Co., Langley, B.C., 1976.

Gilpin, John F. *Edmonton: Gateway to the North.* Windsor Publications Canada, 1984.

Giraud, Marcel. *The Métis in the Canadian West.* Vols I and II, translated by George Woodcock. Edmonton: The University of Alberta Press, 1986.

Hardy, W.G., editor-in-chief. *Alberta: A Natural History.* MisMat Corp. Distributed by Hurtig Publishers, Edmonton, Alta., 1967.

Haestie, Elizabeth. *Ferries and Ferrymen in Alberta.* Calgary: Glenbow-Alberta Institute, 1986.

Helgason, Gail. *The First Albertans: An Archaeological Search.* Lone Pine Publishing, Edmonton, Alta., 1987.

Holmgren, Patricia M. *Place Names of Alberta.* Third edition. Western Producer Prairie Books. Saskatoon, Sask., 1976.

Innis, Harold A. *The Fur Trade in Canada.* Yale University Press. New Haven, Conn., 1930.

Johnston, Alex and Andy den Otter. *Lethbridge, A Centennial History.* City of Lethbrige and Whoop-Up Country Chapter, Historical Society of Alberta. Lethbridge, 1985.

Leonard, David W. *Delayed Frontier: The Peace River Country to 1909.* Calgary: Detselig Enterprises Ltd., 1995

Leonard, David W., and Victoria Lemieux. *A Fostered Dream: the Lure of the Peace River Country 1872 - 1914.* Calgary: Detselig Enterprises Ltd, 1992.

McCullough, Edward J. and Michael Maccagno. *Lac La Biche and the Early Fur Traders.* Joint publication of the Circumpolar Institute, Alberta Vocational College—Lac La Biche Archaeological Society, 1991.

MacEwan, Grant. *Eye Opener Bob: The Story of Bob Edwards.* The Institute of Applied Art Ltd., Edmonton, Alta., 1957.

MacEwan, Grant. *Calgary Cavalcade: From Fort to Fortune.* Western Producer Book Service. Saskatoon, Sask., 1975.

MacGregor, James G. *A History of Alberta.* Hurtig Publishers Ltd. Edmonton, Alta., 1972

_____. *The Klondike Rush through Edmonton 1897 - 1898.* McClelland and Stewart Ltd., Toronto, 1970.

_____. *The Land of Twelve Foot Davis: A History of the Peace River Country.* Applied Art Products Ltd., Edmonton, 1952.

_____. *Overland by the Yellowhead.* Western Producer Prairie Books, Saskatoon, 1974.

_____. *Paddle Wheels and Bucket-Wheels on the Athabasca.* McClelland and Stewart Ltd., Toronto, 1974.

_____. *Vilni Zemli: the Ukrainian Settlement of Alberta.* McClelland and Stewart Ltd., Toronto, 1969.

McCormack, Patricia A. *Northwind Dreaming: Fort Chipewyan 1788 - 1988.* Provincial Museum of Alberta publication No. 6, Edmonton, 1988.

McNeill, Leishman. *Tales of the Old Town: Calgary 1875 - 1950.* Calgary Herald, Calgary, Alberta, 1950.

Morrow, J. W. *Early Years of the Medicine Hat Country.* Revised Edition. Medicine Hat Historical and Museum Foundation. Medicine Hat, Alta., 1974.

Myers, Patricia. *Facing the Land: Homesteading in Alberta.* Friends of the Reynolds-Alberta Museum Society, Wetaskiwin, Alberta, 1992.

Myles, Eugenie L. *Airborne from Edmonton.* Toronto: The Ryerson Press, 1959.

Palmer, Howard and Tamara Palmer. *Alberta: A New History.* Hurtig Publishers Ltd. Edmonton, Alta., 1990.

Palmer, Howard and Tamara Palmer, eds. *Peoples of Alberta: Portraits of Cultural Diversity.* Western Producer Prairie Books, Saskatoon, Sask., 1985.

Parker, James. *Emporium of the North: Fort Chipewyan and the Fur Trade to 1835.* Alberta Culture and Multiculturalism/ Canadian Plains Research Centre, Edmonton, 1987.

Sawchuk, Joe, Patricia Sawchuk and Theresa Ferguson. *Metis Land Rights in Alberta: A Political History.* Metis Association of Alberta, Edmonton, 1981.

Schneider, Ena. *Ribbons of Steel: The Story of the Northern Alberta Railways.* Detselig Enterprises Ltd., Calgary, Alberta, 1989.

Smith, Margot and Carol Pasternak, eds. *Pioneer Women of Western Canada.* Ontario Institute of Studies in Education, Toronto, 1978.

Sparks, Susie, ed. *Calgary: A Living Heritage.* Calgary: The Junior League of Calgary, 1984.

Zaslow, Morris. *The Opening of the Canadian North 1870 - 1914.* Toronto: McClelland and Stewart Ltd., 1971.

This section is designed for the visitor who has a special collecting interest or an interest in visiting museums that focus on a particular theme or topic. All of the following museums are listed in the Index.

1. Agriculture Most community history museums contain artifacts that reflect the agricultural history of their district. However, the following museums either focus exclusively on agriculture or have significant collections pertaining to farming and ranching history.

Acadia Valley Grain Elevator Museum
Battle River Pioneer Museum, Manning
Brooks Aqueduct Provincial Historic Site
Brownvale North Peace Agricultural Museum
Canadian Historical Windpower Interpretive
    Centre, Etzikom
Cochrane Ranche Provincial Historic Site
Echo Dale Historical Farm Museum, Medicine
    Hat
Edgerton & District Historical Museum
La Crete Mennonite Pioneer Village
Museum of the Highwood, High River
Oldman River Antique Equipment & Threshing
    Club, Pincher Creek
Pioneer Acres of Alberta, Irricana
Prairie Acres Heritage Village & Farm
    Equipment Museum, Picture Butte
Reynolds- Alberta Museum, Wetaskiwin
Reynolds Museum, Wetaskiwin
St. Albert Grain Elevators
South Peace Centennial Museum, Beaverlodge
Stockman's Memorial Foundation Museum,
    Cochrane
Western Heritage Centre, Cochrane

2. Art Museums & Collections
Calgary Chinese Cultural Centre
Edmonton Art Gallery
Glenbow Museum
Medicine Hat Museum and Art Gallery
Muttart Art Gallery
Native Cultural Arts Museum, Grouard
Nickle Arts Museum, U of C, Calgary
Prairie Art Gallery, Grande Prairie
Southern Alberta Art Gallery, Lethbridge
U of A Museums and Collections Services
University of Lethbridge Art Gallery
Walter Phillips Art Gallery
Whyte Museum of the Canadian Rockies

3. Fur Trade History
Bonnyville Museum
Fort Assiniboine Museum
Fort Chipewyan Bicentennial Museum
Fort Edmonton Park
Fort George/Buckingham House Provincial
    Historic Site
Fort Vermilion Heritage Museum
Fort Whoop-Up Interpretive Centre
Historic Dunvegan Provincial Historic Site
Fort Chipewyan Bicentennial Museum
Fort Vermilion Heritage Museum
Jasper-Yellowhead Museum
Mackenzie Crossroads Museum, High Level
Rocky Mountain House National Historic Site
Peace River Centennial Museum
Victoria Settlement Provincial Historic Site

4. Industrial/Occupational History

Alberta Association of Registered Nurses
    Museum & Archives
Alberta Forest Service Museum
Atlas Coal Mine Interpretive Centre,
Bellevue Underground Mine
Clay Products Interpretive Centre, Medicine
    Hat
Coleman Journal Building
Crowsnest Museum, Coleman
Diplomat Mine Interpretive Centre
Dr. George House, Innisfail
Dr. Woods House Museum, Leduc
Edmonton Public Schools Archives & Museum
Fort McMurray Oil Sands Interpretive Centre
Frank Slide Interpretive Centre Provincial
    Historic Site
Lacombe Blacksmith Shop Museum
Leitch Collieries Provincial Historic Site
Markerville Creamery Museum
Nordegg Historic Centre
Sexsmith Blacksmith Shop Museum
Telephone Historical Centre, Edmonton
Victoria Composite High School Museum &
    Archives

5. Military & Police Museums
Aero Space Museum of Calgary
Alberta Aviation Museum, Edmonton
Calgary Police Service Interpretive Centre
Canada's Aviation Hall of Fame, Wetaskiwin
Edmonton Police Museum and Archives
Fort Calgary Historic Park
Fort Museum, Fort Macleod
Fort Normandeau Historic Site & Interpretive
    Centre,
    Red Deer
Fort Saskatchewan Museum
Fort Walsh National Historic Site
Fort Whoop-Up Interpretive Centre, Lethbridge
Loyal Edmonton Regiment Museum
Museum of the Regiments, Calgary
Nanton Lancaster Museum
Naval Museum of Alberta, Calgary
RCMP Centennial Museum, Fairview
Vegreville International Police Museum

6. Multicultural Heritage
Barr Colony Heritage Cultural Centre,
    Lloydminster
Beth Tzedec Heritage Collection, Calgary
Calgary Chinese Cultural Centre
Dickson Store Museum
Historical Village & Pioneer Museum at
    Shandro

La Crete Mennonite Museum
Markerville Creamery Museum
Multicultural Heritage Centre, Stony Plain
Stephansson House Provincial Historic Site,
 Markerville
Ukrainian Canadian Archives & Museum of
 Alberta, Edmonton
Ukrainian Cultural Heritage Village, Mundare
Ukrainian Museum of Canada, Alberta Branch,
 Edmonton
Ukrainian Museum of Canada, Calgary
 Collection
Ukrainian Catholic Women's League of
 Canada Arts & Crafts Museum, Edmonton

7. Native History & Culture
Centre Vital Grandin Centre, St. Albert
Fort Calgary Interpretive Centre
Fort Chipewyan Bicentennial Museum
Fort George/Buckingham House Interpretive
 Centre,
 Elk Point
Fort Museum, Fort Macleod
Fort Normandeau Historic Site & Interpretive
 Centre
Fort Walsh National Historic Site
Fort Whoop-Up Interpretive Centre, Lethbridge
Girouxville Museum
Glenbow Museum, Calgary
Head-Smashed-In Buffalo Jump Provincial
 Historic Site
Historic Dunvegan Provincial Historic Site
Lac La Biche Mission
Luxton Museum, Banff
Musee Historique de St. Paul Historical
 Museum
Nakota Institute, Morley
Native Cultural Arts Museum, Grouard
Nose Creek Valley Museum, Airdrie
Oldman River Cultural Centre, Brockett
Provincial Museum of Alberta, Edmonton
Rocky Mountain House National Historic Site
Saamis Archaeological Site, Medicine Hat
Saddle Lake Cultural Museum
Siksika Nation Museum of Natural History,
 Gleichen
Tsuu T'ina Museum, Calgary
Writing-On-Stone Provincial Park, Milk River

8. Natural History
Banff Park Museum
Drumheller Dinosaur and Fossil Museum
Girouxville Museum
Grande Prairie Museum
Helen Schuler Coulee Centre, Lethbridge
John Janzen Nature Centre, Edmonton
Kerry Wood Nature Centre, Red Deer
Kinosayo Museum, Kinuso
Muskoseepi Park, Grande Prairie
Luxton Museum, Banff
Police Point Interpretive Centre, Medicine Hat
Provincial Museum of Alberta, Edmonton
Royal Tyrrell Museum of Palaeontology,
 Drumheller
Siksika Nation Museum of Natural History,
 Gleichen
Sodbusters Archives & Museum, Strome

U of A Mineralogy/Petrology Museum
U of A Paleontology Museum
Waterton Natural History Museum

9. Religion
Basilian Fathers Museum, Mundare
Beth Tzedec Heritage Collection, Calgary
Centre Vital Grandin Centre, St. Albert
Father Lacombe Chapel Provincial Historic
 Site, St. Albert
Girouxville Museum
Historic Dunvegan Provincial Historic Site
Historic St. Bernard Church & Gallery,
 Grouard
Lac La Biche Mission
Ukrainian Cultural Heritage Village
Victoria Settlement Provincial Historic Site

10. Science & Technology
Alberta Science Centre & Centennial
 Planetarium, Calgary
Energeum, Calgary
Edmonton Space & Science Centre
Fort McMurray Oil Sands Interpretive Centre
 Provincial   Historic Site
Telephone Historical Centre, Edmonton

11. Sports & Recreation
Alberta Sports Hall of Fame and Museum, Red
 Deer
Cave and Basin National Historic Site, Banff
Jasper-Yellowhead Museum
Olympic Hall of Fame and Museum, Calgary
Seba Beach Heritage Museum
Whyte Museum of the Canadian Rockies, Banff

12. Transportation
Alberta Railway Museum, Edmonton
Big Valley Station and Museum
Aero Space Museum of Calgary
Alberta Aviation Museum, Edmonton
Alberta Central Railway Museum, Wetaskiwin
Alberta Prairie Railway Excursions, Stettler
Alberta Railway Museum, Edmonton
Big Valley Roundhouse and Interpretive Centre
Calgary and Edmonton Railway Museum
Canada's Aviation Hall of Fame, Wetaskiwin
Canadian Northern Railway Society, Camrose
Fort Edmonton Park
Fort McMurray Heritage Park
Galloway Station Museum, Edson
Heritage Park Historical Village, Calgary
Meeting Creek Station Museum
Museum of the Highwood, High River
Nanton Lancaster Museum
NAR Station, Peace River
Northern Alberta Railway Museum, McLennan
Remington-Alberta Carriage Centre, Cardston
Reynolds-Alberta Transportation Museum,
 Wetaskiwin
Reynolds Aviation Museum, Wetaskiwin
Smithson International Truck Museum, Rimbey

13. Zoos and Botanical Gardens
Alberta Birds of Prey Centre, Coaldale

Calgary Zoo, Botanical Gardens & Prehistoric Park
Devonian Botannic Garden (U of A), Devon
Ellis Bird Farm, Lacombe

Muttart Conservatory, Edmonton
Nikka Yuko Japanese Garden, Lethbridge
Trochu Arboretum
Valley Zoo, Edmonton

Special Collections

Here are but a few of Alberta's museums that have unique or unusual objects and collections. These collections may or may not have a lot to do with Alberta's heritage, but they are a reminder that Alberta is part of a global community.

Alberta Association of Registered Nurses Museum & Archives. A Florence Nightingale Lamp used by Crimean nursing staff. It is one of only three of this design in the world.

Banff Park Museum. A "museum of museums", the oldest natural history museum in western Canada, with collections dating to 1895.

Basilian Fathers Museum. Liturgical books dating from the 15th century.

Bonnyville & District Museum. Exquisite folk art miniatures of people in everyday life.

Bowden Pioneer Museum. One of Annie Oakley's guns

Clay Products Interpretive Centre. Ceramic pieces of Medalta ware, kilns, molds, and machinery

Donalda Lamp Museum. Over 800 industrial and domestic lamps & lanterns

Edmonton Public Schools Museum. The 1881 school was the first public school structure built in what is now Alberta. It now features school classes as were taught in that period.

Edmonton Space & Science Museum. The first international Challenger Learning Centre, a simulated mission control centre and space station.

Fort McMurray Oil Sands Interpretive Centre. Canada's largest land-based artifact, a bucketwheel excavator.

Girouxville Museum. An Autoboggan, early forerunner of the snowmobile

Glenbow Museum. Medieval European & Asian armour & weaponry

Grande Prairie Museum. Mounted specimen of a white moose.

Hanna Pioneer & Village Museum A large buffalo rubbing stone

Heritage Park Historical Village. An early Calgary amusement park, with a carrousel, swings and Ferris wheel.

Holden & District Museum. In situ Masonic Hall and a jail cell.

Kinusayo Museum. Mounted specimen of the largest Great Plains Grizzly from SwanHills.

National Historic Windpower Centre. A variety of windmills from all over North America

Peace River Centennial Museum. Chimney stones and a brass lantern from NWC's Fort Fork. The lantern may have been used by Sir Alexander Mackenzie when he wintered at the post during 1792-93.

Provincial Museum of Alberta. Sacred to Native People, the Iron Creek Meteorite, the largest meteorite found intact in North America.

Trochu Valley Museum. A dress suit once belonging to Louis Bleriot, famous French aviator.

Vermilion & District Museum. "The Button Wall," with over 20,000 buttons

Writing-On-Stone Provincial Park. Prehistoric and historic petroglyths & pictographs

Index

Legacy
Alberta's   *Heritage Magazine*

Does Alberta's past have a future?

Read *Legacy*—filled with stories, news, and ideas about restoring historic buildings, gardens, traditional skills, art—find out how we celebrate and protect our heritage.

Legacy is a quarterly magazine containing fascinating features and regular profiles, history-mystery, how-to, heritage foods, destinations, book reviews and architectural details columns.

SUBSCRIBE NOW

Bring *Legacy* into your home four times a year.

✂ --

Yes, I want a one year subscription to *Legacy* at $14.95 plus $1.05 GST, **17% off** the newsstand price.

Name _____

Address _____ City _____

Province _____ Postal Code _____

I am enclosing a cheque for $16.00 payable to *Legacy* and sending it to:
Legacy, c/o 9667 - 87 Avenue, Edmonton, Alberta T6C 1K5.

(GST Registration #12055 0835)

ALBERTA *Craft* COUNCIL

ALBERTA HAS A COLOURFUL, DIVERSE HISTORY OF CRAFT MAKING. MUSEUMS THROUGHOUT THE PROVINCE EXHIBIT HISTORIC CRAFTS FROM ABORIGINAL, IMMIGRANT AND POPULAR CULTURES. NOW ALBERTA'S HERITAGE CRAFTS ARE AVAILABLE TO YOU THROUGH THE ALBERTA HERITAGE CRAFT COLLECTION.

To celebrate and support the historic and traditional craft skills of Alberta, the Alberta Craft Council (in cooperation with the *Alberta Museums Association*, the *Alberta Historical Resources Foundation* and Alberta's museums) is developing a collection of museum–quality craft products for sale in museum shops and visitor centres throughout the province.

A few examples of craft products you can find in the collection are:

- Traditional crafts still in production in Alberta – Cree bead work, willow baskets, Ukrainian pysanka (decorated eggs), Norwegian embroidery, homestead-style rag rugs, wheat weaving...

- Replicas of historic crafts found in Alberta museums – fur trade wrought iron tools, tatted lace, homestead toys and games, sheepskin slippers, birch kitchen utensils...

- Contemporary crafts which commemorate aspects of Alberta's rich history – jewellery featuring prehistoric rock art images, clay portrayals of historic buildings, model teepees, leaded glass medallions capturing Alberta's wildlife...

The Alberta Heritage Craft Collection represents the best of Alberta's rich craft traditions. You can now collect authentic heritage crafts, like those seen in Alberta museums. Ask for the Alberta Heritage Craft Collection at your favourite museum shops. Or call the Alberta Craft Council at 1-800-DO CRAFT (1-800-362-7238).

pysanka • Christina Koscielnuk
tatted lace • Andrea Wilson
birch scoop • Blaine Askew
woven wheat cross • Grethe Jensen
Cree gloves • Slave Lake Native Friendship Centre

10106 - 124 STREET • EDMONTON, ALBERTA • CANADA T5N 1P6

Other Brightest Pebble books you won't want to miss

Grand Delusions: Henry Hoet and Cobblestone Manor by James Musson is the true story of a great southern Alberta mansion and a reclusive artist from Belgium who spent fifteen years building it for the woman he loved. It is a story of love, obsession, creativity, tragedy, and insanity. It is a story of a monument to the human spirit that now stands as a Provincial Historic Site. This book was partly funded by the Alberta Historical Resources Foundation.

To the Town that Bears Your Name* by *Martin Nordegg is a story that takes place in 1912 when Martin Nordegg, the German-born entrepreneur and early Alberta pioneer who had discovered and developed coal deposits in Alberta's Rocky Mountains, takes his fourteen-year-old daughter, Marcelle, on a journey across Canada to Nordegg, the town that bears her name.

Martin Nordegg wrote this book for his daughter as a souvenir of their journey, that eventually ended on the Pacific Coast. He describes in loving detail the adventures they shared and creates a vivid picture of the country they crossed and a way of life that has already faded into history.

This book was partly funded by the Alberta Historical Resources Foundation.

Zur Stadt, die Deinen Namen trägt

Die Reise eines jungen Mädchens zu Pferde durch die Rocky Mountains im Jahr 1912

Martin Nordegg

Vorwort und Epilog von Maria und W. John Koch

To the Town that Bears Your Name

A Young Woman's Journey to Nordegg in 1912

Martin Nordegg

Translated by Maria Koch
Commentary by W. John Koch

To Order

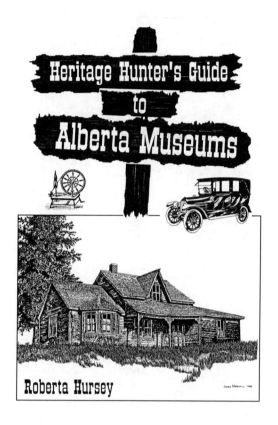

Roberta Hursey

Please send $19.95 to:

Brightest Pebble Publishing Co. Inc.
7604 - 149 Avenue
Edmonton, Alberta, Canada
TSC 2V7

Phone (403) 457-7496   Fax (403) 475-0243
See order forms on the following pages

Please send me the following book(s):

No.	Description	Price	Total
	Grand Delusions	$14.95	
	To the Town that Bears Your Name	$12.95	
	English Edition		
	German Edition		
	Heritage Hunter's Guide to Alberta Museums	$19.95	

Send cheque or money order to:
Brightest Pebble Publishing Co
7604 - 149 Avenue
Edmonton, AB TSC 2V7.
Phone (403) 457-7496 Fax (403) 475-0243

Please add $2.50 to
your order for postage
and handling.

✂ ---

Please send me the following book(s):

No.	Description	Price	Total
	Grand Delusions	$14.95	
	To the Town that Bears Your Name	$12.95	
	English Edition		
	German Edition		
	Heritage Hunter's Guide to Alberta Museums	$19.95	

Send cheque or money order to:
Brightest Pebble Publishing Co
7604 - 149 Avenue
Edmonton, AB TSC 2V7.
Phone (403) 457-7496 Fax (403) 475-0243

Please add $2.50 to
your order for postage
and handling.

Please send me the following book(s):

No.	Description	Price	Total
	Grand Delusions	$14.95	
	To the Town that Bears Your Name	$12.95	
	English Edition		
	German Edition		
	Heritage Hunter's Guide to Alberta Museums	$19.95	

Send cheque or money order to:
Brightest Pebble Publishing Co
7604 - 149 Avenue
Edmonton, AB T5C 2V7.
Phone (403) 457-7496 Fax (403) 475-0243

Please add $2.50 to your order for postage and handling.

✂ --

Please send me the following book(s):

No.	Description	Price	Total
	Grand Delusions	$14.95	
	To the Town that Bears Your Name	$12.95	
	English Edition		
	German Edition		
	Heritage Hunter's Guide to Alberta Museums	$19.95	

Send cheque or money order to:
Brightest Pebble Publishing Co
7604 - 149 Avenue
Edmonton, AB T5C 2V7.
Phone (403) 457-7496 Fax (403) 475-0243

Please add $2.50 to your order for postage and handling.